PENG

MONEY WORKS

Abhijeet Kolapkar is a chartered accountant by profession and has more than two decades of experience in the field of finance. His book *Arthasakshar Vha!* is a bestseller in Marathi. He strives to spread financial literacy through various mediums.

Celebrating 35 Years of
Penguin Random House India

MONEY WORKS

THE GUIDE TO FINANCIAL LITERACY

ABHIJEET KOLAPKAR

PENGUIN
BUSINESS

An imprint of Penguin Random House

PENGUIN BUSINESS

USA | Canada | UK | Ireland | Australia
New Zealand | India | South Africa | China | Singapore

Penguin Business is part of the Penguin Random House group of companies
whose addresses can be found at global.penguinrandomhouse.com

Published by Penguin Random House India Pvt. Ltd
4th Floor, Capital Tower 1, MG Road,
Gurugram 122 002, Haryana, India

First published in Penguin Business by Penguin Random House India 2023

Copyright © Abhijeet Kolapkar 2023

Illustrations courtesy of Prakash Tikare

All rights reserved

10 9 8 7 6 5 4 3 2 1

The views and opinions expressed in this book are the author's own and the
facts are as reported by him which have been verified to the extent possible,
and the publishers are not in any way liable for the same.

ISBN 9780143461647

Typeset in Inter by Manipal Technologies Limited, Manipal

www.penguin.co.in

Contents

Contents

Ten Points to Help You Make the Most Out of This Book

1. This is not 'just another financial planning book'. The key differentiator in this book is its simplicity. It seeks to make the subject easy for anyone to follow, whether the reader is a young person, an adult or a senior citizen. It also takes into account both the individual and family points of view in its approach to finance and aims to make understanding finance easy for everyone.

2. The book has six parts:

    i)   Introduction to Financial Literacy

    ii)   Financial Planning

    iii) Insurance and Debt Management

    iv) Investment

    v)   Shares and Mutual Funds

    vi) Financial Frauds to Beware Of

3. Every topic in this book is explained in simple words. Examples, diagrams, flow charts and illustrations have been used, keeping in mind ease of reading and understanding of the topic. The checklists and smart worksheets are going to be assets in your financial journey, whether your personal journey or the family's.

4. If you are already planning your finances, investments, loans and providing for your risks, this book will be useful to you.

5. Your self-belief—that you can bring about a positive change in your financial life—will be important as you go through this book.

6. After every chapter, ask yourself: 'How can I implement what I have just read?'

7. Highlight the points, concepts or paragraphs that resonate with you so you can revisit them later.

8. To make the best use of this book, review your financial plans every three months.

9. Find a location for this book on your desk or in your library that will enable you to quickly find it whenever you need it.

10. Discuss financial planning with your family members and ask for their advice whenever necessary.

Disclaimer

The information contained in this book is for general informational and educational purposes only and should not be considered as financial advice. The author and publisher of this book are not financial advisers. Readers are advised to consult with a qualified financial professional before making any investment decisions. Always conduct your own research and exercise caution when making financial decisions.

Any examples or case studies of companies or flow charts or graphics mentioned in this book are for illustrative purposes only and should not be considered as endorsements or recommendations. All product names, trademarks, logos and brands are the property of their respective owners. All company, product and service names used in this book are for identification purposes only.

The content presented in this book is based on the author's study, experience and understanding of personal finance concepts at the time of writing. However, financial markets and regulations are subject to regular and rapid change, and the information in this book may become outdated over time. Although the publisher and the author have made every effort to ensure that the information in this book was correct at the date of publication and the author has made sincere efforts to ensure that the book is error-free with regard to the various subject matters covered, the publisher and the author assume no responsibility for errors, inaccuracies, omissions, or any other inconsistencies herein and hereby disclaim any liability to any party for any loss, damage, or disruption caused by errors or omissions, whether such errors or omissions result from negligence or any other cause.

How and Why This Book Was Written

Why such an extensive discussion on finance and a large book to aid financial literacy? Hundreds of books have been written on the topic; why add one more to the list?

I would like to share here a little history of this book. Every day, many blogs on personal finance are published on Arthasakshar.com. In 2019, the team asked me to write a book. To prepare for this, I started reading whatever was available on the topic of investment. Financial illiteracy, although wide, is an ignored topic. This book is a humble attempt to simplify and present the topic of finance so that more and more people can move towards financial literacy. I hope you enjoy reading the book as much as I did writing it.

The following points come to mind as to whether financial literacy is really necessary:

1. **People who are seen as average but are financially literate can become role models in their societies and circles**

   - In a country of roughly 142 crore people, not everyone can become wealthy. The creation of wealth is not everyone's cup of tea either.

   - In a country with unequal distribution of wealth, financial prosperity is somehow considered a benchmark for success.

   - A lot of us idolize wealthy businessmen such as Steve Jobs, Bill Gates, Mark Zuckerberg, Mukesh Ambani or Narayana Murthy. There is a lot to learn from such intelligent, hardworking and visionary people.

   - However, even you can build your fortune and live a prosperous life if you follow certain fundamental rules of financial literacy. Thousands of people in India have done this, but we do not consider them to be heroes and ignore their journeys.

   - Such ignored heroes could be your neighbours staying down your lane or in your housing society. They could be people from your professional networks or from your friends or family circles, and you could be unaware of their financial success. This book will try to decode their thought process—the things they avoid, the things they do and how they do them.

2. **The need for financial literacy**

   - Economics is a complex yet integral element of every country. A few individuals make up a family, a few families make a village, and a village later grows into a city. These cities then, with the villages and towns around them, cohesively form states, which eventually form a country. The economy of each of these units plays a dual role, influencing both the economies of the levels above and below them.

● In the same way that each state contributes to a country's economy, in the long run, the financial literacy of every individual matters.

● Financial literacy does not mean just the creation of wealth but stands for proper planning for the management of wealth.

● Financial planning gives equal importance to income, expenses, loans, savings and investments.

● Finance is not an easy concept to attain literacy in, but that does not mean it is too difficult to follow either.

3. **Accepting reality and working towards improving it**

● Assume that the universe has a software that decides where you will be born. A god is assigned the job of monitoring this, and he is doing this on a big screen, sitting up there in heaven. Say, you are born in a place such as Latur, Parbhani or Malegaon in Maharashtra and are leading a pretty humble life. You believe that your life would have been different if you were born in a bigger city in the state, such as Pune or Mumbai. On the other hand, someone born in these cities thinks the same, wondering if his life would have been different had he been born in London or New York. Now, let us look at another aspect. What if the one working the software in heaven placed you in a country such as Somalia or Ghana, where citizens struggle even for their basic meals? Imagine your life then.

● The life you are living today could be an aspiration for someone somewhere else. So you can leave all your worries aside and strive towards success. Read the previous line again. Don't keep blaming your fate for your financial position. Accept your reality and work towards becoming financially literate; work towards your progress and only focus on the things that you have control over.

4. **The gap between understanding and implementation**

● When it comes to financial literacy, either people understand its importance but fail to implement what they have learnt, or they don't make the effort to understand finance or to work on their misconceptions around it.

- If you notice, the financial frauds that feature in the news follow a pattern. One would think people would by now be familiar with and alert against them. But why is it that so many people still fall prey to them? If you think about it, this happens due to their lack of financial literacy.

- Financial success is measured by how you manage your wealth more than by how much wealth you accumulate, how you invest it the right way and shoulder your responsibilities through proper financial planning.

5. Whom is this book for?

- This book does not talk about 'Three Ways to Get Rich Quick' or 'Becoming a Millionaire in Twenty-One Days'. Rather, it will tell you about the right ways to plan your finances and to honestly earn financial freedom.

- If you are someone who has just started to earn, are not able to track your expenses or have curiosity towards learning financial concepts, this book will be your best friend.

- Since you have read the book up to this page, you seem determined to become financially successful. You want your hopes and dreams to come alive while enjoying a great lifestyle.

- Deciding your financial objectives, saving money, planning your investments and implementing them—are all part of this book.

- The book also contains concepts about investment, insurance and debt, and sheds light on their importance in financial planning. However, no particular scheme, product or brand has been endorsed here.

- Planning your finances based on your personal needs and financial health is what the book intends to motivate you towards.

- Since the reader is going to amass a lot of finance knowledge from this book, I am sure it will always be a handy part of your collection.

- Your feedback on this book is always welcome.

CA Abhijeet Kolapkar
artha.abhik@gmail.com

Part 1

Introduction to Financial Literacy

Money Works

Steps to Financial Literacy

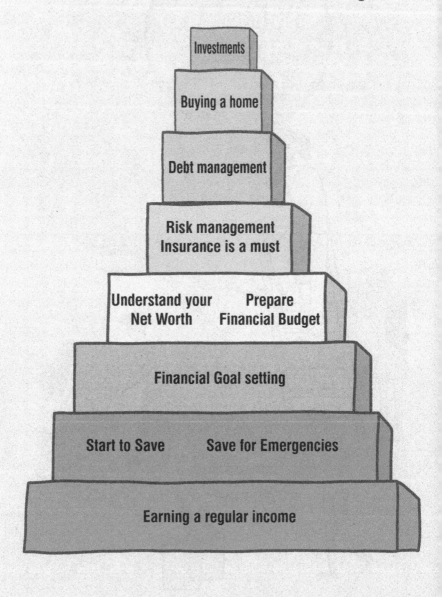

Investments

Buying a home

Debt management

Risk management
Insurance is a must

Understand your   Prepare
Net Worth   Financial Budget

Financial Goal setting

Start to Save   Save for Emergencies

Earning a regular income

Money Works

Evaluate your Money Mindset

- Who am I? What am I made of? There is an innate curiosity in everyone to find answers to these existential questions. The field of psychology has various techniques to assess this. An experiment performed in this regard is particularly noteworthy.

- There is a psychometric test to fetch you answers to your existential questions. You are asked to fill in a questionnaire by choosing from multiple answers. Each answer has a certain weightage in relation to the expected outcome. Based on your choices, you get a fair answer to your existential questions. Likewise, your financial mindset can also be assessed.

- A set of situations is described below. Read them and respond with a Yes/No. Upon completion of the exercise, you will be able to self-assess your financial mindset.

Sr.	Situation	Yes	No
1	I don't have money to pay my bills.		
2	My expenses are more than my income.		
3	I love shopping! That's why my credit card outstandings are always high.		
4	My family members have very high expenses.		
5	I give my children everything they ask for. Because as a child I had to give up many of my desires and I don't want my children to have to do the same.		
6	If I save some cash, it gets spent immediately.		
7	My income from my salary is not enough to cover my expenses. How do I plan my savings, investments and finances?		
8	I cannot afford to pay for my children's preferred higher education.		
9	I am always worried about how to plan for financial emergencies and contingencies.		

Sr.	Situation	Yes	No
10	Since I don't have any savings or emergency funds, I feel like a loser when my colleagues, friends and relatives discuss investments, retirement planning and various financial schemes.		

Conclusion

1. If your answer to eight out of ten questions in the exercise above is Yes, then you have the habit of overspending.

    - You have not understood the importance of savings and investments. You are not bothered about your family's future or about yours. You have failed to make your children understand the importance of savings.

    - Controlling your spending habits is important because you will not be able to face any financial emergencies if you don't do so now.

2. If you have answered Yes to five to seven questions, you have understood the importance of saving money but often end up spending whatever you save.

    - You are yet to plan for any financial emergencies that may arise in the future. However, you can start planning for such contingencies right now and lead a prosperous life.

3. If you have answered Yes to just three to five questions, you seem to have understood the importance of savings. But there may be instances when you feel like overspending and end up spending beyond the limits of prudence.

    - Understand the importance of financial planning and investing, just as you do of saving, and experience a happy life by implementing it.

4. If you have answered Yes to zero to three questions, congratulate yourself. You have well understood the importance of savings, investments and time. You are successful in balancing your income and expenses. Perhaps you can experience a more prosperous future with a bit more financial planning.

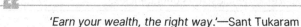

> *'Earn your wealth, the right way.'*—Sant Tukaram

The Flow Chart of Financial Health

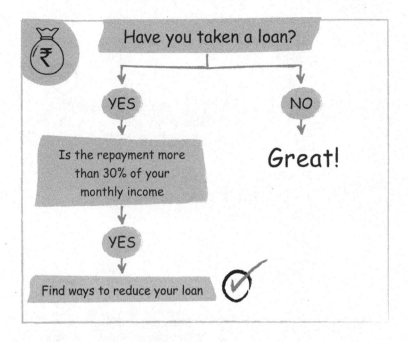

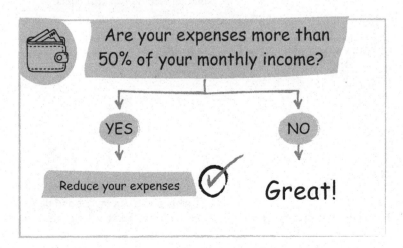

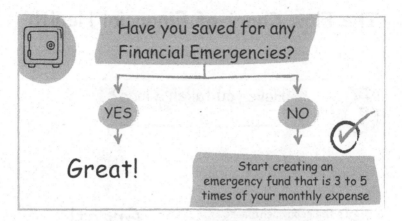

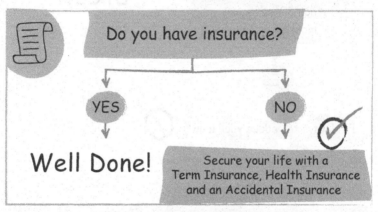

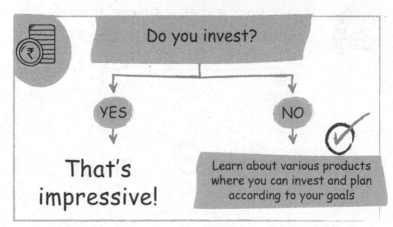

Overconfidence and One's Financial Life

On 19 April 1995, a well-built middle-aged man went to rob a bank in Pittsburgh, USA. He was successful in robbing two banks using his gun. He did not try to hide his face behind a mask or under a cap, unlike other robbers. In fact, he used to give a nice smile when he saw CCTVs. The police caught this man, McArthur Wheeler, the same night. He was confident that he would never be caught. When he was nabbed, he said to the police, 'But I had applied lemon juice on my face. How did you catch me?'

This trick works on paper, where writing made in lemon juice is invisible until the paper is heated up. But McArthur was confident that the same trick would make his face invisible too. You might think he was a fool or a drunkard. But he was found to be neither in the forensic tests that followed.

This robbery received a lot of publicity. David Dunning, a professor of psychology at Cornell University, believed this was more than a fool's attempt at robbery. This came from the belief that one is an expert on a subject when one actually knows very little about it. He published his research paper in 1999 on the phenomenon, which he named the Dunning-Kruger Effect.[1]

The Problem with Overconfidence

- Professor Dunning, with his student Justin Kruger, performed many experiments in psychology. Students were asked various questions, which were to do with grammar, humour and logic.

- When asked how much they would score, the least-scoring students would usually assume they would score the highest.

- As against this, the top scorers did not seem that confident. A few examples from our daily life would parallel this attitude:

  - Bad drivers are usually overconfident about their driving skills and end up having an accident.

  - Some contestants on reality shows are disqualified for lack of skills. Many of them do not believe they don't have the necessary skills and merely make for some entertainment value on the show.

> 'Don't blame God for creating the tiger. Thank him instead for not giving it wings.'—Indian proverb

In general, all of us overestimate our potential in one or other fields. Two problems arise because of this:

- We end up making wrong decisions, based on our limited knowledge and competence.

- We do not agree that we are in error since we do not understand the difference between right and wrong in that particular field.

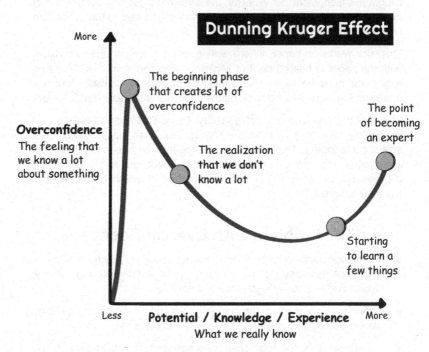

Dunning Kruger Effect

More

The beginning phase
that creates lot of
overconfidence

The point
of becoming
an expert

Overconfidence
The feeling that
we know a lot
about something

The realization
that we don't
know a lot

Starting
to learn a
few things

Less   **Potential / Knowledge / Experience**   More
What we really know

- When you start learning, you realize the mistakes that are due to your ignorance and the ways in which you can rectify them. Of course, the pattern of thinking that one is smarter than one actually is existed before it was titled the Dunning-Kruger Effect.

- Many a time, more than knowledge, it is ignorance that creates overconfidence. It is no wonder that many ancient sacred texts have held that real knowledge means understanding one's own ignorance.

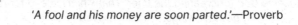

'A fool and his money are soon parted.'—Proverb

A. Our Misconceptions about Finance

Let us look at how the Dunning-Kruger effect plays out in real life:

	Our expectations/our overconfidence	Reality	What you should do
Salary	The field that I work in will see good days in the future. My financial and personal growth are aligned with my company's growth. Hence, I do not think twice before spending money.	When a field starts showing positive signs, everyone jumps into it. This gives rise to competition. Over a period, profitability decreases. People and organizations that upskill themselves stay relevant. Only those who perform get salary increments.	Whatever your income, you should make it a habit to save from the beginning. Unless you earn, you should avoid daydreaming about spending money.
Retirement	I don't need to plan and save for my retirement. My children will take care of me when I retire.	Everyone needs to take into consideration the rising cost of living and expenses while they are still earning.	Your children would definitely be a big support in your old age but avoid being a financial burden on them. They are going to face stronger competition than you did. Plan for your retirement well in advance to live an independent, respectful retired life.

'Empty pockets never held anyone back. Only empty heads and empty hearts can do that.'—Norman Vincent Peale

	Our expectations/our overconfidence	Reality	What you should do
Share market	I saw a video on YouTube of a person who was not well educated but made a lot of money through intra-day trading. I am smarter than him. I can become the next Warren Buffet through trading, while also doing my job/business.	Warren Buffet has been a student of the share market for more than eight decades and has been learning every day. The number of examples of people who have consistently earned money through intra-day trading is small.	Know your financial situation before investing in the share market. Start investing in it only after you have saved enough for your financial emergencies. Investing without knowledge can lead to financial accidents and losses. Do not risk your secure job or business for a small, uncertain profit from intra-day share trading.
Loan	Since my income is always going to rise, I take regular loans for buying new properties, cars, home interiors and foreign trips.	There is no guarantee of a consistent rise in income. But the loans will have to be repaid consistently. Paying interest on loans is like paying rent for buying things that you cannot afford.	Think from all angles before taking a loan. Repayment of loans should not be affected even if there are a few inconsistencies in your regular income.

B. The Usual Financial Misconceptions

Our misconceptions about finance are a major roadblock on our path to financial growth. They can be of various types. We may be completely unaware of them and may not be ready to accept the fact that our notions about many things are misconceptions. Let us look at what these misconceptions are:

1. Misconceptions about Financial Planning

Misconception 1	I do not need to plan my finances as I have a lot of money.
Fact	Everyone needs financial planning. How you plan your finances is more important than how much wealth you have accumulated. Both savings and strengthening of your financial health require financial planning.
Misconception 2	I am always going to grow financially. Why should I bother to plan my finances?
Fact	Although a positive mindset is important, getting a reality check is equally important. Situations such as

the Covid-19 pandemic, which are not in our control, can quickly turn our financial standing upside down. Even if you are in sound financial health, physical ailments, a change in the nature of your work, ever-growing responsibilities and natural calamities such as earthquakes, floods or pandemics can occur at any time. Hence, financial planning needs to be done keeping these contingencies in mind. While it is good to have a positive mindset about enjoying steady growth in the future, having a plan B is always recommended.

Misconception 3 Financial planning is a very complicated exercise. It is almost impossible to find the time to sit and plan.

Fact The things that seem too easy at the start may actually be the toughest to crack later. Conversely, the things that seem tough early on may be easy to achieve. The other important point is: What is the point of earning money with immense hard work, which you hardly have the time to enjoy?

Misconception 4 I earn a lot of money right now and that is enough to take care of my retirement.

Fact Earning money right now does not guarantee a financially secure life post-retirement. If that was the case, we would not have come across 'prince to pauper' examples. Since money is liquid, it needs to be handled with care. The rising cost of inflation devalues your money every day. Therefore, financial planning is essential.

Misconception 5 I will plan for my retirement after my forties.

Fact We retire around the age of sixty. We will enjoy our money right now and start saving for retirement once we turn forty—this is what most of us think. But as we turn forty, we are burdened with family responsibilities and the children's education. In such a scenario, we have to save a lot for our retirement after our forties. If we start setting aside a small sum

> 'You have to learn the rules of the game. And then you have to play better than anyone else.'—Albert Einstein

of money right from the beginning of our career, we can reap the benefits of compounding and can take care of our responsibilities without much to worry about.

Misconception 6	I do not have to worry about finances as my partner takes care of all our family's financial decisions.
Fact	While you and your partner enjoy a great relationship, you should also have healthy financial discussions. The mistakes committed by one can be avoided or rectified through discussion with the other. Many day-to-day expenses need to be curtailed while planning for large expenses such as the purchase of a home or the children's higher education. When you work as a team, you can discuss, plan, decide on and achieve your financial goals in a much better way.
Misconception 7	I do not need to consult financial advisers.
Fact	Almost everyone is capable of making wrong financial decisions. People learn from their mistakes over time. But the monetary losses that wrong financial decisions bring cannot be reversed. Just like we consult different medical specialists for different physical problems, we should consult financial advisers for our financial health and relieve ourselves of our financial ailments. That way, we can excel in our job, business and life.

2. Misconceptions about Investing

Misconception 1	I am not rich enough to invest money.
Fact	The definition of a rich man changes with every person. There are no set rules on how much money you would invest based on your net worth or your monthly income. Rather, you should think about maximizing returns on every rupee saved.

> *'A year from now you may wish you had started today.'*—Karen Lamb

Misconception 2	It is very risky to invest in the share market.
Fact	The share market is a high-risk, high-return investment option and many investors have minted huge profits from investing in shares. This type of investment has also proved to be the one bringing the highest returns over the past few years. This, especially, is a lucrative option for youngsters. But investing in the share market without the right knowledge or based on loose information is too risky and can lead to huge financial losses.
Misconception 3	Investing in mutual funds is not risky and can lead to high returns.
Fact	No investment is 100 per cent secure. It either has a low or a high risk level. Mutual funds are managed by professionally run portfolio houses that are responsible for lower risk and giving maximum returns to their investors. However, the risk factor cannot be completely eliminated. That is why no one can assure investors of returns from mutual funds as the schemes are subject to market risks, and that is why investors are advised to read the offer documents carefully before investing.

3. Misconceptions about Tax Management

Misconception 1	Tax management should be done either at the start of the year or just before the end of the financial year.
Fact	From the point of view of income tax, creating tax-saving provisions either at the start of the financial year or at the end would make no difference. But investing at the end of the year just to save tax could be a hasty decision and one may end up investing in any available scheme. As a good practice, tax management should be done at the start of the

'Adults devise a plan and follow it, children do what feels good.'—Dave Ramsay

year based on one's financial goals, housing loan, insurance and retirement planning.

Misconception 2	Investment in mutual funds is meant for tax saving and management.
Fact	Not all mutual funds are meant for tax saving. But products such as the ELSS (equity-linked saving scheme) can be chosen for tax-saving purposes.

4. Misconceptions about Credit Cards

Misconception 1	I am rich because I have many credit cards.
Fact	Every use of a credit card means taking a loan for a few days without any interest cost. But after a stipulated number of days, you may have to pay heavy interest if the outstanding dues are unpaid. Offers on credit cards make you buy more, and the outstanding amounts go on increasing. You never get rich because you hold a credit card—rather, your financial calculations go for a toss because of unnecessary spending. Instead of making you rich, it works the other way; hence this financial instrument is meant to be used only in emergencies.
Misconception 2	Only the minimum amount due is to be paid while paying credit card bills.
Fact	You postpone your financial downfall when you pay just the minimum amount due. You will have to clear the outstanding dues someday. If you keep paying just the minimum amount due, your outstanding amount keeps increasing, and this habit can lead to even bankruptcy for you.

You have just gone through various misconceptions people have about their personal finances. Even if someone has a vague idea about financial planning, she may fail in it because of a lack of knowledge and effort about the exact actions she needs to take.

> *'If you buy things you do not need, soon you will have to sell things you need.'*—Warren Buffett

There are multiple reasons for this:

1. Misconceptions about finance
2. Mental blocks
3. Fear of financial matters from a young age
4. Low confidence. Conversely, there is also the problem of overconfidence—that you can do everything by yourself—perhaps because someone told you when you were growing up that you would achieve great things
5. Mistakes committed in the past
6. Aggressive parents or partner
7. Unrealistic expectations of oneself after reading a lot of self-help books
8. Laziness, addiction, hatred or stupidity
9. Irresponsible nature—believing that financial planning is the responsibility of one's spouse, parents, financial adviser or the government
10. Overdependence on experts

Being literate means the ability to read and write. Likewise, being financially literate is important too. We will look at what it means to be financially literate in the next chapter.

> 'An investment in knowledge pays the best interest.'—Benjamin Franklin

The Meaning of Financial Literacy

Most of us try to stay away from financial matters. Everyone loves money but does not take the effort to learn the easy steps to making money.

- Financial literacy means understanding how money works.

- Financial literacy helps one take the right financial decisions that lead to the fulfilment of one's dreams and the realization of one's goals. It also helps one prepare for emergencies and lead a prosperous and satisfied life.

- Financial education is not limited to reading financial news. It is okay if you do not understand the country's GDP or fluctuations in the economy but knowing how to keep your financial health in good shape by taking easy steps is essential.

- Financial literacy is an ongoing beautiful journey. On the way, you will have to polish a few skills as follows:

  - A clear understanding of income and expenses—how much money do you earn and where do you spend it?

  - Decide on financial objectives

  - Do budgeting

  - Learn the importance of savings

  - Learn loan management

  - Insure yourself and other key things that need insuring

  - Learn to invest in the right way

  - Be vigilant against being cheated

- When we buy vegetables, we visit at least two or three vendors to get an understanding of the right prices. After that, we select the one that sells the best-quality vegetables at the cheapest rates. If we suspect that the vegetable seller has overcharged us, we find a new vendor the next time.

- If something is free and it holds value, consumers will love it. The seller who makes free giveaways such as curry leaves or coriander

> 'When the student is ready, the teacher will appear.'—Zen thought

has the privilege to charge a bit extra, and yet consumers end up buying from that vendor.

● The alertness we show and the probing we do in the matter of buying our daily vegetables seem to vanish when we take bigger financial decisions. Where do we go wrong?

   - We get attracted by Ponzi schemes and fraudulent plans that lead to financial losses. But we are too cautious when it comes to investing the same money in our children's education and in saving for retirement.

   - We do not learn the facts about a company before investing in its shares. This is essential. Assume that you end up investing Rs 10,000, based on a random tip, and expect it to give 100 per cent returns in a short period of time. This is like driving a car at night with the headlights turned off.

   - We invest in never-before-heard-of multi-level marketing schemes without learning about them.

   - We do not know how much insurance coverage is enough.

   - We take personal loans after getting influenced by aggressive advertising.

   - We buy luxury items—such as a car, a big house, lavish interiors, electronic items, etc.—just to show off.

   - We buy unnecessary items on our credit cards just because they are offered at loans of zero per cent interest rate.

   - We take unnecessary loans.

● Your financial knowledge decides the direction, speed and extent of your financial growth.

● You can spend your time with friends or family or invest your time in pursuing hobbies while you focus on your financial planning.

> 'To attain knowledge, add things every day. To attain wisdom, remove things every day.'—Lao Tse

Why Do We Lack Financial Literacy?

● Schools and colleges do not give importance to financial literacy.

● This topic is not openly discussed at home. The mistakes committed by our elders are considered wisdom for the next generations.

● Even our relatives and friends have limited knowledge that may have been attained through misconceptions. Some of the popular misconceptions include beliefs such as:

- Money attracts money

- Money can be earned only through illegal sources

- I am past the age when I can earn money

- I am not educated enough

- My religion or caste limits my growth

- My family does not support me

- This is a sad world

- I don't trust this country is right for me, etc.

How a Financially Literate Person Evolves

1. By learning the right financial concepts from the family at the right age

2. By learning from educated friends and relatives

3. By reading books and columns written by experts

4. By watching good videos on YouTube

5. By browsing good websites on personal finance

6. By attending discussions and workshops

7. By learning from his or her own mistakes, and

8. By planning finances with the help of a good financial adviser

> 'The one whose mind accepts defeats is a loser,
> one whose mind does not, a winner.'—Saint Kabir

Failure is a stepping stone to success.
But, as said by the wise, don't let it become a slide.

- The mistakes committed in the absence of financial literacy do not just prove to be costly but can also lead to one losing confidence in taking finance-related decisions.

- When many such decisions backfire, you either start avoiding the topic or depend on someone else to take the initiative in the matter of investing.

- Maybe you understand the importance of thoughtfully spending your money, of saving wherever possible, investing in safe options, insuring yourself, not taking too many loans, etc., but there is a difference between understanding and implementation.

- A popular quote says, 'Old habits die hard.' For this reason, we also do not make the required efforts to get rid of our bad habits. Also, if we are surrounded by people who are not disciplined about finance, we are sure to catch the wrong train.

1. Many people hold their parents responsible for their bad attitude in financial matters. 'I was not raised well, my parents were poor, resulting in a lack of financial knowledge on my part,' they may say. This is also true, but only to an extent.

2. Also, many of us keep saying, 'I don't earn enough,' and blame our financial position for our lack of knowledge of the subject.

Let us look at how financial literacy and formal education are correlated.

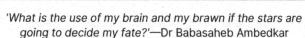

'What is the use of my brain and my brawn if the stars are going to decide my fate?'—Dr Babasaheb Ambedkar

Financial Literacy and Education at School

- Both the institution of school and parents at home showcase their lack of faith in financial literacy. The school thinks this is to be taught by parents, while parents feel exactly the opposite.

- Students are at a financial loss here. The citizens of the future end up making mistakes that cannot be rectified because of their lack of knowledge. This, in turn, is a loss to the nation.

- No parents want their kids to suffer financially when they grow up. In fact, they go to great lengths to make sure that their children are cared for, for as long as possible. In this exercise, they sometimes confidently share their misconceptions about financial matters with their children, as if it is wisdom they are passing on.

- Many a time, parents themselves get their financial knowledge from the wrong sources. What can we expect from young minds, if grapevines and loose chatterers are going to be their knowledge base when it comes to financial literacy?

- One must accept that one's parents' financial knowledge might be limited. This does not mean one should not listen to one's parents, of course. It means, rather, that one should be open to learning from other verified sources too.

- Find out if your parents have the capacity, time and intent to educate you about finance. Even with the right intent and positive will on the part of parents, children can learn the wrong concepts if their parents' knowledge is limited or based on misconceptions.

- You may not be able to bring about a change in your parents or what you learnt at school. But you definitely can self-learn and increase your knowledge of financial matters.

'Anyone who stops learning is old, whether at twenty or eighty. Anyone who keeps learning stays young.'—Henry Ford

What Children Must Be Made Aware of at Every Stage as They Grow Up

1. Ages 3 to 5
   - Identification of currencies, denominations of currency notes and coins and types of cards
   - Management of a piggy bank
   - The importance of money and transactions

2. Ages 6 to 10
   - Comparison of prices of products in the nearby shops
   - What a bank account means
   - Knowledge of school fees
   - The pros and cons of debit and credit cards
   - A bank account must be opened in the child's name

3. Ages 11 to 13
   - The importance of saving—every penny counts
   - Thinking before spending money. Money saved is money earned
   - Understanding different types of bank transactions

4. Ages 14 to 18
   - What does investment mean? Importance of investing
   - Being motivated to invest the money saved by self
   - Importance of compounding interest

5. Ages 18+
   - Use of own debit card
   - Dangers and safety of net banking and mobile banking
   - Importance of financial planning

> 'By far the best investment you can make is in yourself.'—Warren Buffett

Which financial aspects should be taught in school?

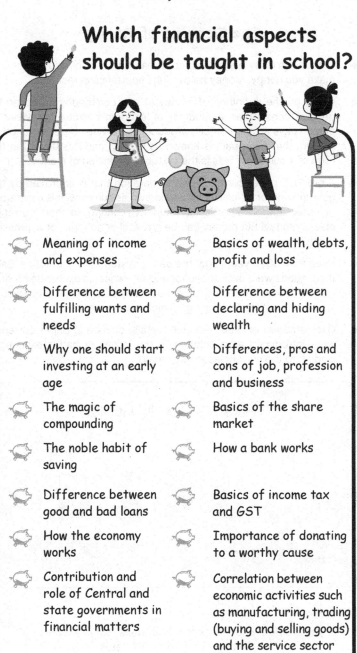

- Meaning of income and expenses
- Basics of wealth, debts, profit and loss
- Difference between fulfilling wants and needs
- Difference between declaring and hiding wealth
- Why one should start investing at an early age
- Differences, pros and cons of job, profession and business
- The magic of compounding
- Basics of the share market
- The noble habit of saving
- How a bank works
- Difference between good and bad loans
- Basics of income tax and GST
- How the economy works
- Importance of donating to a worthy cause
- Contribution and role of Central and state governments in financial matters
- Correlation between economic activities such as manufacturing, trading (buying and selling goods) and the service sector (marketing, transport services, etc.)

The Meaning of Money

- Money can't buy happiness, but it can buy a lot of things that can make you happy. Money holds high importance in real life.

- Going by the definition of money, it is a commodity accepted by general consent as a medium of economic exchange. When a person pays an amount for a product or a service offered by another person, that thing paid is known as money, and it is usually in the form of a currency. This is the textbook definition of money.

- A product, paper currency or a declaration that is approved by the government for official use are all known as currency. It is a symbolic representation of a particular country's economy. In short, currency means money! But money can be physical or notional; or expressed or implied.

- More than 3000 years ago, the barter system was in practice. Back then, goods were exchanged for goods—wheat in exchange for rice, milk for wood, etc. This system had many problems, the biggest of which was not getting the right value for one's goods.

- Over a period of time, valuable metals, coins and paper currency were introduced as a solution to the issues in barter exchange, leading to the currencies in use today.

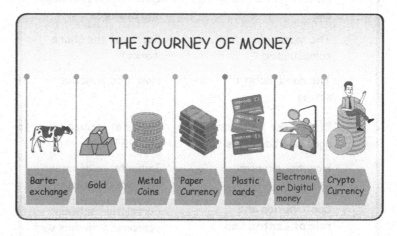

THE JOURNEY OF MONEY

| Barter exchange | Gold | Metal Coins | Paper Currency | Plastic cards | Electronic or Digital money | Crypto Currency |

'If you are born poor, it is not your mistake, but if you die poor, it is your mistake.'—Bill Gates

Are You Part of a Rat Race?

*'The trouble with the rat race is that even if you win,
you're still a rat.'*—Lily Tomlin

- We lead hectic lives. We usually say we don't even find time to sit and think, but in reality, we usually avoid thinking. We blame our lack of time for it. The fact is, we are just running around from dawn till dusk. Sometimes to catch a bus and to find our preferred seat; at other times to complete our targets at work.

- Do we not know about this vicious circle that keeps us trapped, or do we avoid thinking about it? Or, do we say we want to think about it but end up giving the same old excuse of lack of time? This vicious circle will continue until the time we don't stop and make a course correction. The biggest reason why we are always running is money—which pitches us into the vicious circle that makes us run.

- Our situation matches that of Abhimanyu from the Mahabharata, the one who had intent and knew how to enter the Chakravyuha but didn't know how to come out of it.

We Are Stuck in a Vicious Financial Cycle

Income

Last year, there was a message in circulation—'The most powerful words other than "I love you" are "Your salary is credited".' We work as employees or run our own businesses just to earn an income. Our financial life begins from the moment we start earning.

Expenses/Debts

Our income starts getting spent on bills and expenses. In fact, we start spending more than is necessary. A few expenses, such as on electricity and groceries, are essential, while many expenses are non-essential. Only we can control our expenses.

Lifestyle Expenses

We start dreaming of spending money even before we earn or as soon as we start earning. I want to buy an expensive watch, I want to buy branded clothes, let's buy those fashionable curtains for our home, let's change the sofa, let's have dinner at a five-star hotel— we have a lot of dreams and desires to fulfil.

Zero Savings

Our many bills and expenses to achieve our dreams, both old and new, leave us empty-handed. We have zero savings after all this. But 90 per cent of the items on our bucket list are yet to be ticked. Whatever you do in life, this list keeps ever growing, and most of the dreams on it remain unachieved.

Loans

- What do we do when there is no cash in hand and the salary due date is still far away? We look at the red carpet laid out by credit card and personal loan companies. We walk like a celebrity on that red carpet.

- Even though we know that this will lead us into a dark tunnel, we overlook that.

- We realize that we are in the dark tunnel only when we cannot see any light. We then try to get out of the darkness. But how do we get out of the tunnel of ignorance without knowing where to go?

- We need income for this, but we are on a path that traps us in a vicious circle. We have no option but to enter it, and this circle of life continues forever.

- Now think, are you satisfied when you achieve your goals, considering all that you have read above? Not really, isn't it? Why does this happen?

> *'Don't buy things just because you can afford them.'*—Suze Orman

- We should do what makes us happy. More than being too cautious about what people will think, it is important to think about what you really want to do. This way, you will automatically start finding answers to many of your questions.

- What is the use of daydreaming? Life is not a race. Take a pause and reflect on your thoughts.

- Ask yourself: What do I really want to achieve? Where do I really want to go? Is the work that I am currently doing important to reach my goals? More than where you want to go, you must ask yourself why you want to reach a particular destination, and whether you will be satisfied once you reach there.

- Humans have limitless desires. We should be able to distinguish between our wants and needs. The day you see the difference between them, you will be able to find a way out of the vicious circle you may be trapped in.

सन्तोषामृततृप्तानां यत्सुखं शान्तिरेव च ।

न च तध्दनलुब्धानामितश्चेतश्च धावताम् ॥

—सुभाषित

(Satisfaction is a virtue. The peace and happiness that a person gets from the nectar of satisfaction can never be achieved by the one who keeps running after material possessions.)

How can we quit running the rat race? The answer to this will unfold as we read ahead. Please understand—we may get stuck in this rat race even if we earn in lakhs every year. Our lifestyle changes according to our income. If we focus on the wrong things, such as spending on unnecessary things and not investing in the right financial options, we may never be able to get out of the rat race.

> 'Remember that the happiest people are not those getting more, but those giving more.'—H. Jackson Brown

The Mexican Fisherman and the American Investment Banker

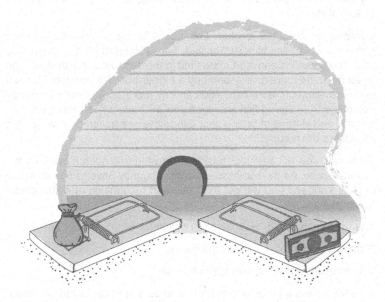

A story about the Mexican fishermen is well known in this context. This story illustrates the difference between needs and wants.

An American investment banker was travelling through a Mexican village. He went to the beach while roaming the countryside. He saw a humble fisherman with his catch of the day. He spoke to the fisherman out of curiosity and asked him a lot of questions about his work and the fish.

The fisherman replied to all his questions calmly. Fishing was easy, it appeared, and the fish was priced high in the market too. After a while, when the fisherman was about to leave, the banker inquired of him, 'It is still time for sunset and will you be catching more fish?'

The fisherman replied, 'The money I will earn from selling these is enough to feed my family.' The banker was puzzled and asked the fisherman,

'It's easier to feel a little more spiritual with a couple of bucks in your pocket.'—Craig Ferguson

'What do you do the rest of the day, then?' The Mexican fisherman replied, 'I wake up late, have breakfast with my family, and leave to catch fish. I return once I have collected enough fish. Then I spend time with my friends and family. I sometimes play the guitar too. I live a simple yet beautiful life.'

Listening to this, the banker was about to burst into laughter but somehow controlled himself. He said, 'I am a Harvard MBA and can help you. You should spend a bit more time in the sea to catch fish. Also, you need to spend more money and buy a bigger boat for yourself. This will help you to catch more fish. You can buy more boats from the money you make from selling fish and soon you will have a fleet. Next, you buy a truck, and instead of selling your fish to the agent, you can transport it directly to the factory.

'This way, you will see your business growing and soon move to a big city in Mexico. As the business expands, you may have to buy an office in New York and you will get the fame and recognition of a successful businessman.'

The fisherman asked, 'How long will it take for all this to happen?'

'Fifteen–twenty years,' replied the banker.

'And what after that?' asked the fisherman.

'You will amass a lot of wealth and retire as a successful businessman. You can then move to a calm and peaceful countryside, and buy a house there. You may wake up at leisure, have breakfast with your family, spend time with your grandchildren, enjoy the sunset with your wife, chat with your friends and pursue some hobby, such as fishing or playing the guitar. In all, you can live a relaxed life.'

The fisherman burst out laughing and said, 'How different is that from what I am doing now?'

What do you learn from this story?

- The Mexican fisherman was spontaneous

- He led a simple and peaceful life

- The American banker told him things about his business world that he already knew

> **"**
> *'If you live for having it all, what you have is never enough.'*—Vicki Robin
> **"**

- What the fisherman does with his business is solely his decision

But life is not as simple as that, and one can wonder what will happen to this fisherman in the case of unforeseen events in his life.

- While being at peace with one's situation is a good thing, one should earn to at least cover one's basic needs

- If the fisherman's boat was caught in a storm, he would face a big financial loss. He might also need money for his children's education. Had he invested for all this, and was he insured? We don't know any of this.

- Being a penny pincher and continuously running after money are two opposite ends of the pole of meaninglessness. Your journey should lie between having no ambitions and being overambitious.

- Money is meant to help you achieve your goals and is not the goal itself. Therefore, you need to be sure of what you really want.

- Decide on your needs. You need to create a framework of what you want to achieve and the way you look at life. Once this is ready, you need to carefully plan your way. This is what we want to suggest to you through this book: Don't spend your life only for earning money; rather, spend money to live the life you have always dreamt of!

> 'Twenty years from now you will be more disappointed by the things that you didn't do than by the ones you did do.'—Mark Twain

Is It True That Money Is God?

त्यजन्ति मित्राणि धनैर्विहीनं पुत्राश्च दाराश्च सुहृज्जनाश्च |
तमर्थवन्तं पुनराश्रयन्ति अर्थो हि लोके मनुषस्य बन्धुः ||

—सुभाषित

(*A man will lose his friends, family, children and relatives in the absence of money, but they will all come back once he earns money. People alienate or befriend others based on the material possessions they have.*)

यस्यार्थस्तस्य मित्राणि यस्यार्थस्तस्य बान्धवाः ||
यस्यार्थः स पुमांल्लोके यस्यार्थः स च जीवति ||

—श्लोक १५, अध्याय ७, चाणक्यनीतिदर्पण

This shloka talks about the greatness of wealth. According to Acharya Chanakya, many want to be friends with people who have a lot of money and wealth. This means a person attracts company when he has money, but if he loses his wealth, the same people will distance themselves from him. No one wants to befriend a poor person. A rich man will be looked after and cared for. Money is synonymous with fame in society.

- Money has become the most important objective in this world. Everyone is running around to make money. Wealth needs to be amassed by whatever means possible. The general notion that money is everything, that money is God, is prevalent. Is money really that important? This itself is a million-dollar question.

- For the children of the 1990s who grew up watching *DuckTales*, you would remember Uncle Scrooge McDuck, the rich cartoon character who would literally swim in a pool of gold coins and would explain the importance of money to his nephews every now and then. Similarly, another popular cartoon character, Richie Rich, showcased how important money is.

- The advertisements you are continually bombarded with, and other media of mass communication such as films and serials, and even

'Many folks think they aren't good at earning money, when what they don't know is how to use it.'—Frank A. Clark

people of significance, such as religious leaders, celebrities, lifestyle influencers, politicians, government officials, social organizations, large healthcare institutions, educational institutions and corporate entities, give prime importance to money.

- A way of life has set in now, where everyone is busy running about building a grand life for themselves. Our minds are constantly doctored, being told that *the more we run, the more money we will make, and then we can buy everything we want using it.*

- What do you really want to do with so much wealth? Money is a means to living; not life itself. We must have read this line a million times before. Money can't buy you happiness, but it can buy you a lot of things that make you happy. If you want to be happy and satisfied, and financially independent, then you need to know the importance of money as a medium of transaction.

- Not everyone in the world can become rich at the same time. People's capacity, education, surroundings and opportunities are different from each other's. Once we are able to meet our basic needs and have saved money for financial emergencies, we can say we have achieved financial independence.

- Prosperity and financial independence may not always be related. They differ according to the individuals and situations concerned.

- How you define the term 'prosperity' depends on the point of view you have built about wealth over the years. If you define prosperity as an expensive car, an expensive mobile, foreign trips and huge loans, then your idea of prosperity is of no use. Because, if at any time you need to sell these possessions to pay off your debts, you will have nothing left in your kitty.

> *'Money is the worst discovery of human life. But it is the most trusted material to test human nature.'*—Buddha

Should Becoming Rich Be Your Goal or Not?

- Goddess Laxmi bears the prefix 'Shree' in our ancient sacred literature. Any name containing Shree is associated with wealth or with someone or something rich (Shrimant). A rich person is one who has amassed a lot of wealth.

- You may experience prosperity in more than one field. If you have a healthy body, close friends and relatives, and make enough money to cover both your basic and lifestyle expenses, you can consider yourself among the richest in the world.

- The definition of 'rich' differs from person to person, and that too is often seen changing.

- Whether your goal is to become very rich or not is your personal choice. We are currently living the best of lives known to humanity in the past 5000 years. The healthcare facilities that we have easy access to were not available even to the king of the kings in the past. The discovery of electricity, the increase in life expectancy due to advances in medical science, the telecom revolution and the Internet have made our lives easy.

- If you are saving enough money to cover your current needs, your expenses in the future, your responsibilities and possible emergencies, then you are on your way to financial independence. Let us look at an example.

  o Akshay is forty years old and his wife, Sukhada, is thirty-eight. Both are employed. Akshay's monthly earnings are Rs 45,000, and Sukhada's Rs 42,000. Their outstanding EMI on their home loan will be Rs 34,000 for ten more years. They have two children, aged seven and five. Akshay's expenses are as follows:

    - Variable expenses: grocery expenses, school fees, extra tuition fees, medical expenses, expenses for discretionary spends during festivals, etc.

    - Fixed expenses: home loan EMI

  o After ten years, Akshay and Sukhada will be free of the home loan. But now that their parents are ageing, their medical expenses might increase. Their kids will be seventeen and fifteen, which means expenses for higher education.

> *'It is not the man who has too little, but the man who craves more, that is poor.'*—Seneca

o Akshay and Sukhada both wish to own a sedan-class car and have dreamt of driving a premium car for many years.

o They both got promoted at work and received Rs 3 lakh as a bonus. Akshay and Sukhada now have the following options:

Option 1	Buy a sedan-class car and enjoy the ride. The car will cost at least Rs 10,00,000; a down payment of Rs 3,00,000 will have to be made and the balance in the form of a car loan will have to be repaid over the next seven years.
Option 2	Pay Rs 3,00,000 towards the pre-payment of the housing loan.
Option 3	Create an emergency fund of Rs 1,00,000 and invest Rs 2,00,000 in a mutual fund for the children's higher education after discussing this with a financial adviser.
Option 4	Invest the entire sum of Rs 3,00,000 in mutual funds.
Option 5	Donate the entire sum towards a social cause and place a placard there with their names on it.
Option 6	Invest Rs 3,00,000 in fixed deposits and think about what to do with it later.
Option 7	Renovate the home. The budget for this is Rs 5,00,000. So, a loan of Rs 2,00,000 will have to be taken for this.
Option 8	Go on a foreign trip and spend Rs 3,00,000.

Akshay and Sukhada could have more options than the ones listed above.

o Many people dream of going on a foreign trip. The pyramids of Egypt, the beaches of Bali, the Eiffel Tower of Paris are on many an Indian's bucket list. However dear this dream is, how will you cover your children's higher education or your parents' medical expenses if you do this foreign trip? This needs to be given a thought.

'One day your life will flash before your eyes. Make sure it's worth watching.'—Gerard Way

o   Akshay and Sukhada should give a careful thought to financial independence. Once the home loan has been cleared, funds must be set aside for their retirement, for the children's higher education and for their marriage. An emergency corpus must be created. After this, they can enjoy foreign trips and even donate to a cause.

o   The definition of happiness changes with every person. It is the same when it comes to the definition of what 'rich' is.

o   Some may feel satisfied after buying a house or gold; for others, a car may bring satisfaction. For still others, it may be sending their children overseas for higher education or staying in luxury hotels.

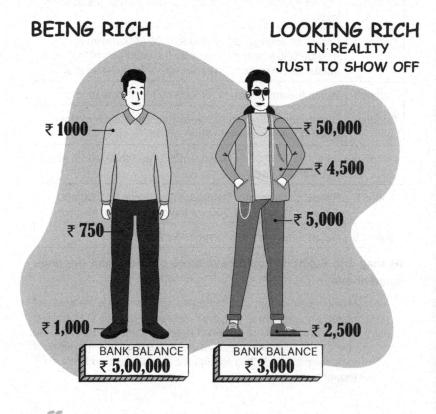

'There is a gigantic difference between earning a great deal of money and being rich.'—Marlene Dietrich

Accept That Someone Will Always Be Ahead in This Race

Success often goes beyond what meets the eye!

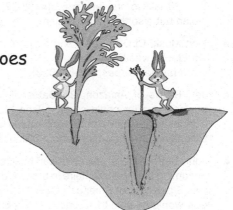

Most of us think the income we earn is not enough. We always have the feeling that we are underpaid as compared to others. Comparing ourselves with others is not good for our financial health. Let us look at an example:

- Sudama works as a teacher at a high school. His monthly income is Rs 30,000. He feels he is lagging behind, as compared to Rahul.

- Rahul has a small tailoring shop in a village. His monthly income is Rs 45,000. Rahul in turn feels jealous about his cousin, Utkarsh.

- Utkarsh is employed in an IT firm in Pune. He earns Rs 85,000 per month but envies his friend Shailaja.

- Dr Shailaja is a specialist and earns Rs 1,50,000 per month. She feels jealous of her neighbour Rajesh Sheth.

- Rajesh runs a furniture workshop in an industrial estate and makes around Rs 50 lakh per month. But he wants to do something big in his life, just like his colleague from the club, Hitesh.

- Hitesh runs a company that is listed on the stock market and is worth Rs 2000 crore and growing at 15–20 per cent every year. Hitesh's

'Do what you love and the money will follow.'—Marsha Sinetar

net worth grows in proportion. Hitesh idolizes Mukesh Ambani, chairman of Reliance Industries.

- Mukesh Ambani's net worth is $94.5 billion, which is approximately Rs 7.75 lakh crore (as on 6 July 2023). He is not just the richest Indian but also the richest Asian.

- Elon Musk, CEO of Tesla and SpaceX is the richest person[2] in the world. His wealth amounts to $248 billion, which is Rs 20.33 lakh crore (as per *Forbes*, 6 July 2023).

- Jeff Bezos of Amazon, Bill Gates of Microsoft or any other big business leader could surpass Elon Musk as you read this book. Curious minds can visit this link https://www.forbes.com/real-time-billionaires/ to know more about billionaires.

- John D. Rockefeller, an American businessman, was well known for becoming the first billionaire in the world. Back in 1913, his net worth was 3 per cent of America's GDP. Finance experts said that no one else would be able to surpass this benchmark in the near future.

- Many kings, queens, royal families, businessmen, merchants and rich people in the world have been recorded as having immense wealth. Many others belong to the list of the richest, but we don't even know their names.

The point is, if you keep comparing yourself with others, you will always find someone ahead in this race. Instead of comparing yourself with others, compare your own present with your past. Instead of putting in efforts to surpass others, find out how much you have progressed from where you were before.

- Ajay's friend, Nilesh, bought the latest model of car. People would automatically turn their heads to see the car when it hit the roads.

- Ajay had the following series of thoughts: *Wow, what a beautiful car! Nilesh must be feeling great while driving this car. I should definitely have one of these so that I can prove my mettle to the world. I will use my Diwali bonus to make a down payment for such a car this year, and the rest will be covered by a loan.*

> 'Money is a terrible master but an excellent servant.'—P.T. Barnum

Let us look at how Nilesh might have got the car:

- Alternative 1: Nilesh took a huge loan for the car. Since he had surety of income, he could opt for the loan as he was capable of paying the EMI on it.

- Alternative 2: He bought the car by paying 100 per cent of the cost upfront. Nilesh had worked hard and saved this money, or had ancestral property at his disposal.

Ajay is unaware of Nilesh's financial position and is therefore blinded by his desire to own such a car.

The same principle applies to most of the luxury items we desire. We are blinded by their shine and overlook what we really want. Our focus should be on earning money, managing money, utilizing it well and living a stress-free life. We should avoid the desire to earn more than someone else.

- Our mind is always ready to compare us with someone along some parameter—financial situation, colour of skin, looks, language, religion, ethnicity, etc.

- Understanding that your mind is trying to compare you with something or someone is the first step to controlling such thoughts. Finding what triggers these thoughts is important.

- What is the first thought that crosses your mind when your friends share news of their promotion? Are you happy for them or do you feel jealous? Both are human emotions and it is natural to experience them. But which emotion you hold on to depends entirely on you. Let your communication display your generosity of spirit. Wish them well with all your heart.

Comparing Yourself with Others Is Mentally Draining

We are slaves to some financial misconceptions, such as poor people remain poor because they do not like to work, people have to do lowly jobs because they are not educated, the reason for that being they do not like to study, etc.

It is easy to generalize and to not understand the facts. Let us look at an example.

Ashok, Dheeraj, Parag and Ashish are four friends. Everyone studied in the same school and are all aged thirty-five.

> *Rich people exercise, poor people take diet pills.*

- Parag works as an investment banker in the US.

- Dheeraj works as an architect and has a successful real estate business.

- Ashok runs his ancestral garments business.

- Ashish is employed as an accountant in a factory.

Conclusion 1

You would have arranged these friends in decreasing order, based on their income, as follows: Parag, Dheeraj, Ashok, Ashish.

We start judging people as soon as they are introduced to us. How do they look, talk and walk? Are they passive or aggressive? What is their sense of fashion? Which mobile phone do they use? Our mind constantly processes such information and draws conclusions from them. Guessing someone's earnings is a regular exercise for many of us. We enjoy judging people in haste, based on incomplete information.

Let us get some more information about the four friends.

Here is a peep into their lives:

- Dheeraj's father was a porter in a shop. His mother used to work as a maid. Dheeraj had to face many hardships as a student.

- Ashish's father was a government officer and he was brought up in a good environment.

- Ashok belongs to a business family. He never faced scarcity in his life.

- Parag's parents were highly educated and renowned lawyers. They gave Parag whatever he asked for.

Conclusion 2

You would have realized by now that Parag, Ashish and Ashok had a strong financial background and had ample opportunities to study and prosper. But Dheeraj belonged to a family where no one was educated, yet he surpassed Ashok and Ashish by working very hard.

Points to note

- Comparing your financial situation with others means you are wasting your time. Everyone comes from a different financial background.

> *'Wealth consists not in having great possessions,*
> *but in having few wants.'*—Epictetus

- You did not decide where you were going to be born. That is your luck. As per UNICEF, more than 60,000 children are born every day in India.[3] Their future depends on a lot of variables:

  o Place of birth: metro city, town, village, tribal area

  o Locality of stay: High-class area, government quarters, middle-class tenement, chawl, slum, roadside shanty

  o Ownership of residence: Self-owned, rented

  o Parents' occupation: Daily wage jobs, regular employment, business, agriculture

  o Parents' financial situation: Rich family background, self-sustained prosperity, higher-middle class, lower-middle class, commoners, urban poor, rural poor, no fixed income, etc.

  o Parents' standing in society: Caste, religion, etc.

- Many of these alternatives come together to determine the upbringing of children, and even their behaviour as they start earning themselves when they grow up to be adults. A few start earning much before most of the others do.

- Before you compare your financial situation with that of others, think about these variables first.

- Everyone starts differently. Their education, parents, environment and available opportunities are all different. Not everyone is born to the same fate.

- How others should act is not in our control, but how we act definitely is. You can bring about a huge change in your financial situation through hard work, experimentation, consistency and constant learning.

Accept your financial reality

Dr Elisabeth Kübler-Ross was studying the behaviour of patients with near-death ailments in 1973. Her research is known by the abbreviation DABDA.[4] Let us look at how her research also connects to us and our acceptance of our financial situation.

D - Denial

> 'Enjoy the little things in life for one day you'll look back and realize they were the big things.'—Robert Brault

A - Anger

B - Bargaining

D - Depression

A - Acceptance

Denial	Refusal to accept your financial position.
Anger	Frustration from comparing one's financial situation with others'. Blaming or being angry at one's parents, relatives, government, society or educational background for not being able to progress financially.
Bargaining	Fooling oneself by saying one's financial position will automatically change by a stroke of luck or by a distant relative leaving behind his wealth in one's name.
Depression	Financial situations don't change because one is not trying hard enough. Also, feelings such as that of being stuck in the same place, sadness, thinking nothing good can happen, or blaming one's luck and not working towards changing one's situation.
Acceptance	Trying to change one's financial situation begins with one's acceptance of it. The four earlier stages that you might have been in cannot bear any fruit. The faster you accept reality, the faster you can start progressing financially.

Accept your financial situation. Take responsibility for making any necessary changes. Many others, just like you, are struggling to progress. You are not alone in this battle.

- What are you doing about it is important! The fact that you have read this book up to this page itself shows your intent to make a positive change, and that is to be appreciated.

- We will look at the various ways of earning money in the next section.

> 'If you want to live a happy life, tie it to a goal, not to people or things.'—Albert Einstein

The Various Ways of Earning Money

Money is the base and the most important element of financial planning. Money means your earnings and you can earn money in various ways.

Some of the common types of income are the following:

- Salary, or income earned from employment
- Income earned from one's business or profession
- Income from property
- Income from investments

Income can be classified in yet another way	
Active income	**Passive income**
Earned by oneself, like a salary from one's job	Income earned as interest on deposits
Income from one's business or profession	Income from dividend on shares
Daily wages—income based on the days worked	Income from property rented out
	Returns on investment—growth in wealth
	Royalty—income from intellectual property

- From the table above, you will understand that you need to work to earn an active income.
- Active income can be further classified as follows:

> 'We have two lives, and the second begins when we realize we only have one.'—Confucius

	Job	Profession	Business
Education/skill requirements	According to the nature of the job	Education and skills are both important (medicine, law, chartered accountancy)	Degree is not mandatory. However, being skilled in multiple fields is important (finance, marketing, technology, etc.)
Investments/ capital	Not required	Comparatively less than for business	Extremely important
Monthly income	Fixed	Uncertain	Uncertain
Risk	Comparatively less	Not high once settled in profession	High
Financial stress/ uncertainty	Comparatively less	Comparatively less	High

- The income that we don't actively work for but earn from investments or indirect participation in something is termed as 'passive income'. It usually starts post-retirement or after a successful stage in one's career.

- You need to earn passive income as it can become your alternative income or second income. To achieve this, you need to work towards increasing your active income, saving it smartly and investing it wisely.

> 'Instead of wondering when your next vacation is, maybe you should set up a life you don't need to escape from.'—Seth Godin

Common dilemma
What should I do? A job or business?

Finding a job after finishing your formal education is a major step in life. But young blood is often attracted towards starting a business. However, very few people have the confidence to start their own venture.

What is easier to do—a job or a business? That is a difficult question to answer because the answer varies from person to person. Every coin has two sides. Similarly, both jobs and businesses have their own pros and cons.

- When you think of a businessman, you visualize a well-dressed person travelling in an expensive car and residing in a huge house.

- We often think businessmen don't have to rush through traffic to reach office in time for a nine-to-six shift.

> *'Quit sharing bad news and gossip; you aren't a garbage truck.'*—Grant Cardone

- But, in reality, running a business has a few downsides too. First, businessmen do not have a monthly fixed income and have to face ups and downs in their business every month. They need to continuously upskill and implement the latest trends in their business to stay relevant.

- On the contrary, an employed person gets a fixed monthly income, a fixed number of holidays and many other facilities.

- In this regard, isn't doing a job an easier option? Not really. There is nothing easy or difficult here. Rather, it is a matter of personal choice, one's skill set and the situation one is in.

The Process of Employment

- Usually, our dream is to get a degree as a student and then find a decent job after graduation.

- Everything feels great at the start. We get to learn a lot in this phase. We start climbing the success ladder by learning and implementing new things.

- As we settle into our lives, we limit ourselves to home and office. At this stage, we then start dreaming about starting our own business.

- A few try to start their own ventures and live life on their own terms. Not everyone becomes successful, but one who takes risks gets many opportunities for sure.

The Process of Starting a Business

- As compared to a regular job, this option gives you more returns in terms of money and success.

- The most important factor in starting a business is investment. You will need financial backing for this. Since raising the required capital all by yourself is not easy, entering into a partnership is sometimes a viable option.

- Since both profit and loss are solely dependent on your skills and the situation your business is in, a business demands more hard work than a regular job.

- A business can generate employment for many others.

> *'Love your job, but never fall in love with your company, because you never know when the company stops loving you.'*—Narayan Murthy

Benefits of running an independent business	Drawbacks of running an independent business
• You are your own boss • The more you work, the more profits you earn • You do not worry about losing your job • You have the mental satisfaction of running your business	• Being your own boss is the most difficult job to do • You have to invest your own money • There is no guarantee of income • There are constant financial responsibilities and constant work pressure

Benefits of Doing a Job

1. Regular employment brings more security than running a business

• The security aspect of being employed is the most important factor. However, experts say that there is no guarantee of employment in today's world. Does that mean it is safer to do your own business? Even that is not true. Comparatively, a job is more secure than a business.

• You can look for a new job in case you lose one, but starting a new business again after facing losses is difficult.

2. Income stability

• For those who do not have the appetite for financial risk, a job is a better option.

• Financial stability is important in today's world. A person who has a good salary and a decent job is considered well-settled. The salary credited at the end of the month brings stability to life.

• Both ITC Limited and Hindustan Unilever are strong competitors. They produce fast-moving consumer goods and are listed companies.

> *Don't aim for job security. It will never happen. Aim for financial security. It is in your control and you can make it happen.*

Both companies are professionally managed organizations. In the year 2021–22, ITC, Hindustan Unilever and United Spirits Limited had 220, 163 and 49 managers, respectively, with annual salaries of more than Rs 1 crore.[5]

- Those who feel jobs don't pay much and that earnings are always limited should check the annual reports uploaded on the listed companies' websites. These reports highlight the details of employees who earn more than Rs 1 crore every year.

3. Less stress

- If reporting to just one or two bosses feels like a headache, imagine what your situation would be if you had to report to multiple bosses.

- For those running a business, customers are just like bosses. As such, they have to face thousands of bosses every day. Therefore, an employed person has less stress to deal with than a business person.

4. Fixed work timings

- Apart from a few situations, an employed person in India works about eight to ten hours per day. The work starts at the same time every day. Even if the time to leave the office is not fixed, the person might be delayed by an hour or two, at most.

- Those running a business do not have fixed working hours. They have to be available round the clock.

- Employees can avoid taking calls while at home, but every call is equally important for a businessman, irrespective of the time and place.

5. Comparatively less responsibility

- Employees are mostly responsible for their own performance and maybe for their department's performance too. But business owners have to take responsibility for every activity in the business.

- Those employed are entitled to a fixed set of days off work. As work at the office does not stop if they take leave, they can really unwind during their holidays.

- However, such is not the case for business owners, as they have to be connected to work even when on leave.

> *Become so financially secure that you forget it's payday!*

6. Opportunity for overall development

- The corporate world is quite dynamic. Here, many new projects and updates take place at the same time, which brings in a lot of job opportunities.

- Various workshops and training sessions are conducted by organizations to give their employees the tools to succeed at work. You can avail of them free of cost, learn about new technologies and upskill yourself. This helps in your overall development.

7. Work from home is possible

- With advancements in technology, it is now possible to work from home even if you are employed somewhere.

- With that, if you have personal problems because of which you are not able to travel to work every day, you can still be employed and work full-time from home.

- Such opportunities are not available for business owners.

8. Bonus and incentives

- In the corporate world, honest and hardworking employees are always appreciated and are suitably rewarded with a pay rise when the organization earns profits.

- Employees may also be rewarded in terms of promotion, bonus and various other incentives. Apart from these, organizations may also provide certain work perks to their employees.

Drawbacks of Doing a Job

1. Lack of ownership

- Some people think that however hard they work, they will always remain employees at their organization.

- However, if you have irreplaceable skills and know how to put them to good use, then you may get promoted or get paid in shares or employee stock options.

> 'Most people work just hard enough not to get fired and get paid just enough money not to quit.'—George Carlin

2. Dependency

- Employees have to act like subordinates and listen to their bosses all the time.

- The salary is their only source of income and must cover all their expenses, right from their daily groceries to their monthly loan repayment instalments.

- Dependency on jobs increases with a rising set of needs.

- However, if the kind of work you do is in demand, then you should think of yourself as an entrepreneur who can provide services to other organizations.

3. No Guarantee of Financial Security

- Just like business owners, even employees have no guarantee of financial security.

- The cut-throat competition of today is too much to handle. Politics at the workplace and too much competition within the organization can drastically affect one at work. One needs to be constantly updated to stay in the race. The use of technology and communication skills are essential for success.

- Sometimes, employees may be sacked without a strong reason.

- Business persons know the scale of their business, but employment brings no financial assurance.

4. Limited income

- An employee mostly earns just a salary as income. Even if one puts in a lot of effort, one will get just one's salary.

5. Workplace environment

- Growing stress at the workplace, cut-throat competition and unrealistic targets are taking away the fun and excitement of work.

- Terms such as deadlines and perfection have converted humans into machines.

- The problems in the workplace environment are equally applicable to employees and business persons.

> ''If you cannot do great things, do small things in a great way.'—Napoleon Hill

6. Decision-making

- Decision-making takes time in many organizations. Everyone has to follow the plan mapped by the management. This affects decision-making at the personal level. Employees often come up with great concepts, but since they do not have the right to make decisions, their bosses get undue credit for their ideas.

- With changing times, a few organizations effectively delegate authority and offer pay raises based on performance.

Benefits and Drawbacks of Running Your Own Independent Business

1. We are the king and we rule here

- Dependence on others feels like a restriction. However, when you run your own business, you are your own boss.

- Being your own boss means the freedom to make decisions and the freedom to decide how many hours to work.

2. Right returns for hard work

- Since it is your own business, the more you work, the higher the returns you can take home.

- On the contrary, the returns are fixed if you are employed. Even if you work hard, you might get promoted or earn a bonus, but overall, your hard work may not always be suitably rewarded.

3. Financial security

- There is no job guarantee in the corporate world. Employees can lose their job without a strong reason.

- One may lose one's job owing to office politics, lack of productivity, slow markets, etc., as opposed to not being under this constant fear when running your own business.

> 'A business that makes nothing but money is a poor business.'—Henry Ford

4. The experience of facing challenges

- Apart from your work areas, you are not exposed to other experiences as an employee. On the contrary, you get to experience all areas of work when running your business, and each facet of experience teaches you a lot.

- With so much experience to bank upon, businesspersons can face business challenges with all their courage.

5. No limit to financial earnings

- In a job, salaries don't significantly rise unless one gets a promotion. On the contrary, a businessman earns a lot if the business is stable.

Conclusion

- Neither doing a job nor running a business can be termed easy or difficult. One decides what to get into based on multiple factors, such as one's personality, educational qualifications, and the positives and negatives in one's own situation and in the family situation.

- Whatever our decision, we have to be ready to face the outcomes, whatever they may be. That is why one should think of finding ways to succeed rather than overthinking things.

- Whether you get a job or run your own business, financial planning is important in both cases. You can lead a prosperous and satisfying life when you plan your finances well. We will learn about financial planning in the next chapter.

> 'If we command our wealth, we shall be rich and free. If our wealth commands us, we are poor indeed.'—Edmund Burke

• Part 2 •

Financial Planning

Debt

Income

Investment

Saving

Budget

Money Works

Your Plan

Reality

Money Works

What Experience Reveals

Most of us live simple and straightforward lives; 90 per cent of our lives follow a pattern—school, college, job, marriage, life after marriage and retirement. We try hard to plan our lives. For example, in our twenties, we plan to finish our studies, buy a home by age twenty-seven, a car by age twenty-nine, and so on.

- Our dreams need to be converted into goals to bring them to life. Pre-planning and execution are essential to achieve these goals. Also, backing our dreams with financial planning is important.

- Most of us realize the importance of financial planning only as we cross our forties; however, if we had realized the need for it in our twenties, a lot of our issues of the present might never have surfaced.

'We do plan our finances but that does not last long.'

'Is financial planning really necessary?'

> 'काल करे सो आज कर, आज करे सो अब ।
> पल में प्रलय होएगी, बहुरि करेगा कब ॥'
> —संत कबीर
>
> *'Do the work today that you are leaving for tomorrow and do the work now that you are leaving for today. Your life will be over in a matter of time, then when will you do so many things?'—Sant Kabir*

'Financial planning is not as easy as it seems.'

We hear such statements about financial planning.

Financial planning is clearly not unnecessary, and it is actually neither difficult nor impossible. It is a simple and straightforward process. What is really needed is to do it with the right intention and make sure you are proceeding with diligence.

How financially illiterate people live their life

| 0-20 | 20-60 | After 60 |

ℂ Birth	ℂ Start earning income	ℂ Retirement
ℂ Childhood	ℂ Being unsure about what one wants	ℂ Complaining about the past and mistakes thereof
ℂ Education		
ℂ College life	ℂ Increasing needs and desires	
ℂ Enjoyment	ℂ Running after money without deciding financial goals	ℂ Being sad about missed opportunities
ℂ Deciding a career	ℂ Working and just working day and night	ℂ Repeatedly talking about what could have been done
	ℂ Thinking about financial stability and peace of mind only once in a while	

Example of an Ideal Financial Plan

- Prahlad was born in a small village sixty-five years ago which had neither electricity nor a school back then. He was the eldest among five siblings. They had a very humble family background, both parents being illiterate. They did not own land in the village and were daily wage earners, barely managing to survive through the month.

- The parents were determined that their children should not remain illiterate like them. Prahlad studied in a local school till class four, after which he moved to a bigger school in town. He was aware of his family's financial condition and was determined to study well and get scholarships in order to continue learning. When in college, he started working part-time to cover his education and living expenses.

- He got placed as a teacher in a local government school. As an earning member of the family, he was responsible for the education of his four younger siblings and the medical expenses of his parents. In the meantime, he got married to his colleague, Vidya. A few days post-marriage, they sat, planned their finances and executed their plans seriously.

- Their workplace was about 25–30 km away from their home. They used to leave their children with their parents or in a daycare facility and travel to work on a two-wheeler, irrespective of whether it was raining or blazing hot. Being in a teaching job at a government school, they were liable to be transferred too. So, at times, they had to travel in two different directions. They avoided purchasing a four-wheeler because they had prioritized saving for their children's education. They bought a home by saving money over the years and by curtailing all unnecessary expenses. Occasionally, they were also able to help their family members with finances.

- Their son got admission to a medical college while their daughter got into an engineering college after their class twelve board exams. Both admissions were impossible to complete without payment of donation fees. The savings they had planned for long back came to their rescue. They paid the donation fees and both children successfully finished their studies and went on to find stability in their careers.

- The speeches given by Prahlad and Vidya at their retirement ceremony were inspiring. They said that instead of looking at what others were doing, they simply planned for how they wanted their lives to be. They earned money, planned their finances well, spent money where required and enjoyed their wealth to the fullest.

> 'Savings without a mission is garbage. Your money needs to work for you, not lie around you.'—Dave Ramsay

Financial Planning—A Continuous Process

Time	✓	✗	✓
Money	✗	✓	✓
Energy	✓	✓	✗

- Many of us feel that financial planning is a waste of time. The reason for this is that we do not have the attitude of 'digging your well before you're thirsty'.

- The ones who plan their finances only to cover emergencies definitely feel this is a useless exercise. Finance management is not temporary or situation based, rather, it is a continuous process.

- We cannot manage our finances until we do not understand our mindset towards expenses and the ways in which we can save money.

- For example, by the time your kids turn eighteen, you will need around Rs 25 lakh per child for their education. You need proper financial planning and investment to achieve that. However, whether you put your money in Sukanya Samruddhi Yojana, where you invest a fixed sum every month, or invest that money in a high-risk high-return equity mutual fund, is entirely up to you.

- Attempting to save money while facing financially turbulent times does not mean financial management. Financial management begins with preparing yourself both mentally and financially to face such emergencies.

- People who plan their finances well can manage to take early retirement from their jobs too.

- That only those born with a silver spoon in their mouth get into business is a grave misconception. Many successful businessmen have started their businesses from scratch. Similarly, being employed in a high-profile job or earning a salary in lakhs are not signs of financial success. In fact, how one secures one's future through planning and by growing one's wealth decides the degree of financial independence one will enjoy life.

When Do You Start Financial Planning?

- A popular quote says, 'Time is money'. You have got to understand the value of time—and in good time. There is no fixed time for financial planning. You should start financial planning at the earliest possible time!

- Life can be broadly divided into four stages—childhood, adolescence, adulthood and old age. Generally speaking, the day you start earning independently is the day you should start your financial planning.

What Does Financial Planning Mean?

- Financial planning is a way of achieving various goals in your life by properly managing your income.

- A well-defined financial strategy helps you control your expenses, save, invest and achieve specific goals within a stipulated time span.

Diversity in Financial Planning

- Financial planning could mean different things to different people because everyone has different goals in mind. For some, their goal could be to build a corpus for retirement, and for others, it would be to send their children to a foreign country for higher education. A few others would want to create an additional stream of income for themselves.

- Financial planning could also mean taking decisions related to your career or getting yourself insured.

- In fact, financial planning is the process of achieving financial goals through a well-defined financial strategy. Since every person and family lead a different life, each should thoughtfully plan their finances in order to fulfil their specific needs and achieve their specific goals.

Financial Mistakes Made at Various Life Stages

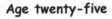

Age twenty-five

- Financial Illiteracy
- Not being serious about repayment of loans
- Casual approach towards retirement planning
- Not giving importance to investments
- Lack of understanding of how compounding works

Age thirty

- Spending money on expensive and often unnecessary things
- Undefined savings
- Short-sighted financial point of view
- Buying unnecessarily large homes
- Investing in homes beyond one's affordability

Age forty

- Not ready to change job/career
- Increasing credit card dues
- Not making a will, thinking it is too early at this age
- Not having enough savings for retirement planning

Age fifty

- Incurring unnecessary expenses while being on the edge of retirement
- Using retirement funds without discipline
- Paying off collateral loans before repaying other loans
- Taking retirement expenses lightly

Saving Money at All Costs Does Not Mean Financial Planning

Spending the right amount of money at the right place and for the right reason and at the right time needs planning. An obsession with savings can be irritating and stressful. Let us look at an example.

- Rishikesh had just started to earn. He had dreamt of owning an iPhone since the time he was a student. A few months into earning, he managed to buy one for himself with the help of some savings, and the rest was financed by a loan. You might feel he is not in his senses. Who buys an iPhone as soon as one starts earning?

- We will now look at the other side of this story. The iPhone that was Rishikesh's constant companion motivated him to work harder. This shows that efforts backed by the right intent can help one earn more.

- You should definitely buy or do something that can boost your morale, even if it is expensive. But you will mess up, the moment you start attaching your ego to every purchase.

- You have two options in the matter of self-grooming—one is to buy branded, expensive clothes and accessories, and the other is to buy clean and right sets of clothes and accessories that are budget buys but look good on you.

- Think about whether the four-wheeler you are about to buy is fulfilling your need and adds to your convenience or is just a product to impress others and show off.

- You need to understand the fine line between the happiness of being able to spend on something that will truly fulfil you and extravagance. Ultimately, it is every individual's decision as to what he will spend his wealth on, and how.

Just Saving Money Does Not Mean Financial Planning

- Just saving money is not enough. Investing the saved money in trustworthy investment options at definite intervals is important too.

- Inflation devalues your money. That is why the value of today's Rs 100 will be reduced by tomorrow. This makes investment all the more important.

- Once you understand your goals and your current standing, you can plan how effectively you can reach your destination.

> 'Even an emperor is no match for a man with no wants.'—Maharishi Raman

Checklist for Successful Financial Planning

1. **Plan your finances as early as possible:** Delaying financial planning is injurious to your long-term financial health. Don't start financial planning when emergencies arise.

2. **Stay away from an extravagant lifestyle:** Always remember: Celebrating with borrowed money is a short-lived joy and a long-term burden.

3. **Avoid overuse of credit cards:** One should use a credit card only when it is absolutely necessary. Using it just to avail of offers should be avoided.

4. **Avoid comparing your situation with others:** Know your limits. Instead of looking at what others are buying, think about whether those items are necessary and affordable for you. Understand your situation before spending.

5. **Prioritize savings over spending:** Expensive cars, gadgets and lifestyle choices may make you look rich, but will not make you a rich person. Prioritize saving and investing your earnings.

6. **Save at least 5–10 per cent of your earnings every month:** The first step in financial planning is to save every month and invest it to provide for emergencies.

7. **Avoid financial investments you don't understand:** It is best to stay away from the type of investments you have no clue about. In case you still want to go ahead, do so with the help of a financial adviser. Practise caution while investing.

8. **Buying an insurance cover is a must:** Insurance is not an investment but a productive tool to financially cover yourself or your family members in emergencies. That is why everyone should get health insurance, accidental insurance and term insurance.

9. **Invest for the long term:** To get the benefit of compounding, invest a major portion of your savings in long-term options.

10. **Regularly re-evaluate and review your financial strategies:** You may have planned a robust financial strategy but failed to implement it or made a few wrong financial decisions. To understand this, you need to frequently review your financial strategies.

    o   **Re-evaluation:** The goals based on which we decided on our investments in the past may change. For example, you may feel that saving money for your children's higher education is more important than buying an expensive car, which was your earlier goal.

o   **Review:** We can re-prioritize our goals based on our current needs, after periodical reviews.

11. **Discuss your strategy with your partner:** Have a healthy discussion with your partner about your financial goals. Whether your partner is an earning member or not, you should consider their point of view as well.

12. **Be ready for change:** Life is full of surprises—be prepared, mentally and financially, to face any unexpected situations that may arise.

13. **Read up on financial matters:** You should regularly engage with financial newspapers, magazines, blogs and social media pages. Also, you should have books on the subject handy in your personal library.

14. **Don't be an emotional fool!** Many a time we make decisions based on our emotions, which may lead to financial losses. Hence, you should stay away from these six age-old enemies of the mind: lust (*kama*), anger (*krodha*), greed (*lobha*), arrogance (*mada*), attachment (*moha*) and jealousy (*matsar*), while making your financial decisions.

15. **Self-confidence is essential:** No one can play your part better than you. That is why you need to study the subject of finance in depth and make the right decisions to get the most out of your wealth.

With this checklist, you can start financial planning based on the goals you want to achieve. All the best!

Financial Planning Flowchart

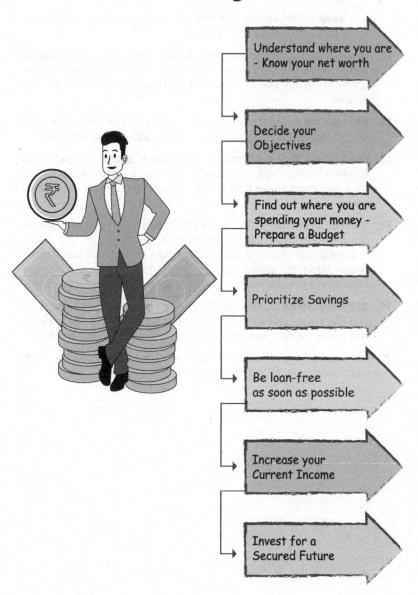

Understand where you are
- Know your net worth

Decide your
Objectives

Find out where you are
spending your money -
Prepare a Budget

Prioritize Savings

Be loan-free
as soon as possible

Increase your
Current Income

Invest for a
Secured Future

What Do You Really Want in Your Life?

यो ध्रुवाणि परित्यज्य ह्यध्रुवं परिषेवते ।

वाणि तस्य नश्यन्ति अध्रुवं नष्टमेव ही ॥

—चाणक्यनीती

(If you leave aside the task that is sure to succeed for the task
that may not, the former is sure to fail along with the latter,
which may go the same way.)

- If you are unsure of where you are heading, you will reach nowhere. That is why deciding on your goals is the most important step in the financial planning journey.

- Our financial goals should cover more than just our basic necessities of food, clothing and shelter. What could be the reasons for our not achieving our financial goals? Where are we going wrong? Are we not trying hard enough? A lot of us find solace in blaming our luck for our situation. But the real reason behind our unfulfilled dreams is our lack of seriousness about them.

- Every task has a predefined timeline at the workplace. You plan your work accordingly. It is only after completing the predefined tasks that you start aiming for goals such as increments, promotions, off-site foreign projects, etc.

- Many of us plan our finances but only a few succeed; those who succeed have plans backed by strong goals and objectives.

- Only we can think up our dreams and goals. Whatever the goals—higher education, foreign travel, buying a home, car, vacations, planning for your children's education, retirement planning, etc.—they need to be prioritized and their financing planned accordingly.

Benefits of Deciding on Goals—Real-Life Examples

Money is important in life as it helps ease many things and opens a lot of opportunities. But in many instances, the power of money fluctuates, based on how we use it. Many are completely unaware of this. Let us look at one illustration of this:

- Both Aditya and Nikita earn a decent income every month. But they are yet to achieve financial stability in their lives. They face a financial pinch towards the end of the month. They have to wait for the next month's salary if they have to buy something. Their disputes would generally revolve around money.

- Why are they in such a situation? The reason—their lifestyle! They frequently buy new gadgets, expensive watches, footwear, furniture and electronic appliances, go shopping, eat out and party, depleting their bank balance. At one time, Nikita got hit hard when she saw zero balance in her bank. That was when she realized her mistakes.

'Some people dream of success while others wake up and work.'—Grant Cardone

- Nikita's debit card was rejected because of insufficient balance at a local grocery shop. The shopkeeper knew her. He gave her whatever she had come to buy and told her she could pay later. She felt bad, but this also brought her to terms with reality. A few similar incidents were enough to make her understand the importance of financial planning, saving, investing, etc. She was now constantly telling herself, 'I will just sit and do financial planning.'

- Nikita told her husband, Aditya, about the situation, and they started taking financial planning seriously. They decided on their goals and started keeping a record of all their expenses.

- Once their financial goals and priorities were set, they started setting 20 per cent of their earnings aside. They curtailed their unnecessary expenses. While planning their investments, they decided to invest 50 per cent of their savings in high-risk equity mutual funds, 20 per cent in recurring and fixed deposits, 10 per cent in gold and 20 per cent for repayment of their home loan.

- Once they were set on their journey, they were looking at newer dreams as they were now backed by savings and investments. Within six months, financial discipline had become an important part of their lives.

- They found it hard to understand the share market and how investing in it worked. But a few ups and downs later, they started regularly following financial news, blogs and websites. A few books on finance made it to their library. They also consulted a good financial adviser to help them with their financial planning.

- It would have been surprising if these efforts didn't pay off! Their financial planning started to bear fruit. Today, fifteen years into it, they have huge investments, a big house, a farmhouse and two cute kids. Both Nikita and Aditya have also planned for their retirement and are now enjoying life to the fullest.

By now you must have understood the importance of deciding on goals. But you need to understand the difference between needs and wants before deciding on your goals.

> *'Our goals can only be reached through a vehicle of a plan, in which we must fervently believe, and upon which we must vigorously act. There is no other route to success.'*—Pablo Picasso

Understanding the Difference between Needs and Wants

Needs	Wants
• You cannot live without fulfilling your needs. E.g.: Food, home rent or home purchase, medical expenses, house maintenance, education, repayment of home loan, etc.	• Wants are not essential to be fulfilled to live a good life. E.g.: Jewellery, interiors, furniture, travel, films, expensive gadgets, accessories, shopping and partying
• Needs do not usually change from time to time	• Wants change according to your situation
• Needs do not usually differ from person to person	• Wants differ from person to person
• Needs are usually limited	• Wants are unlimited

'Money grows on the tree of persistence.'—Japanese Proverb

Understand the difference between **needs** *and* **wants**

01 Which expense is a need and which one is a want? Answer these easy questions to find out.

	Yes	No
a) I cannot live without these expenses		
b) Can I operate without incurring these expenses?		

If the answer to above questions is

 Yes It is a want. *and* **No** It is a need.

02 Prepare a list

 Need

Food, clothing, shelter, home, medicines, cleanliness, education, domestic expenses, loan repayment

Want

Buying an expensive car than what is required, jewellery, interiors, flamboyant lifestyle, travel, expensive smartphones, eating out frequently, shopping, parties

 03 Strike a fine balance between Needs and Wants

How Do You Decide on Financial Goals?

The following steps must be followed while deciding on one's financial goals.

- Step 1: Write down all your goals on a sheet of paper and prioritize them

- Step 2: Decide on the timeline for the goals

- Step 3: Plan for all goals in a SMART way

- Step 4: Decide on a framework

- Step 5: Review your goals regularly

Step 1: Write down all your goals on a sheet of paper and prioritize them

- List all your expenses, income and savings. It is important to think practically while prioritizing your needs and income.

- Example: While choosing between retirement planning and a foreign trip, one would naturally choose planning for retirement.

- Discuss your goals with your partner. If you are married, discuss your goals with your husband or wife. This way, you will find strong support, making your journey easy; it will also lead to a stronger relationship with your partner.

'I saw that it was the artificial needs of life that made me a slave; the real needs of life were few.'—William James Dawson

Financial Goals—Age-Group-Wise

Deciding on goals is very important in financial planning. Your goals and objectives may upgrade or change as you grow in your job or business, or as you grow older. Let us look at the journey of a person's financial goals.

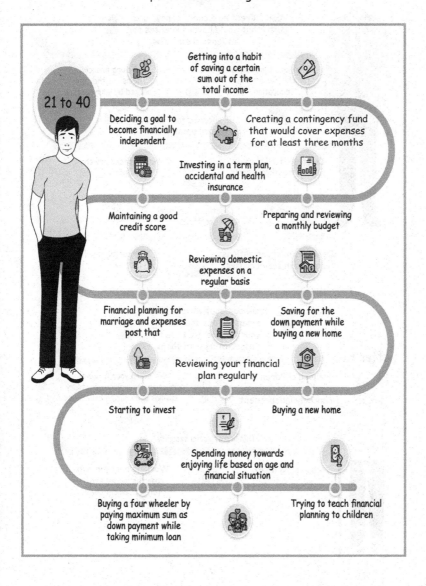

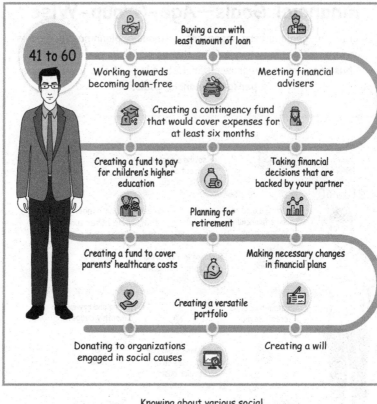

41 to 60

Buying a car with least amount of loan

Working towards becoming loan-free

Meeting financial advisers

Creating a contingency fund that would cover expenses for at least six months

Creating a fund to pay for children's higher education

Taking financial decisions that are backed by your partner

Planning for retirement

Creating a fund to cover parents' healthcare costs

Making necessary changes in financial plans

Creating a versatile portfolio

Donating to organizations engaged in social causes

Creating a will

After 61

Knowing about various social organizations and putting your time to good use by associating with them

Helping children to an extent they become financially independent

Reviewing your financial situation and making necessary savings by reducing expenses

Thinking of social security

Addressing health issues in time

Working part-time in case the money saved for retirement does not seem enough

Step 2: Deciding the timelines for your goals

- It is extremely important to categorize your goals. Goals can primarily be categorized into short-term, mid-term and long-term.

- Mid-term goals need to be considered while planning for short-term goals, and long-term goals need to be looked at while planning for mid-term goals.

- In most cases, long-term goals are not regarded with the same seriousness as the short and mid-term goals. In fact, long-term goals are the most important ones. You may take a certain number of years chasing them. Your ideal timeline to achieve them may change, based on your financial situation, but you will have to decide on the timeline to achieve your goals based on your situation.

a. Long-term financial goals

The most common examples of long-term financial goals are:

- Becoming loan-free

- Buying a home

- Retirement planning

- Financial independence

- Prioritize your goals, depending on which stage of life you are at.

- You may have two or three long-term financial goals, but usually the lesser the number the better. They can be goals such as, 'I have bought a home and am loan-free. Now I am going to put my efforts into planning my retirement and becoming financially independent.'

b. Mid-term financial goals

- Prepare for your mid-term financial goals based on your long-term goals. Most of us commit the mistake of putting in separate efforts to achieve our various goals. 'Divide your goals, not your efforts.'

- Let us look at an example: The base needs to be strong when one wants to construct a high-rise building. While constructing it, the builders do not just think of the first floor but about every floor right up to the top floor. Every floor is designed keeping in mind the goal

> 'Give me six hours to chop down a tree and I will spend the first four sharpening the axe.'—Abraham Lincoln

of building the top floor. You need to plan for your financial goals in a similar way. If the building has twelve floors, the top four are your long-term goals, the bottom four—your short-term goals and the middle four—your mid-term goals.

The table below can guide you in planning your mid-term goals.

Long-term goal	Mid-term goals (based on long-term goals)
Becoming loan-free	• Repaying loans that have higher interest rates • Repaying loans that have smaller outstandings
Buying own home	• Saving for a fund that covers at least 20 per cent of the cost of a new home for down payment • Curtailing unnecessary expenses • Searching for a home
Retirement planning and financial independence	• Saving at least 50 per cent of one's income • Planning for tax savings and investing in options that give good returns

c. Short-term goals

• Your short-term goals should be aligned with your mid- and long-term goals. The first four floors in the example above were short-term goals. The base needs to be strong in order for the building to rise to twelve floors.

• Every goal should be important to us. The efforts at every step should be useful in meeting the next goal too. That helps in saving time, money and effort to an extent.

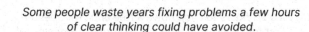

Some people waste years fixing problems a few hours of clear thinking could have avoided.

Step 3: Plan for your goals in a SMART way

Why not plan your goals in a smart way?

A globally used method of goal setting has helped many people set and measure their progress in the accomplishment of their goals.

S.M.A.R.T. GOALS

S SPECIFIC	**M** MEASURABLE	**A** ACHIEVABLE	**R** RELEVANT	**T** TIMEBOUND
Decide every goal with utmost clarity. Find out what you really want to achieve.	Decide on how you would measure the goal. This helps in understanding how much and what needs to be done.	Your goals should be in line with your capacity, experience and present situation.	Are your goals aligned to your dreams and long-term goals?	Decide a timeline to achieve every goal. By when do you want to achieve your goal?

Specific	Decide on every goal with utmost clarity. Find out what you really want to achieve.	
	General	**Specific**
	I want to save a lot	I will save Rs 10,000 every month
Measurable	Decide on how you would measure your progress towards the goal. This will help you understand how much and what needs to be done.	
	Non-measurable	**Measurable**
	I want to buy a home	I want to buy a home for Rs 25 lakh for self-use and will save Rs 2.5 lakh towards a down payment for it.
Achievable	Your goals should be in line with your capacity, experience and present situation.	
	Unrealistic	**Realistic**
	I am going to buy a Mercedes to travel to work in the next year. I watch a lot of motivational videos. I am twenty-five years old and my monthly income is Rs 40,000.	I am going to buy a four-wheeler that I can afford in the next year. Although buying a Mercedes is my dream, I will fulfil that a few years down the line.
Relevant	Are your goals relevant to your long-term goals and dreams?	
	Irrelevant goal	**Relevant goal**
	I have a huge loan to pay off. But I am sure the loan will be paid off by the intervention of some divine help.	I am studying my current situation and am trying to allocate maximum savings towards repaying my loan.

'Don't be afraid to fail. Be afraid not to try.'—Michael Jordan

Time-bound	Decide on a timeline for the achievement of every goal. By when do you want to achieve your goals?	
	Not bound by a timeline	**Bound by timeline**
	• I like to think that I will be investing in mutual funds	• I am going to start a mutual fund SIP of Rs 2500 from next month
	• I want to invest in a retirement fund	• I am going to save 10 per cent of my income and create a fund for my retirement
	• I keep thinking of becoming loan-free	• My wife and I are going to repay an additional 10 per cent of our EMI and pay off our loan in the next five years

Step 4: Decide on a framework

● Make a list of all the things you will require to achieve your goals.

● For example, your actions could be as follows: Start saving money in a savings account, which will earn interest for the next fifty-two weeks. Choose a bank for it and set auto-debit instructions to deduct an amount for saving.

Step 5: Review your goals regularly

● Your efforts and planning need to be reviewed on a regular basis to understand if you are on the right track.

● The more you focus on your goals, the more your mind will work towards achieving them. With regular reviews, you can get a sense of the progress you are making, leading to more excitement on your part towards achieving your goals. Regular review is also important to remain excited about your goals over a longer period of time.

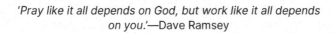

'Pray like it all depends on God, but work like it all depends on you.'—Dave Ramsey

● Look at the table below:

Financial goals	Timeline for achievement	Review
Long-term	Five+ years	Yearly
Mid-term	One to three years	Quarterly
Short-term	Less than one year	Monthly

Points to remember during your review process:

1. Do not avoid reviews. They are important to find out whether your financial planning is being executed the right way and within the right time frame.

2. Our goals may change according to our needs. The time it may take to achieve a goal may also change. Avoid being stubborn while reviewing your goals. Be ready to accept changes, if required. However, frequent changes should also be avoided.

3. Don't be afraid to commit mistakes. A few decisions might not go your way. But not taking any action to avoid committing mistakes would be a bigger mistake. This is termed 'analysis paralysis'. It is important to understand that perfect decisions cannot always be taken.

4. Don't keep crying over financial mistakes. There is no life without mistakes, and a wise man accepts that and moves forward.

> 'We don't have to be smarter than the rest. We have to be more disciplined than the rest.'—Warren Buffet

Think about your goals and objectives and sort them according to the table below:

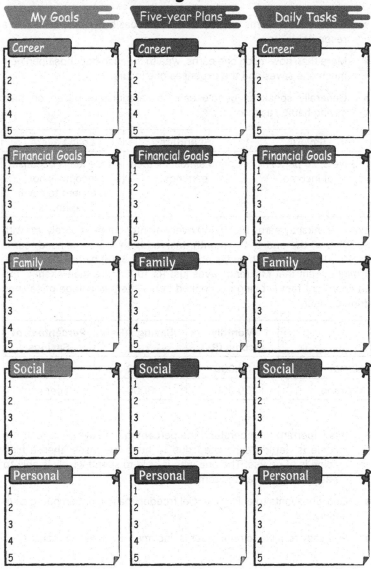

My Goals	Five-year Plans	Daily Tasks
Career 1 2 3 4 5	**Career** 1 2 3 4 5	**Career** 1 2 3 4 5
Financial Goals 1 2 3 4 5	**Financial Goals** 1 2 3 4 5	**Financial Goals** 1 2 3 4 5
Family 1 2 3 4 5	**Family** 1 2 3 4 5	**Family** 1 2 3 4 5
Social 1 2 3 4 5	**Social** 1 2 3 4 5	**Social** 1 2 3 4 5
Personal 1 2 3 4 5	**Personal** 1 2 3 4 5	**Personal** 1 2 3 4 5

Where Is Your Hard-Earned Money Being Spent?

- Every person earns money to fulfil his basic needs and to live a respectable life.

- More than how much one earns, wealth creation depends upon how much one saves and the expenses one incurs.

- Generally speaking, people can be categorized, based on their saving habits, as follows:

Savers	Spenders	Loan Lovers
Save 5–20 per cent of income	Spend almost all their earnings	Take loans because income is not sufficient to cover expenses

Example: Akshay earns Rs 50,000 every month, but he is barely left with Rs 2000 at the end of the month. Makrand, on the other hand, earns Rs 30,000 every month and is able to save Rs 3000 by the month-end. It might seem that Makrand saves just Rs 1000 more than Akshay, but an important fact is being overlooked here—the percentage of savings done by each.

	Monthly income (Rs)	Savings (Rs)	Percentage of Savings
Akshay	50,000	2000	4 per cent
Makrand	30,000	3000	10 per cent

- It is important to understand the percentage of savings here. If the income is getting exhausted due to huge expenses, then a high income is of no use. The one who is able to spend wisely is able to create wealth in the long term.

- One who wants to enjoy financial freedom has no option but to save and invest.

- The easy formula to remember is: Income – Savings = Expenses

'When I had money, everyone called me brother.'—Polish proverb

- Savings can be increased by either reducing expenses or by increasing income. Earning income is dependent on multiple factors and may need additional effort at times. In comparison, reducing expenses may seem easy.

- Spending only as much as is needed is the basic rule of savings. Many of us are now used to increasing our expenses based on our future income by way of credit card use and easily available personal loans. In such a scenario, reducing expenses may seem a difficult task.

- Today, people are focused on finding ways to spend rather than on finding ways to save. Thomas Jefferson said, 'Never spend before you earn.' But today we see many offers for all kinds of products and services, which lead to unnecessary expenses.

- Example: Ganesh had just got his job appointment letter. He was supposed to join after three months on a decent salary. Ganesh spent a lot of money on branded clothes, shoes and watches to create an impression at his future workplace. But the company cancelled all new appointments because of the coronavirus pandemic. Forget savings, Ganesh had spent even before he began to earn.

- You literally have a thousand ways to spend, but the same is not true in the case of earnings. That is why you need to think of your budget, savings and financial goals.

- Why, where, on what and how much to spend would depend on the person in question. Having said that, if you keep in mind your income and savings, you will not feel the burn of expenses.

> *'Money is not the most important thing in the world. Love is. Fortunately, I love money.'*—Jackie Mason

How to Become Poor

Why do some poor people remain poor forever? These are some of the reasons:

- Not looking for any ways to earn more

- Not putting your skills and potential to use

- Spending money without thinking

- Always finding the need to take a loan

- Blaming others

- Thinking money making is a job of greedy and selfish people

- Living a flamboyant lifestyle without earning or investing enough

- Ignoring financial education

Reasons Why People Do Not Save

1. Inability to Save

- We have a huge group of people that are unable to save any money owing to their meagre earnings. This group often finds it hard to save anything.

- Lifestyle expenses cannot go below a certain level. Increasing income is the only available option here.

> 'That man is richest whose pleasures are cheapest.'—Henry David Thoreau

2. Competition and Envy

अर्थनाशं मनस्तापं गृहे दुश्चरितानि च ।

वञ्चनं चापमानं च मतिमान् न प्रकाशयेत् ॥

—चाणक्यनीती

(A wise man never talks to anyone about his wealth, anger,

family issues and bad people around him.)

- Social media trends have led to people wanting to flaunt their wealth in the virtual world, even if that means taking loans and adding to their financial debt. Envy of the other has been around for ages, and social media has further fuelled the feelings of envy and struggle among people. Many spend just to make others envious.

- Example 1: Purchase of a fancy car

  o When a friend buys a car and shares a photo of it on social media, we are afraid we might be left behind in the race and become desperate to buy a similar or bigger car.

  o In this case, questions such as 'do we need this car', or 'do we have enough savings to afford one' take a back seat.

  o You will end up buying a similar or bigger car on a loan if you are envious of your friend. Instead, you should be happy for your friend.

- Example 2: Activity of neighbours

  o Your neighbours are renovating their home. They have chosen bright paints and the latest designs in furniture. You suddenly feel your home looks old and outdated, despite the fact that you renovated it just two years back.

  o In fact, you should appreciate your neighbours and feel happy for them. Instead, you feel the urge to do something in your own home out of envy.

  o You spend a big sum on a new couch or television. We do not know whether the neighbours planned for financing their renovation, took a loan or got some money from the sale of ancestral property. But we jump to the conclusion that they are spending money freely and want to feel equal or better than them. And we end up spending too.

> *We don't buy things with money, we buy them with hours from our lives.*

- People are too conscious about the image others have of them. We are always trying to create a particular image of ourselves in the minds of others.

- We label others as misers, hoarders, generous, philanthropists, studious, avid readers, humorous, boring, etc. Similarly, we spend a lot to show our 'class', 'status' and 'standard of living' and to maintain our 'image'.

- We think others will reject, avoid or stop thinking about us if we don't spend money, leading to losing the race of life. This leads to our getting stuck in the vicious circle of buying unnecessary, expensive items, replacing perfectly working TVs and refrigerators with the latest ones, bought on loans.

- Thomas Cooley was a renowned nineteenth-century judge in the US. His thoughts echo well here:

  - I am not who you think I am;

  - I am not who I think I am;

  - I am who I think you think I am

3. The Family's Wrong Point of View about Money

- Parents always make sure they teach good things to their children. A few children, however, are self-taught in many matters. Some things children learn through observation too.

- Children observe their parents' approach to money too. If the parents are frugal spenders, the children mostly become the same way when they grow up.

- Parents are neither wrong nor right in their financial planning every time. Their decisions are based on their situation and experience. How you react to a similar situation is more important than blaming your parents for the outcome of your choices.

- Financial wisdom and knowledge gained from age and experience should be used to get rid of old opinions and form new ones.

4. Unnecessary Buying

- You feel nice when you use your favourite shopping or e-commerce app or enter your favourite shop or mall. You may buy more online than at a physical store. You are more desperate when you buy online than when you make a physical purchase.

> *'If you're saving, you're succeeding.'*—Steve Burkholder

- The brain releases a chemical known as dopamine,[1] also known as the happy hormone. Once it gets a dopamine high, the mind wants to go through a similar experience, and we start spending more.

- Never buy things without making a list of what you need to buy. This way, you can avoid unnecessary buying and not cross your monthly budget.

Should You Buy It?

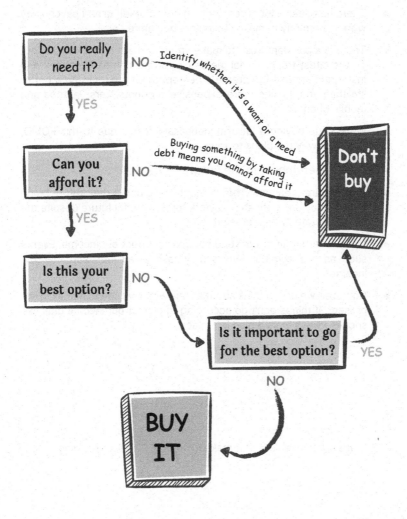

5. Lack of budgeting or planning

- It is difficult to assess the expenses we have incurred if we don't plan or budget for our daily expenses. Instead of 'Income – Savings = Expenses', it is 'Income – Expenses = Savings' for us.

- You will be more aware of the expenses you can avoid if you list your daily expenses in a book or an app. You can also understand which of your expenses are essential and which are not.

6. Expenses Incurred Towards Freedom from FOMO (Fear of Missing Out)

- There has been a lot of research on how marketing and psychology work in harmony to make customers buy more.

- There is a constant push to make you fear that you are missing out on the latest trend. Social media platforms such as Facebook and Instagram are used to create a perception of others living a better life than you, buying more expensive products, cars, laptops and mobile phones.

- We end up buying a lot of unnecessary things due to this FOMO, pushing away our plans to save.

7. Overdependence on the Future

- Humans are dreamers. They are optimistic about their future being bright. They are motivated to work for a beautiful future despite the dreadful state of their present.

- Many factors that are beyond our control affect our income. Events such as war and pandemics may take away jobs and thereby, incomes.

- However, we do not think about all this when we spend money in the present. If things don't go according to plan or our income dips, we should always have a plan B in place.

'It's not your salary that makes you rich, it's your spending habits.'—Charles A. Jaffe

Stay Away from these Financial Mistakes

Lack of financial planning

Spending a lot whenever you get a chance

Buying a more expensive car than you can afford

Always trying to impress others

Buying a more expensive home than you can afford

Making no attempt to become financially literate

8. The Attraction of Branded Products

- It is constantly advertised that a particular brand's usage will create for you a certain image in society.

- We spend more on expensive brands thinking they will take us forward somehow, and this sends our budgets haywire.

- Many brands enjoy a trustworthy, satisfactory and top-graded image in the minds of customers. Our expenses increase and our savings go down when we do not give any thought to whether we can afford or need a branded product before buying one.

9. Instant Gratification

- When you buy grapes, the fruit vendor will offer you a few to taste. If we like the taste, we may buy a bunch of grapes from the vendor. On the contrary, we would not have bought them if they were kept in a sealed box.

- Similarly, we are bombarded with offers, like grapes, all the time. People forget about their savings and budgets and run behind these offers. In such a scenario, we should think of the future benefits of financial planning. This helps us avoid future financial problems.

10. Marketing

- We get to read stories of how celebrities reward themselves with expensive cars, houses and foreign trips.

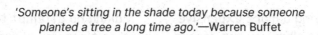

> 'Someone's sitting in the shade today because someone planted a tree a long time ago.'—Warren Buffet

- Advertising has taken over the entire world. We look at advertisements throughout the day on multiple media such as apps, newspapers, television, the Internet, hoardings, malls, bus stops, railway stations and the radio.

- The advertisements say you need to flaunt your wealth. Many a time, if you have had a childhood filled with hardships, you develop a mentality where you want to showcase your achievements to the world, just as depicted in the advertisements.

The following catchphrases and terms make people buy things:

- **Free/Complimentary:** People love to get free stuff. The products that have FREE written in a large font tagged to them usually get sold faster. The quality of this free stuff usually goes unnoticed.

- **Exclusive offer/Special offer:** People do not usually give a second thought when they see these phrases, as they believe that what is on offer will benefit them for sure.

- **Premium quality:** When a product's name is prefixed with the term 'Premium Quality', people think the product really is of high quality. But the reality might be very different.

- **Limited period offer:** This means you have to buy the product without any delay and might lose a huge discount if you do not. People forget that such offers come up every two months under a different name. Examples: Diwali Offer, Women's Day Offer, Independence Day Sale, etc.

- **Offer till stocks last:** This means the offer will only be available on limited stocks of the item and you will have to shell out more money for the same after the offer ends. So, buy immediately and save your money! People take this too seriously and go on stocking unnecessary things.

- **Save value:** Selling the product at a lesser price than its MRP. Example: If a soap costs Rs 10, it is sold at Rs 8. The Rs 2 discount catches the attention of customers. But the weight of the product might also have been reduced, from 100 gm to 80 gm, which might go unnoticed. If you look at the offer closely, there will be no savings in this transaction.

> 'We buy things we don't need with money we don't have to impress people we don't like.'—Dave Ramsay

- Check if you are buying unnecessary things just to get a discount. The new-age shopping malls are designed in such a way that you will get to see a lot of new products displayed, and that pushes you to buy them even if they are not necessary. Example: Displays of chocolates and sweets next to billing counters in the supermarkets.

- **Act Now:** Your brain works faster when you see or read 'Act Now' in an advertisement. Similarly, a few other terms have a psychological effect on us—Powerful, Immediately, More, New, Secret, Effective, Best, Limited, Hurry, Bonus, Deadline, Fast, Cash Offer, First, Greatest, Instantly, Final, Gift, Last Chance, Now, Pay Zero, Final, Effective, Hurry, etc.

11. Easy Availability of Loans

- These days, loans can be availed of easily. Previously, only a handful of banks and financial institutions would give loans, that too at high interest rates. Arranging for the required documents seemed an uphill task. One had to visit a local bank to withdraw money only during stipulated hours. Even items of daily use were bought with hard cash.

- Today, you can spend money whenever and wherever—using debit cards, e-wallets and UPI. With credit cards, one can easily avail of an instant loan of Rs 50,000 to Rs 1 lakh for a forty-five-day interest-free credit period. Gradually, we get used to this.

- Spending money just because 'you have a lot of it' is a grave mistake in financial planning. Using credit cards sparingly and thoughtfully is fine, but their unnecessary use leads to bankruptcy for many financially illiterate people.

The points above will help you spend your income wisely, help you track your expenses and develop the habit of saving. Following these over the long term will be beneficial in wealth creation, in living a happy retired life and in being ready for contingencies.

'Rich people have small TVs and big libraries, and poor people have small libraries and big TVs.'—Zig Ziglar

Small Savings, Large Benefits

Your savings can be seen in your body language. You radiate confidence and positivity when you are backed by savings.

- If you avoid unnecessary expenses and save that money, you will be able to build a large corpus that would be helpful in the future.

- Example 1: Nisha and Pankaj's Sunday started with pen and paper. They made a list of new furniture that needed to be bought. They were setting aside a part of their salaries for a few months towards renovating their home.

- Example 2: Raghu, a daily-wage earner, seems happy today. He has got a room on rent and is now going to live there with his wife and children who are currently staying back in the village. He will spend only on what is necessary and save the rest in a bank, as his boss has advised him to.

- Whether it is Nisha-Pankaj or Raghu, they could spend more than what their daily requirements called for. How did that become possible? That is because they had set aside some money from their earnings and had refrained from spending their entire earnings earlier.

अनालोक्य व्ययं कर्ता ह्वानार्थः कलहप्रियः ।

आतुरः सर्वक्षेत्रेषु नरः शीघ्रं विनश्यति । ।

—सुभाषित

(*The one who spends without thinking, fights without asking for help and hurries in everything loses everything quickly too.*)

In simpler words, setting aside a portion of one's earnings as savings and not spending all of one's income is important. Not spending all that you earn and having something left over after your expenses is savings. This equation is applicable in many situations—whether the item in question is money, time, food or water. The formula for savings is universal.

> '*Annual income twenty pounds, annual expenditure nineteen six, result happiness. Annual income twenty pounds, annual expenditure twenty pound ought and six, result misery.*'—Charles Dickens

Why Should We Save?

First Federal Savings and Loan Association, based in the USA, had published an advertisement in the 1960s. It talked about the impact of savings on our daily habits and lifestyle. Whichever period of time or country we come from, the timeless wisdom the advertisement contained will make us save and motivate us to lead a happy and satisfied life.[3]

Living Your Life on Your Terms

- Who doesn't want a quality lifestyle? But to live that, savings are absolutely important.

- You might not believe this, but your savings define the way you stand, walk and speak, and your lifestyle and self-confidence say a lot about it.

- One who does not save is always running around. He has to keep running to make ends meet. He has to take the first available job he gets. He is always full of fear, since any contingency or emergency may derail his life and enslave him.

- Without savings, one is always undertaking favours from someone or the other. While gratitude is a virtue, being helpless and constantly asking for help from someone is a dreadful situation to be in.

- One who has huge savings can live his life on his own terms. He can fulfil his financial needs without haste. He can approach any situation with poise after weighing it and making educated decisions.

- One who saves regularly can give up his job if it is making him go against his principles. But such people usually work towards the betterment of the organization they work for and do not need to quit their jobs.

- One who is constantly thinking of fulfilling his daily needs such as food and rent can never think about his career prospects. He has to sprint towards financial opportunities. Without savings, one leads a life of hurry and haste.

- One who loves to save can steer clear through an emergency and also help his friends and family through their difficult times. That person can face friends, strangers and even enemies with equal confidence. This positive energy helps to shape his personality and character.

- People find an easy escape by saying, 'We don't earn much to save.' But frankly, savings are not dependent on the quantum of earnings.

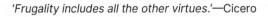

'Frugality includes all the other virtues.'—Cicero

Many people who earn high incomes are seen running around as if they are exercising forever on a treadmill—whatever the number of steps they take, they always find themselves in the same place.

• J.P. Morgan, the dean of American bankers, once said, 'Take waste out of your spending; you'll drive haste out of your life.'

• Even when you are not going to need money for education, a home or for your retirement, you should still save to boost your self-confidence. Your savings are directly proportional to the way you live life on your own terms. Your status in society also depends on how much you have saved.

• Read the lines above that highlight the importance of savings. Print them out if possible and place them on your desk or in your bedroom.

Have You Got Your Formula for Savings Right?

• What is the simplest equation for savings? The amount you save after deducting your expenses from your monthly income, meaning, Income – Expenses = Savings.

• We use our monthly income to cover our monthly expenses. The balance is considered to be savings. What might happen here is that the entire income gets exhausted. What are you left with then?

• Here, in this thought process, your focus is more on expenses than savings. We spend as we want, and the balance, if any, is put into our savings. This way, we are not able to save much and our total savings hardly increase. This is where the flaw lies. 'Income – Expenses = Savings' is a flawed approach.

• The ideal formula with which to approach this matter is **Income – Savings = Expenses**

• We will start saving only when we handle our income based on this formula. How does that work? Before spending the income we get every month, we must set aside a specific sum towards savings. Say, you kept 10 per cent of your income aside as savings; you now have to cover all your expenses with the balance 90 per cent of your income. This way, you will save at least 10 per cent of your income.

> *If you look after the pennies, the dollars will look after themselves.*

- Once you realize that you have only 90 per cent of your income to spend, your spending patterns will change too.

- You will become more cautious while spending, and this will lead to gradually increasing your savings.

- Although increasing your income is important to increase savings, consistently reducing expenses is equally important.

- For example, if you earn Rs 25,000 and want to save Rs 4000, you may start a SIP of Rs 2000 and can invest Rs 2000 in a fixed deposit as an emergency fund. You will be left with Rs 21,000 for your expenses. This way, you can automate both your savings and your investments.

॥ प्रभूतं कार्यमल्पं वा यन्नरः कर्तुमिच्छति ॥

॥ सर्वारम्भेण तत्कार्यं सिंहादेकं प्रचक्षते ॥

—सुभाषित

(*Just the way a lion does, irrespective of whether the task is small or huge, if a man is desirous of doing it, he should put his best into it from the beginning till the end.*)

—Chanakya Niti, Chapter 6, Shlok 16

Saving Rules!

◯ How ordinary people look at saving

Income ▬ Expenses ▬ (SAVINGS)

◯ How extravagant spenders look at savings

Income ▬ Expenses ▬ (LOAN)

You will be debt-ridden as expenses will be higher than the income.

◯ How financially literate and responsible people look at savings

Income ▬ Savings ▬ (EXPENSES)

◯ How financially independent people look at savings

Income ▬ (Investments) ▬ Expenses

Income earned from investments then becomes the capital to cover expenses and is re-invested for future income.

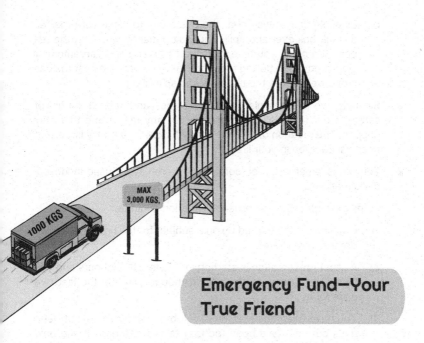

Emergency Fund—Your True Friend

You are the head of the department that constructs bridges. This is going to help in regulating traffic in a big way. You are supposed to decide the weight-bearing capacity of the bridge so that it can handle traffic of 10,000 tonnes every day.

● Will you plan for a weight of 10,001 tonnes or 10,201 tonnes? The traffic could increase on some days and the bridge might weaken, so its capacity might have to be increased to 15,000 tonnes.

● Considering the margin of safety, engineering experts say the capacity of the bridge pool must be 30,000 tonnes when built. The margin of safety concept is built upon the knowledge of engineering and quality control studies.

● We can use the margin-of-safety concept in our daily lives too.

   o   Example 1: You reach the bus stop five minutes early for the 6 a.m. bus. To get there on time, you wake up early, get ready quickly and leave your place at 5.30 a.m.

> 'A simple fact that is hard to learn is that the time to save money is when you have some.'—Joe Moore

- o Example 2: You wait near the gas stove to make sure the tea doesn't boil over and spill. You wait patiently watching the tea boil. At a point, you take it off the flame and add cardamom or cinnamon to the boiling tea. You make sure you are near the gas stove well before the tea boils and spills over.

- Similarly, we need to plan well in advance and keep a margin of safety in our financial life to provide for any misfortune that may happen. The creation of an emergency fund will be a very important financial decision in your life.

- The terms 'emergency' or 'contingency' are usually used in 'do-or-die' situations.

- Some examples of an emergency situation could be:

  1) Opening a book to read up on a subject for the first time a night before one's exam.

  2) A client presentation is starting in the next three hours and you haven't prepared anything for it though you had the last two days for it.

  3) You have been complaining of a toothache for the past fifteen days but you have been too lazy to visit the dentist and now there is a lot of pain.

- We all have to face financial emergencies in our lives. Whomever you may be and whatever you may think of yourself, you will have to face such a situation one or the other time.

- Financial Emergency Fund = Contingency Fund.

1.   The following situations could make for financial emergencies:

- Not getting the expected pay rise.

- Health issues. Accepting low-income jobs due to constant backache caused by the earlier one. Having to find a new job due to the constant strain on the eyes from prolonged use of computers at the current job.

> 'Doing a budget means learning an ancient and powerful
> word: NO!'—Dave Ramsay

- Accidents
- Physical ailments

One should set aside some money to tide over emergencies.

- The following situations are not included in financial emergencies:

  o   Expenses that can be pre-planned, such as the purchase of a home, new car, children's education, etc.

  o   Monthly expenses on medicines to manage lifestyle diseases such as diabetes and hypertension, a laser surgery to get rid of spectacles, hair weaving to cover up one's baldness—these call for pre-planned expenses and are not financial emergencies. One needs to set aside some money from the monthly budget for these expenses.

  o   Last-minute surprise trips to Dubai or Bangkok just because one's friends are insisting. These are not financial emergencies but need to be covered using your monthly budget.

2.   Do you really need emergency funds?

- Creating an emergency fund is the first step in facing a financial crisis.

- Since these crises do not come with a warning, they come along with a few smaller problems too. No one had thought our jobs would be at risk because of the Covid pandemic, or that salaries would not be credited on time and we would have the unforeseen expenses of Covid treatment.

- Since you are not ready to face these crises, they create mental pressure and the problems seem bigger than they really are.

- You should create an emergency fund for yourself, your family and the ones you care for. It is easy if you decide to do it wholeheartedly.

- If you create and review your 'personal budget' regularly, you will be constantly aware of your income and your average monthly expenses.

- Your friends, relatives and seniors will come forward to help in a crisis. But what if everyone is affected by the same crisis? Whom do you look to for help, then? Also, if you are frequently getting into a

A penny saved is a penny earned.

financial crisis, even those who have helped you earlier might start avoiding you.

- You might think you don't need emergency funds if you have a credit card. You could use it in an emergency, but the spends on credit cards are a type of loan and not your own money.

- Emergency funds are your own reserve force that is useful in financial wars.

3. How much should be saved as emergency funds?

Your emergency fund should suffice to buy three to four months of essentials and other expenses.

- These essential items would include milk, groceries, domestic help wages, home rent, school fees, healthcare, insurance, various EMIs, etc.

- You should prepare your list of expenses with honesty. You can prepare this list yourself. You can do it right now too—keep aside this book for a while and list all your expenses on a piece of paper, an app or a spreadsheet.

- **Insufficient funds:** If your emergency fund is less than what is required, it will be exhausted very soon. Only when the fund lasts till the emergency has passed will the objective of the fund's creation have been met.

- **Excess funds:** Also, it won't be right if you are too cautious and have created an emergency fund enough to cover expenses for nine to ten months. Emergencies arise only in exceptional circumstances. That is why investing a large sum in low-return investments can be a loss-making proposition.

4. How to save for emergency funds

- Every drop makes an ocean. Even if this saying is true, do not implement it by allocating very small sums to your emergency fund!

- You cannot create an emergency fund to cover three to four months' expenses overnight. For example, if your monthly salary is Rs 30,000 and you set aside Rs 1000 towards your emergency fund

'You won't always be motivated. You must learn to be disciplined.'—Denzel Washington

every month, it will take you 120 months to save Rs 1,20,000. Also, there is no point in putting aside a huge sum, say Rs 25,000, in an emergency fund every month.

- Emergency funds cannot be created out of the blue. Creating an emergency fund is the first step towards savings, which means controlling your monthly expenses. The Diwali bonus or the amount by which your salary has been raised can initially be used for this purpose.

- Remember this—emergency funds are meant only for emergencies. You should avoid using it every now and then. Never use it for unnecessary expenses or for buying things just to show off.

5. Where do you invest emergency funds?

- The answer to this could be different for different people. But a few fundamentals stay the same for everyone. When you invest in emergency funds, the investment should have an aspect of liquidity.

- Examples: recurring deposits, savings accounts, sweep-in savings accounts, ultra-short-term mutual funds, etc.

- Not everyone will face an emergency situation. That is why one should never keep this fund idle, in an instrument from which you will not get anything in return.

- Not every situation will be a financial emergency. It could just be a temporary financial struggle. The solution to this could be to expand your income sources and reduce expenses wherever possible.

You will discover what your financial position is when you calculate your net worth. We will look at net worth in the next section.

What Is Net Worth?

Net worth means the wealth owned by you! Just knowing the destination is not enough. We also need to know where we have reached today in the journey.

- Our net worth is a measure of our financial health. It shows what we will be left with if we sell all our assets and clear all our liabilities.

- Our financial decisions should help us increase our net worth. This means we should try to increase our assets or reduce our liabilities.

Many net worth calculators are available on the web today, which help you understand what your net worth is. But it is always better to calculate it yourself instead of relying on borrowed wisdom. You need to understand what net worth really means.

● How do you calculate net worth? Scan the QR code to download a spreadsheet.

Visit this page to read various examples of what net worth is, to get references and to download various spreadsheet formats.
https://arthasakshar.com/book

> '*Games are won by players who focus on the playing field, not by those whose eyes are glued to the scoreboard.*'—Warren Buffett

Part 1: Make a list of all your assets and their probable market value

Assets	Amount
Amount saved in bank accounts • Savings • Fixed deposits **Market Value of Investments** • Shares • Bonds • Market value of these **Market Value of Fixed Assets** • Home • Shops • Office • Land (market value would depend on the type of land—non-agricultural/residential/reserved, etc.) • Vehicles **Market value of gold/silver and other precious items**	
Total	

Avoid counting possessions that cost less than your vehicles as your assets.

Example: The amount in your savings account, according to your bank statement. The market value of other assets, such as homes built fifteen years before, needs to be approximated.

When you're having money problems, the first thing to do is quit spending on all things that don't produce money.

Part 2: Make a list of all your liabilities

Liabilities	Amount
Balance of loans Home loan Car loan Personal loan Outstandings on credit card Loan taken from cooperative banks and other financial institutions Money borrowed from others	
Total	

Add all the liabilities to get your total liabilities.

Part 3: Do the Maths

Particulars	Amount
Total Assets	
(-) Less	
Total Liabilities	
Net Worth	

'No one is going to come to your house and make your dreams come true.'—Grant Cardone

Calculation of One's Net Worth

Example 1: Mahesh

Mahesh is thirty-five years old. He has a home worth Rs 22 lakh and an outstanding of Rs 12 lakh on his home loan. A two-wheeler he bought three years ago is worth Rs 20,000 now. His credit card outstandings are Rs 6600. He had borrowed Rs 1,00,000 from an uncle for his mother's medical treatment. He has about Rs 55,000 in his savings account and owns 10 grams of gold.

Assets	Amount (Rs)
● Home	22,00,000
● Two-wheeler	20,000
● Savings account bank balance	55,000
● Gold 10 gm (Rs 55,000 per 10 gm, as per current market value)	55,000
Total assets	23,30,000
Liabilities	
● Outstanding home loan	12,00,000
● Outstanding credit card payment	6,000
● Borrowed money	1,00,000
Total liabilities	13,06,000
Net Worth [Total Assets (-) Total Liabilities]	**10,24,000**

'Without continual growth and progress, such words as improvement, achievement and success have no meaning.'—Benjamin Franklin

Example 2: Neha

Neha is forty-two years old. She owns a home worth Rs 52 lakh. Her home is jointly owned by her husband, and the home loan outstanding is Rs 22 lakh. According to her, the car she bought four years ago, for Rs 8 lakh, is worth Rs 2 lakh now. But her husband thinks the car has been lying around after an accident and will fetch only around Rs 25,000. Neha does not have any other loans or liabilities. She has about Rs 15,000 in her savings account, investment in shares of Rs 2.50 lakh (market value of Rs 1.80 lakh), and investment in mutual funds of Rs 1.50 lakh (market value of Rs 2.80 lakh). She has 40 gm of gold.

Assets	Amount (Rs)
• Home (half of it)	26,00,000
• Four-wheeler	25,000
• Savings account	15,000
• Investment in shares worth Rs 2.5 lakh	1,80,000
• Investment in mutual funds worth Rs 1.5 lakh	2,80,000
• Gold 40 gm (assuming cost of 10 gm at Rs 50,000)	2,00,000
Total assets	33,00,000
Liabilities	
• Outstanding home loan (half of it)	11,00,000
Total liabilities	11,00,000
Net Worth (Total Assets (-) Total Liabilities)	**22,00,000**

> 'Believe you can and you're halfway there.'—Theodore Roosevelt

Example 3: Rahul

Rahul is thirty-five years old. He stays as a tenant. He had taken a loan of Rs 6 lakh to travel to the Himalayas. He bought an expensive mobile phone a year back on a loan of Rs 50,000 and the buy-back cost of it is Rs 0 as the phone is not repairable. Rahul's credit card outstandings amount to Rs 45,000, and money borrowed from friends is Rs 2 lakh. He has about Rs 2000 in his savings account. He has no other assets, loans or liabilities.

Assets	Amount (Rs)
● Money in Savings Account	2,000
Total assets	**2,000**
Liabilities	
● Outstanding personal loan—Himalayan tour	6,00,000
● Outstanding personal loan—mobile phone	50,000
● Outstanding credit card payment	45,000
● Borrowed money from friends	2,00,000
Total liabilities	8,95,000
Net Worth (Total Assets (-) Total Liabilities)	**(-) 8,93,000**

We understand the following aspects when we summarize the three examples we have looked at.

Person	Net Worth (Rs)	
Mahesh (age 35)	10,24,000	Net worth is positive since assets are more than liabilities

> *'One definition of maturity is learning to delay pleasure.'*—Dave Ramsay

Person	Net Worth (Rs)	
Neha (age 42)	22,00,000	Net worth is positive since assets are more than liabilities
Rahul (age 35)	- 8,93,000	Net worth is negative since liabilities are more than assets

What is Negative Net Worth?

● Some people occasionally calculate their net worth and get frightened when they see a negative net worth. For some, their negative net worth is due to their being at the start of their career. For some, it is due to the wrong financial decisions they have made or due to some unfortunate incidents, such as medical emergencies, etc.

● Your net worth will be negative, i) if the loan you have taken to buy your home is greater than the current value of the home, ii) the rate of growth in that home's market value is less than the total interest paid on the home loan till date.

● Loans taken just for fun activities and personal pleasure may lead to reducing your net worth.

● But don't worry! Calculating your net worth is the first step towards financial growth.

● If you control your expenses and save money, that could help you repay your loans faster. Also, you will be left with more money to invest. If you have taken a home loan from a bank, you can pre-pay more than your stipulated monthly instalments and save on future interest expenses.

How Many Times Should I Calculate My Net Worth?

● You should ideally calculate your net worth every three or six months. Your objective should be to increase your net worth. Instead of calculating it just once and forgetting about it, being honest and doing this exercise quarterly or half yearly will definitely help you.

'The greater danger for most of us isn't that our aim is too high and miss it, but that it is too low and we reach it.'—Michelangelo

What Is a Personal Budget?

You might be imagining our finance minister walking with a laptop bag when you hear the term 'Budget'. The best and the most fundamental way to increase your net worth is by preparing your personal budget. Many people avoid such an exercise because they are scared to face reality.

● Creating a personal budget means planning for your personal income and expenses.

● Your budget tells you exactly where you have spent your money instead of letting you wonder about it.

● If you have variable income, you can calculate the average of the last six to twelve months' income and take that as your monthly income. Knowing your average monthly income is important in calculating your personal budget.

● You can stay away from unnecessary expenses and save yourself from depleting your savings.

Who should make a budget? And why?

Everyone should prepare a budget to become loan-free, to plan for retirement and to achieve their financial goals.

How to make a budget

| 1 | Decide to initiate a budget | For someone who lives a financially flamboyant lifestyle, the decision to make a budget is a big thing. Prepare yourself mentally to create a budget. Congratulations on making the first decision towards this exercise. |
| 2 | Check your monthly income | People employed in a job have a fixed income, but those running a business do not! Therefore, business persons should consider the minimum fixed income they make while preparing their budgets. |

'If you aim for nothing, you'll hit it every time.'—Zig Ziglar

3	Calculate your net worth	Once you understand your net worth, you need to focus on how to increase your assets or reduce your liabilities. Example: If you own a home, a plot of land or a flat that is not occupied, you can rent it out to earn additional income, which can be used to repay your loan.
4	Budget your monthly expenses	Categorize your monthly expenses while making your budget ● **Domestic expenses:** Groceries, electricity, medicines, milk, newspapers, domestic help wages, gym, yoga classes, etc. ● **Educational expenses:** School and tuition fees, stationery, school trips, projects, etc. ● **Socializing expenses:** Meeting friends, parties, weddings, birthdays, gifts, etc. ● **Vehicle expenses:** Fuel, small repairs, major repairs, vehicle insurance, etc. ● **Other expenses:** Unplanned expenses such as trips, restaurants, movies, etc. Make a list of fixed and variable expenses after this. ● **Fixed expenses:** Rent, electricity bill, wages for domestic help, home loan EMI, vehicle loan EMI, mobile-DTH-Internet charges, average groceries bill, daily commuting expenses etc. ● **Variable expenses:** Entertainment, gifts, medical expenses, etc. This will not only help you in making your budget but also in understanding your expenses and the areas where you can reduce them.
5	Put this information to use	Compare your budget to your financial situation. You may do this comparison on a sheet of paper, a spreadsheet or an app.

'More important than the will to win is the will to prepare.'—Charlie Munger

6	Review every month	• You will just need ten to fifteen minutes every week to review your budget. What is expected here is 'knowing what you are doing in reality'.
		• This has many long-term benefits. You start accepting your reality and live in the present moment. You keep trying to match your budget even if your expenses exceed it for a few months.

Benefits of Making a Personal Budget

1. You can find a balance between your income and expenses, leading to savings for you. You can fix your financial goals and start putting in efforts towards achieving them.

2. You understand the value of your total wealth.

3. You are better prepared for both planned and unplanned expenses arising in the future.

4. Your family's health gets better as you worry less.

Personal Budget

Monthly Budget of Mrs and Mr _____			
Sr. no.	Income/Source of income (your money comes from here)	Budgeted amount (Rs)	Actual Amount (Rs)
1	Income from salary/business/profit/fees		
2	Interest on savings or term deposits		
3	Interest/dividend/income from investments		
4	Other income		
A. Total Income			
Sr. no.	Expenses/Types of expenses (This is where your money goes)	Budgeted amount (Rs)	Actual Amount (Rs)
1	Daily expenses (groceries, fuel, commuting, rent, etc.)		
2	Personal expenses		

3	Major expenses		
	- Entertainment/Travel		
	- Gifts/Socializing expenses		
4	Emergency expenses—Medicines and Healthcare, etc.		
5	Important liabilities		
	- Car		
	- Insurance		
	- Loan EMI/Credit card bill		
	- Saving for an emergency fund		
	- Other important expenses		
6	Other monthly expenses		
Scan the QR code to download personal budget spreadsheet	**B. Total expenses**		
	Gain / Shortfall (A - B = C)		

Types of Personal Budgets

Preparing a budget is not a difficult task at all. Once you understand it, you can easily prepare both your family and personal budgets.

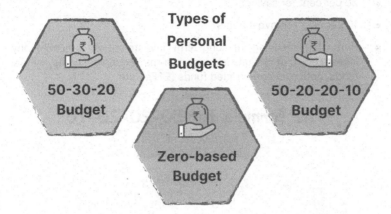

1. The 50-30-20 budget

● Your income is divided into needs, lifestyle and savings in a 50-30-20 ratio.

● Daily needs: 50 per cent of your income goes towards daily needs, such as daily expenses, home rent, groceries, loan EMIs, utility bills, etc.

● Lifestyle needs: 30 per cent of your income goes towards gym, club membership, shopping, eating out, Internet, partying expenses, etc.

● Savings: 20 per cent of your income is set aside for not just savings but also for investments, emergency funds, insurance, etc.

This type of budget accounts for your needs, wants and future needs too.

2. The 50-20-20-10 budget

● This is similar to the 50-30-20 type of budget. In both, 50 per cent is allocated towards daily expenses. But out of the rest, only 20 per cent is allocated to lifestyle expenses instead of 30 per cent and the 10 per cent that remains is left for long-term investments.

In this type of budgeting,

- 50 per cent is for needs
- 20 per cent for wants
- 20 per cent for savings
- 10 per cent for investments
- Here, the meaning of long-term investment is primarily any investment that is high-risk, high-returns. Example: shares, mutual funds, gold exchange traded funds (ETFs), etc.

The formula for 50-20-20-10

3. Zero-based budgeting

- In this type, nothing is left at the end because it is ensured that your total income, minus your expenses, equals zero. Once all the needs are met, the balance amount is used for future planning, investment, social work, enjoyment, etc.

- Every rupee serves the purpose because you're telling every single rupee where to go.

- This type is popular in Western countries and is pretty successful.

You choose the type of budget that you want to make and plan for it accordingly.

Do You Have Fights with Your Partner over Money?

- Today, family members have started to distance themselves from each other. The rising cost of living, cut-throat competition and unrealistic ambitions and dreams are leading to physical and mental pressures in our lives or adding to them.

- Husbands and wives do not find time for each other while chasing their own lives. And if they fight during the little time they do get to spend with each other, then they feel disconnected because of money. Let us look at two examples of this.

- Example 1: Riya and Rohan are a happy couple. Their income is in lakhs, they have a lavish three-bedroom home in the heart of the city, a premium car, a row house in an upcoming premium housing society outside the city and multiple individual investments. Their parents have retired from senior positions and are living self-dependent lives. Yet, both Riya and Rohan have frequent arguments, and the reason is usually Rohan's flamboyant lifestyle. Rohan invests huge sums in the share market without consulting with financial advisers. Riya, on the other hand, chooses traditional options for investment. They end up having disagreements over this.

> 'If something costs $1000, and it is on sale for $750, and then you decide to buy it, you did not save $250. You spent $750.'—Vala Afshar

- Example 2: Sameer and Sonali are a middle-class couple with decent salaried jobs. They used to stay with Sameer's parents in a home owned by his father. A few tussles are expected in a joint family. But his parents would take a step back and incline towards Sameer's views since he was an only child. That was why everything was going well. They had good savings too as they did not have to pay any rent or EMI. But Sonali wanted to live with Sameer in their own home. She was trying to achieve her dream. Although her objective was not wrong, she was a bit overemotional about it. She was acting too cold and practical at times because of this, keeping track of every small expense, thinking of money all the time, even when small amounts were involved. This was not appreciated at all by Sameer. On the other hand, his spending money on his parents and gifting people expensive things for their weddings seemed an issue to Sonali. Their small fights have now turned into a full-fledged war.

- These were a few fictional examples. But almost every couple has these financial arguments at home.

- We will discuss the financial elements that become the strong pillars of the family. Rohan's investments in the share market had become a big headache while his love for online shopping and rising credit card bills were adding more fuel to the fire.

- In the other home, Sonali's stringent expense tracking and fussiness about saving every penny was irking Sameer. Also, Sameer's expenses on his parents seemed to be a problem for Sonali.

- Money is at the centre of the differences between the couples in both of the above examples. The common reasons for arguments among partners over money could include:
  o One partner's high spending or frugal attitude
  o One of them giving money to his or her relatives
  o One hides financial transactions from the other
  o One or the other not taking the partner into confidence before making an investment

> 'It's good to have money and the things that money can buy, but it's good, too, to check up once in a while and make sure that you haven't lost the things that money can't buy.'—George Lorimer

o One or the other partner hiding his or her present financial situation from the other

o Absence of healthy financial dialogue between the couple

- Arguments over financial matters can easily be avoided. Both partners need to understand each other's points of view and discuss their thoughts with each other. This can be achieved by means of the following:

1. **Regular healthy discussions:** One word that describes today's lifestyle is 'busy'. We are active on social media but do not find time for our partner or family. Even if we spend half of our social media time with them, we can solve many of our problems, understand each other better and strengthen relations. Many a time, even small discussions can solve big problems. Arguments over investments, loans, credit card use, etc., can be resolved by means of healthy discussions.

2. **Accepting each other's nature:** Both being a high spender or an extremely frugal person are issues related to one's mentality. Sometimes, the person does realize their ways but cannot help being what they are. At other times, we spend just to impress others or go against our will and do not spend at all. Discussing your nature with your partner and accepting your mistake or getting to understand your partner can solve many issues.

3. **Relatives and financial transactions:** Many a time, interference by relatives in financial matters or help offered to them may lead to arguments between a couple. Some relatives interfere on purpose. In such instances, discussions instead of indulging in blame games can solve problems. Don't borrow from anyone or lend to anyone. Banks are designated to do that. Help your relatives for sure if they are in need, but only after discussing it with your partner.

- Don't hide financial matters from your partner.

- Prioritize your partner and family over everything else.

- Although you cannot ignore that money is an important element in your life, remember that you are incomplete without your partner. That is why you must spend on what is necessary and plan your finances with each other's support.

> *'A journey of a thousand miles must begin with a single step.'*—Lao Tzu

Record-Keeping

Dinesh had parked his bike on the street. A tanker came from the opposite direction and hit his bike, breaking it into pieces. It appeared that Dinesh would have to spend a huge amount on the repair of the bike.

He had saved every penny to be able to buy this bike three years ago. He felt extremely sad to see the condition of his bike; and there would be the load of expenses on repair, on top of that. The only support he had was the bike's insurance policy. But he had completely forgotten the whereabouts of the policy documents since he was busy with his office routine. He turned his home upside down and finally found the papers. But to his bad luck, the policy had lapsed two months ago. Ignoring one small matter now meant he'd have to spend two-and-a-half months' salary to repair his bike.

We come across many situations in life where we have to spend a lot of time and money unexpectedly. Many of us realized only after getting admitted to hospital for Covid treatment that we had not paid the premium for our health insurance. That is why remembering important dates is extremely important.

1. Review your income (where it comes from) and expenses (where your money goes).

2. Record all important dates related to your assets (property, savings, investments, insurance, etc.) and liabilities (credit card bills, home loan, education loan, car loan, etc.).

3. Collate all the information about your budget, savings, investments, taxes, etc.

4. Keeping a record book or file to note down or maintain proofs of financial transactions, such as repayments on loans, new property purchase, deposits in bank accounts, etc. They will come in handy if a discrepancy arises later.

5. Documents such as insurance policy papers and warranty cards help in a smooth claims process. Even after-sales services can be easily availed of when you have the documents handy.

'All your dreams await just on the other side of your fears.'—Grant Cardone

6. At least one person in your life should know about all your financial transactions.

Record-keeping plays an important role in financial planning, for both your present and your future. Record-keeping means keeping all your important documents together and tracking all the important dates.

There are two ways of record-keeping

1. Identifying important documents

- File all your documents in a sequence, including new documents such as renewed policies and annual maintenance contracts (AMCs). Not all documents need to be stored for always. Discard the documents that have expired or are no longer required.

- Arrange all your important documents chronologically, i.e., according to their date of purchase, warranty or validity.

- Keep the file handy in such a way that you can access it any time you want. You can use a paper file, a safe box or a briefcase for this.

- Keep a record of where you have stored all the information on a sheet of paper, mobile or your personal computer.

- Create a simple calendar for payables. (Example: Due dates for payment of credit card bills, insurance premium, deposits, repayment of loans, etc.). You may use a Google spreadsheet or Microsoft Excel, enter the details on a sheet of paper, click a picture of the document or send an email to yourself so that you never lose it.

2. How to keep records

A list of important financial records and documents is given below. You can use this to create your personal and family's list of documents. You can use a basic filing system, such as paper or electronic records, for this.

- Account book: Record your daily income and expenses, future expenses and financial review planning in this.

- Income and work record: Payslips, payment slips, experience certificates.

'Put your heart, mind, and soul into even your smallest acts. This is the secret of success.'—Swami Sivananda

- Income tax records: Records of taxes paid, deductions, receipt of taxes paid, paid tax, exemptions, etc.
- Insurance policy and premium receipt.
- Bank records: Bank statements, updated passbooks, deposit slips, chequebooks, ATM debit cards, credit cards and their PINs.
- Loan records: Terms of agreement, repayment proofs.
- Credit card records: Transaction details of payments done by credit card will help while checking statements.
- Purchase records: Bills (especially of high-end products), warranty cards, customer care numbers, service numbers, etc.
- Investment and property purchase details.
- Your financial objectives, financial resolutions and plans.

You can save these records digitally too.

We will look at the importance of a financial adviser in the next section.

'Perfection is basically a symptom of procrastination.'
—Grant Cardone

Adviser Zaroori Hai!

- In the past, the seniors in the family would be considered as wise persons in financial matters. Later, the role of financial adviser expanded to include post office employees, bank officers, insurance agents and highly educated family members.

- Over time, the scope of investments widened and the importance of financial planning came to light. An independent stream of financial advisers came into existence and the provision of financial advisory services became a profession.

- A good financial adviser helps his clients to become financially literate. When highly educated people lack financial literacy, you can imagine the plight of relatively less educated people.

Do you feel you need a financial adviser?

If the answer to this question is no, then you are yet to understand the importance of a financial adviser.

- Many people hesitate to meet a financial adviser. What different thing will he say? Our money will remain as it is, they think.

- But we are happy and always ready to visit a restaurant and spend thousands. We easily spend Rs 500 on a pizza or a burger, but we are reluctant to pay the financial adviser a small fee.

- You should not be so negative about the professional who is going to plan your finances, which consist of your hard-earned money.

- Many of us have misconceptions about what a financial adviser really does. We think only rich people need an adviser or that the adviser just helps clients in making investments.

- In fact, middle-class people need a good financial adviser more than rich people do, because experience, family background and money-handling habits among the middle class are different. We need expert planners even more when our property and income sources are limited.

'The successful warrior is the average man, with laser-like focus.'—Bruce Lee

The Scope of Financial Planning

We usually hold the misconception that financial planning is needed only while planning our investments. But the scope of financial planning is much wider than that. It is not just for investments, but planning should be done in the following matters too:

● Income and savings

● Understanding the different investment options and their special features

● Understanding the difference between investments and savings

● The risks involved in investing and how to handle them

● Loan management

● Retirement planning

● Tax management

● Emergency funds

● Effect of inflation

● Compounding interest and its benefits

● How much returns can be expected, and many such fundamental things are taken care of by a financial adviser on behalf of her clients.

Who Needs a Financial Adviser, and When?

● You should start financial planning as soon as you begin to earn. Once you save enough money, you need a financial adviser to plan your management of money wisely.

● If you have never asked for a financial adviser and have made some wrong financial decisions, you can still visit a financial adviser and not be hesitant about it.

● A financial adviser can help you in managing your wealth, in tax planning and in investing the lump sum you receive in the form of a bonus, salary raise or similar income. A wrong decision at such a time can lead to financial loss. That is why you must always seek a financial adviser's help in such a scenario.

'Rich people invest. Poor people spend.'—Grant Cardone

- You will also need a financial adviser to manage finances for your family, children and for your life after retirement.

- A financial adviser's job is comprehensive and all-encompassing.

- A lot of people think, 'Why spend money when we can plan for ourselves?' and turn to insurance agents or bank employees for free advice. Nothing in this world comes for free. These agents make money or a commission from the expensive products they sell to you.

- Advice from a financial adviser is beneficial from the investor's point of view in many ways. Example: There are more than fifty mutual funds in India and more than 1000 plans to choose from. Similarly, there are more than twenty-five health insurance companies, and the same is the story with their coverage plans as with mutual funds. You can easily get confused about which plan would be right for you. Your financial advisers help you find a way through the chaos.

- Many people try to make their own financial decisions based on information they get from the Internet. We cannot take all our decisions just on our own merit. The Internet can give you a lot of information, but this does not necessarily mean you have gained knowledge of the financial world. In fact, excess information can be confusing and can lead to wrong decisions on your part. Navigating the financial storm safely is no easy task, but with a financial adviser by your side, the journey becomes hassle-free and a lot more beneficial to you.

- A financial adviser can also help in bringing discipline to your investments and boost your self-confidence during tough times.

A fee of a few thousand charged by an expert financial adviser can help you save lakhs. Look at it as a type of investment and don't hesitate in asking your adviser for help.

> 'Nothing is more difficult, and therefore more precious,
> than to be able to decide.'—Napoleon Bonaparte

Will and Nomination

'मरे एक त्याचा दुजा शोक वाहे।
अकस्मात तोही पुढें जात आहे।।'

—समर्थ रामदास स्वामीं

Speaking about death, Saint Ramdas Swami mentions an incident from the Mahabharata: Yaksha once asked Yudhishthira, 'Which is the most surprising thing in this world?' Yudhishthira replied, 'Many people die in front of our eyes. Yet, the ones that are alive think of themselves as immortals and never even have the slightest thought of death.'

Even we avoid talking or thinking about death, which is inevitable and at times sudden. We always procrastinate giving a thought to what will happen to the wealth we have earned throughout our lives or have inherited, after we are gone. 'I am not going to die any time soon. I will think about it later,' is the reason why we tend to push it for later.

However, Yamraj, the god of death, is least concerned about what you think. Once you take your last breath, Yamdoots, the angels, descend to take you away. They don't ask, 'Uncle, did you create your will? If not, please do it, we will come back in another ten days.'

You should decide to make a will well in time so that your rightful heirs don't fight over the division of your property or someone else does not claim rights to your property. The ones who do not have children also should definitely do this at the earliest.

Important Points about Making a Will

Division of self-acquired property

- A will is a legal document that records the division of property, rights of heirs, guardianship and caretaking of minor children, and provisions made for their future.

- When should you create your will? You should do it as early as possible, when you are physically fit and have an active lifestyle. You may change it in the future if you feel the need to do so. The last will always prevails.

'Stay committed to your decisions, but stay flexible in your approach.'—Tony Robbins

- **How do you create it?**

  o   Put in the details about yourself, your family and how you have accumulated your wealth.

  o   Since the wealth you have amassed has come from your hard work, you have the sole right to decide how it will be divided. However, you can bequeath your undivided share in the ancestral property as per section 30 of the Hindu Succession Act.

  o   The will should have a detailed statement of your earnings, a well-formatted description of each income head and legal information.

  o   A clear picture of both the movable and immovable properties in your possession is expected to be added to the will.

  o   Example: 'My home, situated at the address: 23, Lane 15, Prabhat Road, Pune, shall be transferred to my elder son, Suresh, after my death and the 10-acre land bearing the address: S. no. 23, A/P Nagaon Village, Thane, shall be transferred to my younger daughter, Shreya, and all my investments in shares shall be transferred to my wife, Sunita.'

  o   Savings accounts, term deposits, shares, mutual funds, etc., should be listed clearly.

  o   You may also donate your wealth to a social organization or to a person outside your family too.

  o   You can create provisions for the upbringing and the securing of the future of minor children, specially-abled children or other members of the family. Likewise, you can provide for family members from your other marriages, if any, too.

  o   There have been instances of wives living lives of neglect after the demise of their husbands, the head of the family. To avoid that, the wife should be given priority, followed by the children, when a man prepares his will.

  o   Towards the end, that the will was created thoughtfully and independently, and in a sound state of mind, should be clearly mentioned.

- **Signature of the person creating the will**: The signature of the person creating the will is of utmost importance. If the person is not able to sign for any reason, he/she may put his/her thumb impression and the same needs to be ratified by other persons.

> 'Success is walking from failure to failure with no loss of enthusiasm.'—Winston Churchill

- **Signature of the witness:** Once the will is ready, two people known to you must testify the document with their signatures and have to enter their name, age, address, date, day and place. The witnesses should preferably be younger than the person creating the will so that they are able to visit the court to testify if needed. The beneficiaries of the will cannot be the witnesses. The testator and witnesses must sign in the presence of each other, which is the legal requirement. The witnesses are not supposed to know the contents of the will.

- **Doctor's certificate**

  o Attach a doctor's certificate to the will, even if it is not required as per the law.

  o A doctor's certificate helps to certify that the person creating the will was physically and mentally fit while creating the will. The doctor should sign, stamp and add their registration number alongside.

- **Registration**

  o It is not legally binding to register a will. However, a registered will is backed by the judicial system and hence cannot be easily challenged. That is why it is important to get your will legally registered.

  o You can get it registered at a registrar's office through a lawyer. No stamp duty is levied on this.

- **Probate**

  o Probate means a certified copy of the will by a competent court. As per the Indian Succession Act, probate is mandatory only in metropolitan cities like Mumbai, Chennai and Kolkata. In other places, it is not mandatory.

- **Keeping the will**

  o The will needs to be kept in a secure place. The law does not say with whom the will should be kept.

- **Can you make changes to the will?**

  o You can make as many changes or updates as you want. These changes may happen due to the transfer of property, death, marriage or divorce of a person mentioned in the will, the birth of children or grandchildren, etc.

o   You can attach a codicil (supplement) at any time to the will. The codicil also needs to be executed in the same fashion a will is executed.

o   The person needs to be physically and mentally fit while preparing a new will or while editing it, or else the additions will not be considered.

o   'The previous will was created on this date _____', should be clearly mentioned while discarding it and creating a new will.

o   If a person has multiple wills, the latest will is considered, according to the law.

o   If a registered will is changed, the new document should also be registered. Otherwise, the changes are not considered.

Other Information

- The will comes into effect when the person making it dies.

- The law does not say that the will has to be read aloud.

- If a property is caught in some legal matter, consult a legal adviser before adding it to your will.

- Always seek legal help while creating a will.

- The appointment of executors is also not mandatory.

Important

- Disclosure of the information in the will to your children should be decided based on the situation. You could be mistreated, or feuds or animosity could arise between them if they are not happy with what has been allocated to them. That does not mean you avoid making a will, but you can inform your close ones when you do so that they are aware of its existence.

- You have the following alternatives at your disposal:

    o   Distributing your wealth among all your rightful heirs while you are alive. (They might not value you after they get their money, in this option.)

    o   Have your wealth distributed after your demise. You will need to leave proper instructions for this distribution if you are not making a will.

    o   Find a fine balance between the two alternatives given above by utilizing your wealth for your family, friends and society while you are alive. This way, you can be of great help when others need it, and you will find immense satisfaction from it too.

Nomination

- Nomination is treated as a stop-gap arrangement in law. It does not give ownership rights to the nominee. The courts have held that nomination is not the third law of succession.

- Whether you want to open a bank account or get an insurance policy, you have to fill up a nomination form. This is required even when you invest money. Many applicants avoid filling up the nomination form as they feel it is a mere formality. But it is an important element in a financial transaction.

- Nomination is a legal facility meant for our benefit. The nominee acts as a trustee and even if money is transferred to the nominee, the legal heirs don't lose their rights. The will/succession prevails over the nomination.

- The full name, age, address and relationship of the nominee with one must be declared in the nomination form.

Why is Nomination Important?

- In the unfortunate event of one's death, one's family members have to face financial problems. Many a time, the money in the deceased person's account lies idle with the bank if the nomination process is incomplete.

- This corpus can only be availed of by showing documents establishing your relationship with the deceased person, the death certificate or court order. This process can take a long time to complete, and you may end up spending a lot too.

- We should complete nominations for all our accounts so that our family members can use our wealth.

Important

- If the deceased person does not leave a will and has no rightful heirs, the wealth is transferred in the nominee's name, and he holds it as a trustee.

- If the deceased person does not leave a will but has a rightful heir who has claimed his property, the nominee will only get that wealth where he has been named specifically. However, ownership of that property remains with the rightful heir when no person is formally nominated.

Conclusion

● People work hard to accumulate assets for their families but often neglect to consider what will happen to their assets and who will inherit specific properties. To avoid conflicts and misunderstandings among your loved ones, it is critical to write a will and make nominations.

> 'विद्येविना मती गेली। मतिविना नीती गेली।
> नीतिविना गती गेली। गतिविना वित्त गेले।
> वित्ताविना शूद्र खचले। इतके अनर्थ एका अविद्येने केले।।'
>
> 'Without knowledge, wisdom was lost; without wisdom, morals were lost; without morals, development was lost; without development, wealth was lost; without wealth, shudras are ruined; all these disasters are due to lack of knowledge.'—Mahatma Jyotiba Phule

• Part 3 •

Insurance

Money Works

Money Works

What Is Insurance?

When people are asked where they have invested their money, a common reply is: 'I have invested in insurance to save taxes,' There are three distinct concepts contained in this statement.

1. **Buying insurance coverage to mitigate risks**

2. **Investing**

3. **Tax-saving**

These are three important but distinct concepts.

● There is always a probability of encountering financial losses, which is beyond our control. The concept of insurance came from the idea of covering risks and providing for financial losses.

● The main reason for getting a property insured is that the insurance company will pay for the loss of the property or damage to it in case of unforeseen events.

● Insurance can be further classified into:

   o   Life insurance: Insurance of human life

   o   General insurance: Insurance of possessions or for contingencies other than life. The following would be covered by general insurance

      ■ Home, vehicle, property, theft, accident

      ■ Health

      ■ Travel, etc.

History of Insurance in India

● Insurance in the country was a private business at first. On 1 September 1956, the Life Insurance Corporation of India was established.

● In 1972, a law to nationalize the general insurance business came into effect, and insurance companies were nationalized.

● Private companies were allowed to enter the insurance business in 1999, and in the next year, in 2000, the Insurance Regulatory and Development Authority of India was established.

'The art is not in making money, but in keeping it.'—Proverb

- Insurance agents had to work hard to make people understand the importance of insurance in the early years of insurance in India.

- People were so ignorant about insurance that it was a huge challenge to convince them to spend a small sum to cover a larger risk. LIC tried everything—from marketing gimmicks and attractive advertising to highlight the savings people would make—in order to get them to understand the importance of insurance.

- People who had purchased insurance policies here, when inflation was under control, benefited from buying insurance. LIC's business grew multi-fold and they had a monopoly in the market.

- After the privatization of the insurance industry, people started buying insurance policies since the competition had led to long-term and sufficient insurance coverage at low premiums.

- The most successful products were the life insurance schemes. We will look at a few of them.

What Is a Life Insurance Policy?

- A life insurance policy is an agreement between the insurance policyholder and the insurer or the insurance company.

- The policyholder's family gets a fixed sum upon his death or upon completion of a stipulated tenure, or in certain situations. The policyholders have to pay premiums regularly to keep their policy active.

Before Buying a Life Insurance Policy

Life insurance is important. It creates a provision for and covers the financial needs of the policyholder's financial dependents upon his or her demise.

The following questions need to be considered before getting a policy.

1. Do you need insurance?

    -   You don't need life insurance if no one is financially dependent on you.

> 'Whatever your income, always live below your means.'—Thomas J. Stanley

- Young children do not require life insurance since no one is financially dependent on them. Mutual funds and SIPs could be better options to provide for their education or marriage expenses.

2. If insurance is required, how much should be the coverage? The policy coverage or sum assured should be in proportion to the current income of the person buying the policy.

3. What should the tenure of the insurance policy be? Until what age, or after what age of the policyholder, should the policy be kept going? That must be decided.

One should get a policy that offers maximum coverage for a minimum premium from a reliable insurance company which has a good track record of claims settlement.

How Does the Insurance Business Work?

- You have to pay a fixed sum for a fixed tenure (period) to the insurance company. Against this, the insurance company pays the assured sum to your nominee or family members after your demise.

- The insurance company decides on the sum assured based on your current and future income, your health, your current and future responsibilities, and the rate of inflation.

- The premium is based on the sum assured, the policyholder's age, health, insurance plan and the riders in the policy.

- You have to pay an insurance premium regularly, as per your agreement with the insurance company. Your coverage lapses if you pay once and then stop paying before the end of the stipulated tenure.

- Assume your age is thirty-five. You should choose a policy based on the following factors—family's yearly expenses, projection of expenses in the future (assuming an 8 per cent rate of inflation), current wealth, loans, financial goals, etc.

Types of Life Insurance Plans

There are different types of life insurance policies, based on their maturity, tenure and other benefits.

 'The more you learn, the more you earn.'—Frank Clark

1) Policies that offer bonuses/profits

    a) Endowment insurance plans—Insurance + Savings

    b) Money-back insurance plans

    c) Unit-linked insurance plans

    d) Whole-life plans

    e) Term insurance

    f) Child plans

    g) Retirement plans, etc.

Types of Life Insurance Policies

1. Policies that offer Bonus/Profit

- Apart from security, these types of policies set aside a part for investments. The policyholder gets either a bonus or assured returns. These types of policies are popular with people looking for insurance, investment and tax saving in a single product.

- Insurance companies choose low-risk investments to pay fixed returns to their customers. At times, in the long term, the returns from these policies are less than the returns on mutual funds.

- As compared to the term plans, the policies that offer bonuses or profits offer less insurance coverage.

- For those who do not save any money, these policies help them develop the habit of saving in the long term.

a. Endowment plan: Insurance + Savings

- Both objectives, insurance and savings, are met here. You may get a bonus after a stipulated time period.

- Endowment Plans are like Unit Linked Insurance Plans (ULIP), where a plan is a mixture of insurance and savings. The premium on the policy is invested and the bonus is declared each year after deduction of expenses.

> 'Life insurance is the only tool that takes pennies and guarantees dollars.'—Ben Feldman

- The bonus and the assured sum are paid to the policyholder upon completion of stipulated tenure or to the legal heir upon the death of the policyholder.

- This is a low-risk policy as compared to ULIP.

b. **Money-Back plan**

- As the name suggests, this plan offers the money the policyholder put back in stages, as stipulated in the policy, and the balance amount plus the bonus is paid at the end of the policy tenure. The policyholder gets insurance coverage as well.

c. **Unit Linked Investment Plan: Insurance + Investment Opportunity**

- Insurance cover and investment are both offered by a ULIP. The policyholder has to pay a premium for a stipulated period of time.

- A part of the premium is used to buy insurance cover and the rest is invested in debt funds, equity funds or government bonds, as per the policyholder's preference. The risk of these investments is borne by the policyholder.

- Some ULIPs are specifically designed to cover expenses towards specific health issues.

- You will have to study the policy before investing in a ULIP since it is complex in nature.

- Even though a ULIP can be terminated after five years, the policyholder may have to bear losses. That is why it is advised to continue with a ULIP for at least ten years to benefit from it.

d. **Whole-Life plan**

- Just as the name suggests, this is lifelong insurance.

- The policyholder gets a cover till he turns 100 years old or till he survives. Since the tenure is long, the premium paid is also comparatively higher.

- The premium has to be paid for a stipulated tenure, and a fraction of the money can be withdrawn after a certain period.

> 'Wealth is not about having a lot of money; it's about having a lot of options.'—Chris Rock

2. Term insurance

- The most affordable type of insurance is term insurance. The main objectives and the need for getting life insurance will be met here.

- Everyone should get term insurance as soon as they start earning. The assured sum is paid to the heir upon the policyholder's death.

- A long-tenure and a large-cover term insurance would be beneficial since it costs less. It can be purchased both online and offline.

- The policyholder will not get any money back once the tenure of the policy is over in a basic term insurance policy. Term insurance policies that provide a refund of premiums are commonly referred to as 'Term Insurance with Return of Premium' (TROP). In this type of policy, the insurer returns the premiums paid by the policyholder if they survive the policy term.

- Your cover should be at least twenty times your annual income. This can be changed from time to time.

3. Child plan

There are a few insurance plans for children. This takes into account the child's future expenses, and the child gets a stipulated sum every year once he turns eighteen, or a lump-sum payment that can cover education, marriage expenses, etc.

4. Retirement plan

As per the agreement, a stipulated sum is paid after a certain period to the policyholder as retirement pension.

A combination of or amendments in two or more of the above policies is done to create different types of policies.

Insurance and Tax Saving

- Section 80C permits certain investments and expenses to be tax-exempted. Payments made towards life insurance premiums are covered under section 80C of the Income Tax Act. The taxpayer has to opt for the old tax regime to avail these deductions. A maximum of Rs 1.5 lakh is allowed as total deductions under sections 80C, 80CC and 80CCE.

- Insurance policies taken for oneself, husband/wife or dependent children, or for parents, can be claimed as deductions under section 80C of the Income Tax Act 1961.

Under section 10(10D), the proceeds of the sum assured and any sum received as bonus paid on the death of the insured, surrender of the policy or maturity of the policy, are tax-free as per the Act.

Important Points about Section 10(10D)

The following payouts are not tax-free, as per the Act:

- Except for the death benefit, no other benefits are tax-free in the case of policies issued between 1 April 2003 and 31 March 2012. One does not get tax exemption under section 10(10D) if the amount paid towards premium during the policy period is more than 20 per cent of the sum assured on maturity.

- For life insurance policies purchased from 1 April 2012 onwards, exemption cannot be availed of if the premium payment exceeds 10 per cent of the sum assured.

- Exemption can only be availed if the premium is not more than 20 per cent of the sum assured for policies issued before 31 March 2012.

- For policies issued after 1 April 2012, tax exemption is available only if the premium is not more than 10 per cent of the sum assured.

- In the case of policies issued after 1 April 2013, a disabled person can avail of exemption on premium for not more than 15 per cent of the sum assured.

- Hindu undivided families can also claim exemptions under section 80C as per the Income Tax Act.

> *Life insurance is like a parachute. If you don't have it when you need it the first time, there is no second chance.*

Avoid These Mistakes when Buying a Life Insurance Policy

A very small number of people in India have life insurance cover as compared to people in developed countries. Don't buy policies going by blind faith or just because your agent asked you to do so. Also, you are not free to do whatever you please just because you have a life insurance policy. Let us look at the mistakes that can be avoided.

Common mistakes made while getting a life insurance policy	Precautions to be taken
1. Not understanding the difference between multiple types of policies.	You should understand the difference between term insurance, bonus-linked, endowment, money-back, ULIP and whole-life policies. Only then will you be in a position to decide which one suits your requirements.
2. Not deciding your goals before getting a policy.	• You should give serious thought to why you are getting a life insurance policy. It can cover you for accidents, sudden health conditions, etc. • Avoid getting a policy just to save tax or because everyone else is getting themselves insured.
3. Delaying the decision to get a policy.	• Insurance is of utmost importance to cover those dependent on you after you are gone. The longer the time for which you are uninsured, the longer the time for which they are unsafe. • The insurance premium is less for a younger person. Start early with the right insurance policy.

> 'You don't buy life insurance because you are going to die, but because those you love are going to live.'—Anonymous

4.	Not doing enough research before getting a policy online.	• There is stiff competition between websites trying to sell insurance policies with the highest coverage and at the lowest cost. • While buying a policy online, consider your age, health, physical complaints, habits, needs and financial ability to pay the insurance premium. • The kind of insurance that must be taken varies from person to person. It is not necessary that a policy similar to the one that your friend or family member has purchased is suitable for you. • Often, online portals do not give you as much information as an insurance adviser can in an in-person meeting.
5.	Not reviewing the policy after a period and not making the necessary changes.	• The sum assured should be reviewed, based on one's age, changes in the number of family members and one's financial growth. • Maybe you could afford a term insurance of just Rs 10 lakh at the start of your career. But now that you are more settled, you can increase the coverage to Rs 1 crore. You need to review your insurance coverage for this.
6.	Depending on the policy drawn by your employer.	• Organizations offer insurance coverage to employees to retain them, just like they offer salary and incentives. • You should find out whether the insurance covers your and your family's needs when they arise and get additional coverage on your own if needed.

'A man who dies without adequate life insurance should have to come back and see the mess he created.'—Will Rogers

7. Thinking that a habitual smoker or a diabetes patient cannot get an insurance policy.	• Insurance companies charge additional premium if the person has the habit of smoking or is diagnosed with diseases such as diabetes. This is because they know that the probability of a claim arising for such a person is high. • It is a wise decision to pay additional premium and get an insurance cover than to not get a policy and be at 100 per cent risk.
8. Surrendering the policy before the stipulated tenure.	• Your policy is an agreement between the insured and the insurer. The insurance companies charge a heavy sum if the policy is surrendered before the stipulated time. • You should consider ways to pay the stipulated number of premiums and not surrender the policy unless it becomes absolutely essential.
9. Getting a policy whose tenure is too long-term or too short-term.	• You should decide upon a term based on your age, family responsibilities, need for insurance coverage and the premium amount you can afford.
10. Buying a random insurance policy just to save taxes.	• According to section 80D of the Income Tax Act, insurance can help save 10–30 per cent of tax. But if you choose a policy without considering your needs, you will lose 100 per cent of the amount paid as premium.
11. Not being aware of the riders.	• Riders, along with health insurance, are essential to cover for accidents and terminal diseases.

'You don't need to pray to God any more when there are storms in the sky, but you do have to be insured.'—Bertolt Brecht

General Insurance

Many types of essential insurance plans are included in general insurance. Let us look at the types of general insurance offered by the government and private insurance companies.

Highlights of General Insurance

- The tenure of this insurance is usually one year but can be two or three years in some cases. Some plans are to be bought by default, while the rest are essential, yet optional.

- This insurance brings no fixed returns. If the policyholder has a mishap covered under the policy during its active tenure, he may be paid a part or the full sum agreed, based upon assessment of the damages.

Types of General Insurance

1. Health insurance

- The Covid-19 pandemic forced us to understand the true importance of one kind of insurance—health insurance.

- A serious illness can turn a prince into a pauper, depleting his life savings. A health insurance policy can help avert that, to an extent.

- Health insurance can be taken for oneself or for one's family. Many organizations offer individual or family policies to their employees. The terms of a corporate health insurance policy differ from those of individual policies.

2. Accident insurance

- Personal Accident insurance provides financial protection to policyholders in case of death, permanent or temporary disability caused because of an accident.

- Death due to any reason other than accident is not covered in the policy.

'Whatever excuses you may have for not buying life insurance now will only sound ridiculous to your widow.'—Anonymous

3. Travel insurance

● A delay in scheduled travel, loss of passport or luggage and sudden health conditions are covered under this type of insurance.

● Usually, people travelling abroad take this insurance policy.

4. Motor insurance

● Insuring your vehicles is mandatory by law. Vehicle insurance can be classified into two types.

● One covers the loss to another person and their property, which is covered under third-party insurance. The other type covers the breakdown of one's vehicle or its parts.

● The coverage is decided based on the value of the vehicle, its date of purchase and its use.

5. Property insurance

● Loss to one's property due to fire, burglary or natural calamities is covered under property insurance.

● Movable and immovable assets such as a house, factory building, jewellery, home appliances, and raw and finished goods are covered under this.

● The insurance company pays a stipulated sum if the event mentioned in the policy takes place.

Apart from this, strikes, lockouts or losses incurred due to an employee's wrong decision can be covered under fidelity insurance. Also, it is popular in the corporate world for leaders of organizations to be insured. Farmers can opt for agriculture insurance.

> 'Fun is like life insurance; the older you get, the more it costs.'—Kin Hubbard

Difference between Insurance and Investment

Insurance, savings and investments are all different from each other.

- An insurance policy is a provision to cover your family or yourself from financial problems arising out of accidents or adverse health conditions. Human life is invaluable and cannot be measured in terms of money. But policies help to financially support you and your family members in unforeseen circumstances.

- **Importance and Need of Investments**

  o It is important to save money and invest it wisely to fulfil your medium- and long-term goals, including children's education, your retirement and the purchase of a home.

  o Investment in term deposits can help you get fixed though comparatively less returns, whereas investments in equity shares and mutual funds can give you variable yet higher returns.

  o The main reason to make investments is to lodge your saved money in the right products to get good returns.

- The main reason for taking life insurance is for financial support of the family members in case of an accident or death of the family member who is insured.

- The goal of life insurance should not be to get rich while one is alive; rather, insurance is supposed to cover your family's financial needs once you are gone.

The Confusion between Insurance and Investment

- Lack of financial literacy and the bombarding of consumers with insurance advertising leads to people believing that both are the same.

- A mix of both is available in options such as endowment and money-back policies and ULIPs. But hybrid policies are not able to both insure and give good returns at the same time.

> 'A policy of life insurance is the cheapest and safest mode of making a certain provision for one's family.'—Benjamin Franklin

- Example: The sum assured in a ULIP is ten times the premium. The insurance policyholder gets a cover of only Rs 5 lakh for a yearly premium of Rs 50,000. This payout is insufficient to cover a family's financial expenses. Against this, a thirty-year-old can get a cover of Rs 50 lakh for an annual premium of Rs 7000–Rs 10,000 if he opts for a term insurance policy.

- Insurance and investment goals should be independent of each other.

'You may not control all the events that happen to you, but you can decide not to be reduced by them.'—Maya Angelou

What Insurance Should You Get?
The Traditional Insurance Policy vs Term Plan

Let us look at some examples that can illustrate which insurance you should opt for.

Example 1

- A healthy thirty-year-old intends to get a policy with a term of twenty years and a sum assured of Rs 25 lakh.

- Options of premium (annual):

  o   Endowment plan—Rs 1.45 lakh

  o   Term plan—Rs 6000

- There is a big difference in the premium amounts. The premium paid towards the term plan does not come back. As against this, the premium paid for an endowment plan comes back, along with a bonus.

- In our example, the amount saved by choosing term insurance is Rs 1.39 lakh. It can be invested in mutual funds (Rs 1.45 lakh less Rs 6000).

- The annual returns from an endowment plan are about 4–6 per cent, whereas mutual funds may give higher returns.

- In short, the insurance cover of Rs 25 lakh can be obtained by paying just Rs 6000 in a term plan as against Rs 1.45 lakh in an endowment plan.

- If you feel a cover of Rs 25 lakh may not be enough, you can get a Rs 1 crore cover at a premium of Rs 16,000–20,000 with ease.

Example 2

- When one gets an insurance cover of Rs 25 lakh, the annual premium would be Rs 1.44 lakh.

- If the same person opts for a term plan of Rs 1 crore, the annual premium would be Rs 16,000.

> *'The only thing a man can buy on the instalment plan, on which his widow won't have to finish the payments after he dies, is life insurance.'*—Anonymous

- The difference in the annual premium of these two plans is Rs 1.28 lakh, and the coverage is four times higher in the term plan.

- On maturity of policy:

	Endowment Plan	Term Plan + Equity Fund (Assuming annual returns of 12 per cent)
Insurance cover	Rs 25 lakh	Rs 1 crore
Total premium paid	Rs 29 lakh (20 years X Rs 1.44 lakh)	Rs 3.2 lakh (20 years X Rs 16,000)
Amount policyholder gets on maturity (insurance policy)	Rs 60–70 lakh	0
Amount receivable on maturity (Investment)	0	Assuming 12 per cent average rate of return, Rs 92 lakh on an annual investment of Rs 1.28 lakh

If the policyholder dies while the insurance policy is active:

- 1.25 times the sum assured plus a bonus is paid under the endowment plan. In the above example, the claim could range between Rs 31 lakh and Rs 60 lakh. This amount will vary depending on when in the twenty-year term of the policy the death occurs.

- In the option of term plan plus equity fund, the nominee will get Rs 1 crore. The amount invested in equity funds will also go to the nominee named for them.

Conclusion: The returns from a term plan plus equity fund are higher than from an endowment plan. Also, one gets four times higher insurance coverage at a premium that is ten times less.

What Insurance Will You Take?

- Insurance and investment are two distinctly independent and important things. Do not mess up your financial planning by mixing up these two.

Don't fear failure. Fear being in the exact same place next year.

- Traditional plans offer full money back if you are alive at the end of the term. On the contrary, most of the term plans do not offer the same benefit.

- As compared to traditional plans, term insurance policies can offer high coverage at low premiums.

- If you have had a traditional insurance policy going on for less than three years, you can stop paying the insurance premium on it. You may have to bear the short-term loss from doing this. However, if you choose term insurance plus investment in equity mutual funds, you will get much better returns plus higher insurance coverage in the long run.

- If your traditional insurance policy is more than three years old, you can opt for policy surrender or policy paid up, and stop paying future premiums. The amount received from this transaction can be invested in a high-return equity scheme, and you can get a new term plan based on your income.

- If the maturity date of your policy is close, do not stop the policy. Get additional term insurance to cover for any shortfall.

- Remember! Do not ignore life insurance. It is a financial provision to cover your family's financial needs after your death.

'Wealth is largely the result of habit.'—John Jacob Astor

Health Insurance

Many of us feel that we are fit and healthy. Why do I need health insurance? Of course, the Covid-19 pandemic made a lot of us give a second thought to this. People of any age group on any given day may fall sick or catch an infection. You may also have an accident for no fault of yours. That is why health insurance is essential for everyone, irrespective of their age or background.

Health Insurance of What Amount?

● In the past few years, medical inflation, meaning the rate of increase in medical costs, has been about 8–14 per cent.[1]

● While deciding on your health insurance, you should think of the costs you will have to bear for five or six days of in-patient hospitalization.

● You can get to know the costs of high-end surgeries with a bit of inquiring or from the web. This can help you decide on the approximate coverage you will need.

● A coverage of Rs 5 lakh if you reside in a big city, and Rs 3 lakh if you reside in a smaller town, is recommended.

● The cost of treatment varies according to your health condition, and so should your health insurance coverage.

Cashless Health Insurance Policy

● **Cashless family health plan:** One person pays the premium and his immediate family members are covered under the same cashless health insurance plan.

● **Cashless health plan for senior citizens:** Ambulance hire, medical tests, in-patient hospitalization and other such expenses are covered under the plan. This health insurance plan may come with many terms and conditions. Also, the policyholder needs to declare all his current health conditions to the company.

● **Corporate cashless policy:** An employer insures his employees as part of employee benefits through this insurance plan. The employer pays a premium that covers hospitalization, recovery and medicine expenses.

● Corporate policies also cover female employees for maternity expenses. A few insurance companies also offer coverage for pre-existing diseases upon payment of additional premiums.

> *'If there is no struggle, there is no progress.'*—Frederick Douglass

How Does a Cashless Hospitalization Facility Work?

- Insurance companies tie up with hospitals in various cities. They do their research and look at the facilities offered by the hospitals before onboarding them.

- The term for such facilities is 'network hospitals'. If the insured person gets admitted to a network hospital, he does not have to bear any expenses. A person appointed as a third-party administrator looks into the case and submits all the details to the insurance company. Based on this, the insurance company pays the bills on behalf of the insured person.

- The insured person often knows beforehand about his admission to hospital. In such a situation, the insured person can go to a network hospital of his choice and submit his insurance policy documents to the hospital before getting admitted. It is important to inform the insurance company or third-party administrator well in advance.

- Sometimes, the insured person needs to be admitted on an emergency basis. In such a situation, the person gets to understand the importance of the cashless policy. The policy details need to be submitted to continue to avail of treatment. The cashless procedure can begin within a few hours of admission, saving the patient a lot of mental stress. Hospital authorities need to be informed that it will be cashless payment once the treatment starts.

- The cashless claim may be rejected if the insured person has not declared any pre-existing diseases, or has a particular disease or avails of a treatment that is not covered by the policy. It may also be rejected if the hospital is not part of the insurance company's network.

Renewal of Health Insurance

Vikas and his wife were salaried individuals and hardly found time for each other. The only day off they had was Sunday, which was spent on household work. The renewal date for the health insurance policy that Vikas had taken was close. The insurance company had notified him about it by phone, email and SMS. His wife had particularly asked him to renew it in time, but he forgot to do so, owing to his busy schedule.

A few days later, his wife had to be admitted to hospital as she developed a health problem. The date of renewal of their policy had long

> 'You have to believe in yourself before anybody else believes in you.'—Ray LaMontagne

passed and their health insurance was of no use now. Luckily, all her reports were normal and they did not have to spend a huge sum towards hospitalization, but this incident made Vikas very alert and cautious. He decided to renew his health insurance policy immediately. Due to the late renewal, he had to let go of the no-claim bonus he had received on his previous policy. Learning from his mistake, he opted for the right insurance policy. The next year, he made a note in his diary to remind him about the timely renewal of the policy. He also updated his email calendar to remind himself about the date.

Health insurance is very important, for both yourself and the family. It saves you from spending a huge sum towards expenses related to hospitalization. But you cannot forget about health insurance once you get it. You need to renew it every year by following a simple process. However, you need to note certain points while renewing your policy.

While renewing a health insurance policy:

- You get a 'grace period' even after the end of the policy period. But know that the insurance company does not offer any coverage or security during the grace period. That is why you should renew it in time.

- A health insurance policy can be renewed both online and offline. You need to submit your details on the insurance company's website to renew your policy or contact an insurance agent or the nearest branch of the insurance company to renew it offline.

Confirm the following while renewing your health insurance policy:

- You can opt for a different plan or take a plan from a different insurance company while renewing your existing plan.

- Check if expenses such as medical tests, ambulance charges and in-patient expenses of all kinds are covered under the plan you choose.

- Many insurance companies cover post-hospitalization medical expenses (usually up to two months) as a part of the plan. Are these covered in your policy? If yes, what is the nature of the coverage?

> 'Getting insurance is YOUR responsibility to your family and loved ones. You may hate it but it is your responsibility.'
> —Jeremiah Say

Are the rules the same as last year or have they changed? Clarify these doubts at the time of renewal.

- Compare your policy with those of other companies. Think of opting for those companies that offer high coverage at low premiums and offer a no-claim bonus.

- Think of the facilities and coverage offered by the policy as against your needs. You may also get a few add-ons to match your requirements.

- The term 'utmost good faith' mentioned in your insurance policy is of high importance. It is said that you should not hide anything from your doctor and your lawyer. The way you would inform your doctor about your health conditions, you are expected to inform the insurance companies too of any new health conditions through a declaration form.

- If your insurance agent has overlooked or forgotten to mention a health condition, you should do it at the time of renewal.

- Non-declaration can lead to a lot of hassles in the future, and also lead to claims getting rejected or the policy being terminated.

- It is important to understand the claim settlement ratio and the time required for that. The claim settlement ratio is a percentage of claims that the insurer has paid out against the number of outstanding claims during a financial year.

- The hospital needs to have a tie-up with the insurance company. Since the cashless facility is only available in network hospitals, verifying this at the time of renewal is important.

- The insurance policyholder might have some pre-existing health conditions even before getting his policy. The policyholder has to give a declaration notifying the insurance company about it. A few insurance companies cover pre-existing diseases only after four years of policyholding with them. That is why it is important to find out if pre-existing diseases are covered under your policy or not.

Free Medical Check-ups

Health check-ups are important. You must get your health check-up done at least once every year. Almost all insurance companies offer free medical check-ups for their policyholders. Make the best use of it.

A wealthy man with poor health is always poor.

When an insurance claim is rejected:

- You can raise a complaint with the insurance company's Grievance Redressal Officer if your claim is rejected.

- The insurance companies may change their decision in their review and may ask for additional information.

- If you don't find a solution, you can raise a complaint with the Insurance Ombudsman.

- The Insurance Regulatory and Development Authority (IRDA) is the government authority that regulates the insurance business in India.

- IRDA has their own complaint redressal centre. You may raise a complaint with them by email. Mention all the details when you send an email.

- If you do not find a solution from either of the ways given above, you can take legal action as the last resort by filing a case in a court of law.

How to Avoid Common Mistakes When Getting Health Insurance

Common mistakes	Precautions to take
1. Getting a low-premium health insurance that does not cover you adequately.	• A policy that does not sufficiently cover your health insurance will not help in covering your hospitalization and medicine bills in an emergency. • Get an insurance that will adequately meet your medical needs.
2. Getting a random health insurance policy just to save tax.	• Although health insurance can help to save 10–30 per cent on taxes under section 80D of the Income Tax Act, a policy that does not cover your needs leads to a 100 per cent loss of the premium amount.

> ❝
> 'As an athlete, I understood the value of my health insurance. I knew that in my profession, injuries were common and could happen at any time.'—Magic Johnson
> ❞

Common mistakes	Precautions to take
3. Declaring wrong or incomplete health information to insurance companies.	• Insurance companies have many ways to find out about your lies. • Hidden or misleading information can be responsible for the rejection of claims. • Even if you need to pay a higher premium, it is important to disclose the existence of conditions such as diabetes and hypertension, and habits such as smoking.
4. Not taking the riders into consideration.	• Considering the riders is important, to cover for accidents and major illnesses.
5. Not getting enough information about health insurance policies.	• Reading your insurance policy's terms and conditions is important. • The difference between the communication from an insurance agent, your understanding of it and the actual details mentioned in the policy can lead to problems when you file the actual claim.
6. Not comparing different policies.	• Health insurance needs differ from person to person. You need not get the same policy that your friends or relatives have got.
7. Getting insured for more than what is needed.	• Being overcautious may sometimes lead to your getting a policy that has a higher-than-required premium. • The policy that covers all diseases is usually priced higher. You should consider whether this additional premium is affordable for you or not.

> 'Without health insurance, getting sick or injured could mean going bankrupt, going without needed care, or even dying needlessly.'—Jan Schakowsky

• Part 4 •
Debt Management

Money Works

Money Works

अग्निशेषम् ऋणशेषम् शत्रुशेषम् तथैव च |
पुन: पुन: प्रवर्धेत तस्मात् शेषम् न कारयेत् ||

—सुभाषित

*(Even a small fire, loan or enemy has a tendency to grow quickly. That
is why it is important to get rid of them completely.)*

Let us understand a few fundamental aspects of debt.

How Does the Loan Business Work?

Most of us opt for loans to fulfil our life goals. A loan is a facility for which one pays a price in the form of interest towards its usage.

Everyone takes loans. You can advance towards achieving your financial goals when you make the right use of loans. But the same loan seems like a burden leading to financial problems if you are not making the right use of it. Don't go for a loan just because it is available with ease, since every loan is a financial risk.

How Do Banks or Financial Institutions Earn Profits?

No one makes others earn profits by bearing losses. Similarly, banks and finance companies would not offer loans if they didn't see a profit component in them. These institutions think about themselves while offering loans. Let us understand the thought process behind the loans business.

Why Do People Take Loans?

1. **To fulfil needs:** Loans can be availed of for constructing a home, buying a home or a vehicle, higher education, travel, home furnishings, personal needs, business growth, etc.

2. **To ease financial difficulties:** Loans help when one has not created an emergency fund or if the fund is insufficient to cover one's expenses. Example: All schools started online classes during the pandemic. If you had two children, you would have needed two laptops, tabs or mobile phones, for which many of us would not have saved money. Many parents would have got these electronic products against loans.

3. **Just because everyone takes them:** It is a common thought process that we progress when we take loans since we will 'run' more and work hard to repay them.

4. **For tax planning:** Repayment of the premium and interest on home loans as EMIs is allowed as a tax deduction. The interest on loans taken for business purposes can be recorded as a business expense and can help the business save tax. If the interest on the loan amount is, say, Rs 1000, and the tax saving is 30 per cent, even then, Rs 700 would be an additional expense. If you don't need funds, it is best to not take loans.

> *A moneyless man goes fast through the market.*

5. **Just because banks give attractive loan offers:**

- Banks offer loans as a part of their business. Getting money from depositors at a low rate of interest and lending the money to those who need it at a higher rate of interest is their way of conducting the banking business.

- Banks are always on the lookout for people wanting to take loans. Being eligible for a loan is not a big thing. You are just a customer for the bank.

- For some people, it can be an ego issue, and they make emotionally-driven decisions and take loans as soon as banks offer them.

Classification and Types of Loans

Loans can be largely classified as secured and unsecured loans. They can also be classified based on the tenure of repayment.

Secured loans: Loans taken against property, gold, term deposits, etc., where collaterals are mortgaged, are secured loans.

Unsecured loans: Sometimes, banks or financial institutions are ready to offer loans without any collateral security. Their offer is based on the credit score or creditworthiness of the borrower. This type of loan is an unsecured loan.

Revolving loans:

- Credit card spends is an example of a revolving loan.

- The loans repaid in the form of EMIs are known as term loans. The repayment term and monthly instalments are pre-planned in this type of loan.

Common Types of Loans

1. Home loan
2. Car loan
3. Education loan
4. Personal loan
5. Business loan
6. Gold loan
7. Mortgage loan, or loan against property

> *'Beware of little expenses; a small leak will sink a great ship.'*—Benjamin Franklin

Important Concepts Underlying the Loan

1. **Income:** While giving a loan, the first thing banks or financial institutions check is the ability of the customer to repay it. Income is the biggest factor in the credit appraisal of the customer by the lender. The higher the income, the higher the loan offered.

2. **Age:** A person of a young age who has been employed for a few years has more chances to get a loan easily than one nearing retirement or a new joiner.

3. **Down payment:** This is the contribution by the applicant towards the purchase for which the loan is being taken. Example: If you are planning to buy a home worth Rs 1 crore and the bank is ready to offer you a loan of Rs 80 lakh, the balance Rs 20 lakh is your down payment amount. This is to be self-arranged by the person opting for the loan. The higher the down payment, the better it is for the borrower.

4. **Tenure:** It is the total time permitted by the bank for repayment of the entire loan amount. If you miss or delay the repayment, the banks can charge a penalty or seize the property against which you have taken the loan.

5. **Interest:** This is the price you pay for borrowed money. The rate of interest changes according to the type of loan, the collateral security provided and the customer's credit score. You can opt for a fixed or floating rate of interest.

6. **EMIs:** Equated monthly instalments are the part repayments of the loans and are made every month, as the name suggests. This includes parts of both the principal and the interest.

Benefits of Taking a Loan

1. **Helps in fulfilling one's financial goals:** You need financial assistance in fulfilling your objectives, such as buying a home, car, higher education, etc. You can fulfil your dreams when you take loans.

2. **Covering emergency needs:** You can apply for a loan if an emergency arises. You can also plan for emergency expenses such as treatment for major diseases and family or social programmes by taking a loan.

3. **Financial flexibility:** A loan helps you manage your financial needs or expenses that arise all of a sudden. You have money at your

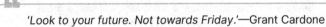

'Look to your future. Not towards Friday.'—Grant Cardone

disposal through loans, you are not stuck due to a lack of money, and can easily plan to buy property or create provisions for major expenses.

4. **Easy process:** Many loans can be disbursed in just forty-eight hours, subject to the collateral securities that are provided, while some loans are based on the income and financial history of the borrower.

5. **Preferred tenure:** The tenure of a loan is dependent on the bank and the loan amount. You can decide the tenure based on your ability to repay. It could range from twelve to sixty months or longer.

6. **Tax saving:** A few loans can help one save tax as per the provisions of the Income Tax Act. Example: Repayment of principal and interest on home loans, interest on business loans, etc., are allowed as deductions in calculating your taxable income.

Before Applying for a Loan

Taking a loan is a major financial decision. You need to know a few things before you take one:

1. **Credit score:** Checking your credit score before applying for a loan is important. Your credit score shows your financial ability. Banks can check your loans and repayment history through this, and it explains whether you are capable of repaying the loan or not. Banks rely on the credit score of their borrowers to ascertain their creditworthiness. Usually, a 750+ CIBIL credit score is considered excellent.

2. **Rate of interest:** Check the actual rate of interest before applying for a loan. Loans that require collateral security carry a lower rate of interest than those which do not.

3. **Processing fee:** When you apply for a loan, the banks will ask you for a few documents. They charge a fee to process these documents. This fee is different for each bank and for each type of loan.

4. **Best rate of interest:** Compare the rates of interest offered by different banks. Also confirm the processing fees, EMI, tenure and other charges.

> *'A bank is a place that will lend you money if you can prove that you don't need it.'*—Bob Hope

What are EMIs (equated monthly instalments)?

- EMI or equated monthly instalment is the amount you need to pay periodically as part of your loan repayment, i.e. monthly, quarterly, etc. It is based on the loan amount, tenure and rate of interest of your loan.

How is EMI Calculated?

EMI depends on three major factors.

1. **The loan amount:** The total loan taken from the bank is the most important factor. The EMI increases if the loan amount increases.

2. **Rate of interest:** Loans of different types have varied rates of interest. The interest can vary based on the borrower's income, age, repayment capacity, designation, credit history, etc. The number of instalments in which it is to be repaid would be less if the rate is low.

3. **Tenure:** The repayment tenure for a loan is fixed at the time the loan is taken. You can request the bank or the financial institution to revise this. The tenure affects the EMI in a big way. The longer tenure, the less the EMI.

- The EMI primarily consists of two parts—principal and interest.

- Interest is charged on the principal amount, and it is divided by the number of instalments in which the repayment will be done during the given tenure.

- During the initial period of repayment, interest forms the major part of the EMI.

- As the tenure nears its end, the principal component in the repayment amount grows bigger than the interest component.

- If you have taken a loan for a longer term, try to opt for pre-payment of the loan—meaning, paying more than the EMI. This will help you to reduce the tenure of repayment and save on the interest you pay.

Can the EMI change during the tenure of the loan?

The EMI may change in the following circumstances:

1. Choosing a floating rate of interest

- If you choose a floating rate of interest, banks can change the interest rate according to their policies, leading to a change in the interest on the loan and its EMI too.

- You may opt for a fixed rate of interest when the rate of interest is low.

- If you opt for a fixed rate, then even if the rate of interest changes as per the RBI repo rate, your EMI remains the same. If you have not missed a single instalment or have not done a prepayment, your EMI will remain unchanged for the complete period of the loan.

2. Prepayment of loan

- Your EMI changes if you have done a pre-payment towards your loan. Pre-payment also helps to reduce the principal owed and save on interest.

- This means, if you want to repay your loan at the earliest, you should think of reducing your tenure instead of the EMI. You can also think of keeping the EMI intact and repaying before the stipulated tenure by way of pre-payment.

3. Tenure

- Your EMI will be reduced if you request your bank to increase the repayment tenure.

- But you should understand that an increase in the tenure will also increase the interest you will be paying.

How is EMI Calculated?

Rohan purchased a car worth Rs 5.95 lakh and paid Rs 1.50 lakh as a down payment. The balance amount of Rs 4.45 lakh was taken as a loan at 12 per cent rate of interest per year with a four-year repayment tenure. Rohan is currently paying an EMI of Rs 11,718. He feels the EMI is high compared to the loan amount. But he does not know how to find out whether it is actually so.

Many of us, just like Rohan, are confused about the EMIs we are paying because we are not sure about how EMI is calculated. Let us understand how EMI is calculated.

1. Excel spreadsheet

- The easiest way to calculate EMI is by using an Excel spreadsheet. You can easily calculate the EMI by using the PMT formula.

'Tell me to what you pay attention and I will tell you who you are!'—J.O. Gassett

- You need to know three things for this—the interest rate, tenure (number of periods, or NPR) and principal value (PV).

- The formula to be used in Excel will be: EMI = PMT (Rate, NPR, PV)

- Let's check Rohan's EMI using the above formula. Please note that the rate needs to be calculated for one month since the 12 per cent given in the example is the annual interest rate.

- Monthly rate = 12 per cent/12 = 1 per cent or 0.01

- Tenure = Total number of EMIs to be paid

- EMI = PMT(0.12/12, 4*12, 445000) = Rs 11,718

Example 2

Assume that Ravi is paying a quarterly instalment on a loan of Rs 10 lakh over a tenure of twenty years at an interest of 12 per cent. In this situation, you have to divide the interest rate by 4 instead of by 12 and multiply it by 4 to find the number of instalments that will be paid.

EMI = PMT (0.12/4, 20 × 4, 10,00,000) = Rs 33,111

2. Using the equation to calculate EMI

Not everyone will be comfortable using the Excel spreadsheet. You can use the mathematical formula you must have learnt in school to calculate EMI. You can use a calculator.

- EMI = [P x R x (1+R)^N]/[(1+R)^N-1]

- EMI = [Principal x Rate of Interest (1+R)^N] / [(1+R) ^ Total instalments - 1]

- If the annual rate of interest is 11 per cent, then 11/12 × 100, and N will be the number of instalments.

- You will get the same result as you would using an Excel spreadsheet.

'It's easy to meet expenses—everywhere we go, there they are.'—Anonymous

If a person takes a loan of Rs 10 lakh for a period of one year at 9.5 per cent interest, then the EMI for twelve months would be Rs 87,684.

The EMI table is prepared as follows:

Month	Principal	Interest	EMI	Balance Amount
1	79,767	7,917	87,684	9,20,233
2	80,398	7,285	87,684	8,39,835
3	81,035	6,649	87,684	7,58,800
4	81,676	6,007	87,684	6,77,124
5	82,323	5,361	87,684	5,94,801
6	82,975	4,709	87,684	5,11,826
7	83,632	4,052	87,684	4,28,194
8	84,294	3,390	87,684	3,43,901
9	84,961	2,723	87,684	2,58,940
10	85,634	2,050	87,684	1,73,306
11	86,312	1,372	87,684	86,995
12	86,995	689	87,684	0

- In EMI repayment, the proportion of interest is more than the premium in the initial instalments. The reason is, the interest to be paid will be dependent on the balance loan amount. The more you pay towards principal repayment, the less the interest charged.

- You have now understood how EMI is calculated. We will look at good and bad loans in the next chapter.

'If Plan A fails, remember there are twenty-five more letters.'—Chris Guillebeau

Good Debt	Bad Debt
Home Loan	Car Loan
Education Loan	Home Essentials Loan
Business Loan	Credit Card Outstanding
	Personal Loan
Rate of Interest	
Comparatively lower rate of interest	High rate of interest
Final Use	
Good debts lead to creation of assets or investments	Bad loans are generally used for spending on things meant to show off

- The debt that helps you to increase the value of your assets which get income for you is good debt.

- As against this, the debt that lets you buy unnecessary things which are beyond your current affordability levels, becomes a roadblock in creating wealth in the long term or makes you poorer slowly and gradually, is called bad debt.

What is Good Debt?

Good debt helps you grow your assets.

- **Home loan:** You can buy a home with a home loan or an office space using a business loan. The valuation of this home or office space can increase in the future. If you have not purchased it in haste and have taken a thoughtful decision in buying it, its value can increase.

- **Education loan:** This type of loan can help you finish your higher education, after which you can get a good job. The interest paid on an education loan is a kind of investment. One should try to pursue an education that will help one earn a high salary in the long run. But we should give some thought to whether the loan is actually going to help us in the future, as people sometimes take unnecessary loans for their children's overseas education or to acquire unnecessary degrees for them due to social pressure.

- **Cash credit loan:** This helps a business manage its cash flow. Example: When you take a loan of Rs 10,00,000 at an interest of 12 per cent per annum, you will have to pay Rs 10,000 as interest every month, considering the rate of interest as 1 per cent per month. If you are earning Rs 50,000 every month, then Rs 40,000 is your profit from using cash credit. Note that you will be at a loss if you are earning less than Rs 1,20,000 as income every year by using a Rs 10,00,000 cash credit.

Even good debt comes with an element of risk: We always think of a bright future when we opt for good debts. We take loans assuming that our income and assets will rise and our expenses will come down. But, as they say, *'Umeed pe duniya kayam hai* (Hope keeps the world afloat)'; our assumption may not always come true. We recently saw how many organizations were brought to their knees during the coronavirus pandemic.

> *'It has been my philosophy of life that difficulties vanish when faced boldly.'*—Isaac Asimov

Example: Just getting a reputed degree by taking an education loan does not guarantee good employment. Similarly, a business loan does not assure growth in business. An element of risk is always associated with every type of loan.

Remember this!

● The rate of interest on a good debt should be fixed and must not be rising. Your monthly instalments should be in tune with your monthly budget.

● The instalments should be paid without any fine, additional interest or other charges.

What are Bad Debts?

A loan that brings you instant gratification by helping you make extravagant purchases of products or services is called a bad debt.

Bad loans are usually taken to buy the following things:

● Things that depreciate over time. Examples: vehicles, electronic items such as television, refrigerator, mobile phone, etc.

● Things that do not have a replacement cost. Examples: garments, restaurant meals, cinema tickets, vacations, etc. These are purchases or expenses made just to show off or to experience things that are highly priced.

Once you have set aside a sum towards your emergency fund, what you do with your savings is entirely your own decision.

● Should you always keep saving, without making any additional expenses towards enjoying life? This is a valid question. However, would it be a wise financial decision to take a loan to enjoy life? That too is a valid question.

● You work hard, earn money and save. You ought to be appreciated for this, and this is going to help you in the long run. However, when you are running short of funds, you are bound to think of taking loans.

'We can't change the direction of the wind, but we can adjust the sails.'—Indian proverb

1. Vehicle Loan

Why is a vehicle loan a bad debt? Let us find out.

- A loan for buying a new vehicle can be availed of at a relatively low rate of interest. The vehicle's value depreciates as soon as we buy it. You might say your dream of owning a vehicle will never be fulfilled if you go by this theory. First and foremost, you should give some thought to whether you really need the vehicle or are buying it just as a status symbol.

- In the time of cab services such as Ola and Uber, is it really necessary to stress yourself every day by driving a vehicle in ever-increasing traffic? Of course, if you do not have a good public transport network, you should definitely think of getting a vehicle.

- People look at vehicles as a 'status symbol' and end up buying a bigger-than-required car for themselves. The vehicle dealers are the best at sales in their line of business. They can easily convince you about how the higher variant of the vehicle you intend to buy will suit you better.

- If your budget is Rs 6 lakh, they may talk of how the 'high-end model' is loaded with features and specifications that suit you, and convince you to go for a vehicle model worth Rs 10 lakh, without you even noticing the jump in your budget.

- Just because getting a loan is easy or the EMI over ten years is less than that on a three-year tenure, you may end up paying a lot more as interest.

- Many businessmen fall prey to the notion that a bigger and high-end model of a vehicle will help them impress their customers, leading to higher profits for themselves. If you are able to provide quality products and services at a reasonable cost, your customers will hardly care what vehicle you drive. In fact, an expensive vehicle may create a perception that your product or service may also be priced too high.

2. Personal Loan

- A type of loan offered at a high rate of interest for a short tenure without any security or checking of the end use is called a personal loan.

Lend your money and lose your friend.

- Except in an emergency, you should try to control yourself from taking unnecessary personal loans or avoid them altogether. Example: You might need to take a personal loan to cover your emergency medical expenses if your health insurance is not sufficient to cover them. Avoid taking a personal loan to renovate your home just because the bank is offering it. If you do want to renovate your home, you should save a small sum every month and set aside a budget for it instead of taking a personal loan and showing off to people. This is not a healthy financial practice.

3. Credit Card Outstandings

- These days, credit cards are considered a basic need, just like food, clothing, shelter, education and the mobile phone.

- Offers on credit cards orbit all around you. You come across them at banks, ATMs, bank websites, etc. Even your monthly savings bank account statements have credit card offers printed in them, and you unknowingly get drawn towards them.

- Why do credit card tele-callers call us multiple times a day? The reason is huge profits. Let us look at how they make money and how we can make good use of this process.

The Credit Card Concept

- Everyone wishes to buy a product or a service they desire. Sometimes we do not have the required money with us when we come across such an item. We cannot use our debit card since we do not have the required amount even in our bank account. At such times, the credit card comes to our rescue.

- We can easily buy our desired product or service using a credit card, irrespective of whether we have money or not. We can even buy an expensive product or a service on instalments using a credit card.

- However, we need to be cautious while using it, as overuse of credit cards may lead to one getting caught in a debt trap.

Why Use a Credit Card?

1. **Easy availability of credit:** The biggest benefit of a credit card is that one can use it to easily access funds up to a certain limit. In

> *The house is owned by the bank until the home loan is fully repaid!*

short, you can transact up to a limit even if you do not have money at that point.

2. **Repayment tenure:** Credit card users are given a stipulated time within which to repay outstanding dues. This could generally be twenty to fifty days. You can repay your outstanding dues any time during this period without any interest levied on them.

3. **Easy purchase on instalments:** A credit card helps when you are planning to buy an expensive product or a service and do not have sufficient funds for it.

4. **Multiple offers:** Credit card companies often make offers to lure their customers to use their cards. You can save money using these offers and also get reward points, which can be redeemed later. These offers are a decoy to make you use the card frequently.

5. **Help in emergency situations:** If you need hard cash in an emergency, you can use your credit card at an ATM and get cash. But you are subject to paying a high interest on it. That is why you should avoid using a credit card to withdraw money.

6. **Good credit score:** If you are using your credit card wisely and making timely repayments, your credit score is going to be good. That will help you increase your credit rating, and you can benefit from this when you apply for a loan.

7. **Useful while travelling:** Credit cards are handy when you travel as they can be used in emergency situations. In 2013, during the floods in Uttarakhand, many people were stuck in small villages in the state. They took to social media to describe how they ran out of hard cash in a few days and how people who had credit cards could use them to meet their needs.

Problems with Using a Credit Card

1. High rate of interest

- Credit card statements highlight the minimum amount due, meaning the least amount to be paid by a given period of time. You have to pay an interest of 3–3.5 per cent per month as interest on the balance amount if you use the option of paying only the minimum amount due.

> *'Every time you borrow money, you're robbing your future self.'*—Nathan W. Morris

- Read the previous statement again. The interest mentioned is per month and not per year, which translates to 36–42 per cent per annum. While the rate of interest on home loans is 7–12 per cent and on business loans 10–15 per cent, credit card outstandings carry an interest of 36–42 per cent per annum. Choosing this option to spend can lead to financial loss.

- What should you do? You must pay the outstanding credit card amounts on time. Saving interest is saving money. The best way to save is to avoid unnecessary expenses like high-interest payments.

2. **Increase in unnecessary spends**

- We start buying more when we have a credit card at our disposal. At such times, we may buy more than what is necessary and add to our expenses.

- If our payments are made on time, the credit card companies increase the spending limits on our card. This might lead to more spending.

3. **Cheating**

- We may fall prey to cheating and fraud by scamsters, even if this is not a common practice.

- Fraudsters may also get access to our personal information by using technology and use our card details to make their own purchases on it.

- Someone may use a stolen or lost credit card. We are responsible for all the transactions made on our cards till we inform the bank about our lost or stolen card, or about unauthorized purchases made on it.

- It is important to read the monthly credit card statements sent by the bank. If you find erroneous transactions, inform the bank immediately.

4. **Hidden charges**

Although credit cards may seem easy and straightforward to use, they are usually loaded with hidden charges.

1. **Late payment fee**

- If you miss the due date, you have to pay both interest and late fees. The larger the outstanding you have on your card, the higher the late fee. Example: Generally, a late fee of Rs 300 is charged for an outstanding of Rs 10,000 on your card. However, if your outstanding amount is Rs 25,000, the late fee would be Rs 600.

- If you miss the due dates regularly, then your credit limit will be reduced. Your credit score will also be affected, causing problems when you make loan applications in the future.

- What should you do? Maintain a sum in your bank account that will pay at least the minimum amount due. Please understand that you had to use the credit card because you did not have any money in your account. After having spent money when you don't have it, at least ensure timely payment of your dues.

2. Registration and annual charges

- You are usually charged Rs 500 to Rs 2500 as registration or annual fees on your credit card. To attract customers, banks may give them a fee waiver for the first year. Thereafter, a fee is charged annually.

- Some banks waive your annual fees if you spend more than a certain threshold amount on your card in a year.

- What should you do? Learn about the annual fee you will be charged when you register for a credit card.

3. Fee on withdrawal of cash using a credit card

- You are allowed to withdraw cash up to 20 to 40 per cent of your credit card limit from an ATM. This is a type of unsecured loan given to you by the bank. Banks usually charge around 2.5 per cent on it as fees.

- Example: If your credit card's limit is Rs 50,000, then you can withdraw Rs 20,000 from an ATM using your card. You will be charged Rs 500 as a convenience fee for this transaction. Apart from this, you pay 36–42 per cent interest annually on this amount, as it can only be repaid once all your other dues on the card are cleared.

- What should you do? Avoid withdrawing cash using a credit card.

Forgetting a debt does not pay it.

4. Overlimit fee

- If you attempt to spend more than your prescribed limit on your card, either the transaction will be declined or will be accepted with a hefty overlimit fee.

- This is to the tune of Rs 500 or 2.5 per cent of the transaction amount, whichever is higher.

- What should you do? 'Know your limits.' Don't overuse your credit card. Many banks increase your credit limit without your asking for it. Understand your needs and decide on what your credit card limit should be.

The Right Way to Use a Credit Card

1. Read all the rules before getting a credit card

- We fill out a physical form or click on a link shared by the bank to apply for a credit card. In this process, we tend to not read the rules.

- From the rules you will be able to find out the different types of charges levied by the bank. We often get a credit card through some offer and thus ignore the rules and regulations thereof.

2. Pay dues within the stipulated time

- Paying the dues before or on the due date will be beneficial. You will save on the additional interest and fees charged by the bank, and this will also help increase your credit score.

3. Keep track of your transactions

- We use the credit card for a lot of transactions. It will be useful to keep track of all these expenses and put a limit on our additional expenses.

4. Read your credit card statement carefully

- We often do not care to read the entire credit card statement. We just see what the payable amount is and keep the statement aside.

> *'Life is really simple, but we insist on making it complicated.'*—Confucius

- The statement clearly mentions the payable and the total outstanding amounts. But since the total outstandings are mentioned at the bottom of the page, we may just pay the minimum due and be charged interest on the balance.

5. Do not spend more than your credit limit

- Banks decide on a credit limit for every card before its issue. There are no interest or overlimit charges until the limit is crossed. If the user crosses this limit, a fixed charge is levied for this. That is why you must avoid using the card for amounts above the stipulated limit.

6. Don't withdraw cash on your credit card

- You may use the credit card to withdraw cash in case of an emergency only. Banks charge a heavy interest on this. Avoid using credit cards to withdraw cash as much as possible.

7. Avoid unnecessary expenses

- Banks refine our credit limit based on our usage pattern. We may use a card more often if our credit limit is increased. In such a scenario, if we are not able to pay the dues, we may be stuck in a debt spiral.

- Also, the charges and fees on late payment or non-payment of outstandings are unnecessary expenses. If you realize that you are using the credit card more than is necessary, you can request the bank to reduce your credit limit.

Many personal finance experts hold that any loan, of whatever kind, is bad. That is because it depletes your hard-earned money. We will look at signs of bankruptcy in the next chapter.

> 'The decision to go into debt alters the course and condition of your life. You no longer own it. You are owned.'—Dave Ramsay

Signs of Bankruptcy

Nilesh is very happy today. One of his dreams is getting fulfilled today, and that was to become debt-free. The moment he pays Rs 1 lakh to the bank, tears start to roll down his cheeks. When he reaches home, he offers a box of sweets to the gods and gives one to his neighbour, Shinde. Because if it wasn't for Shinde, Nilesh would never have been able to come out of the vicious circle of debt he had got tangled in.

Fifteen years ago, Nilesh had decided to quit his job and started his own business. He expanded his business over the next two or three years, and it was growing. He was blessed both with knowledge and money. But his lifestyle started to change too. He sold his flat and bought a new one in a premium locality. He started spending extravagant amounts on expensive cars, branded clothes, eating out, travelling and expensive gym and club memberships. He got his children admitted to the most expensive school in the city. While everything was going well, he had a major business loss and had to face a financial crunch.

He was finding it hard to clear his pending bills, bank instalments, employee salaries and other such expenses. He was under a lot of mental stress. His wife advised him to quit the business and move to a stable job. This became a reason for arguments between them. Their quarrels kept growing. One day, Nilesh's car was hit by a vehicle approaching from the wrong side of the road. Nilesh was not at fault here. He got out of his car and started arguing with the other driver. At the same time, Shinde was witness to all this. He intervened and solved the issue right then and there.

Shinde had known Nilesh from the time he was a smart, dedicated child and was shocked to see him in this condition. He took him home. Nilesh ended up telling Shinde everything about his state of affairs. Shinde felt bad for him.

Nilesh was shocked to hear the term 'bankruptcy' from Shinde. Suddenly, he recalled all his childhood lessons and decided to become debt-free at the earliest.

He cancelled his expensive gym and club memberships. As suggested by Shinde, he sold his premium flat and moved to a rented flat to pay his office expenses and the children's school fees. By doing this he could save both time and fuel expenses. He sold his premium car and got a new mid-size car. His family supported him in all his decisions. He worked harder than ever before and got the business back on track. But this time he was cautious. He fully understood the importance of financial planning. He followed Shinde's advice and planned his finances with the help of a good financial adviser. He first started by planning for repayment of the loan he had taken and salvaged his lost image gradually.

- Taking on debt has never been respected in Indian culture. Our forefathers have always taught us to work hard, save money and stay away from debt in order to be happy.

- But in the recent past, Indians have started to spend more, and flamboyant lifestyles have started to take root in Indian soil. The Internet and social media have shown us how people in other countries live their lives and have fun. In an attempt to copy their 'cool way of living', we have forgotten the simple-living-high-thinking philosophy of our Indian culture. People started to take loans for every type of expenses.

- 'Is taking a loan a good or bad thing?' This is a complex question to answer, and the answer itself would differ depending on the situation and the person in question.

- If you have a strong financial standing, no one will care how, where, why and how much you spend, because that is your personal choice. However, the mindset of always getting into debt to celebrate is self-destructive. Stay away from it.

> 'Rather go to bed supperless than rise in debt.'
> —Benjamin Franklin

THE DEBT SPIRAL

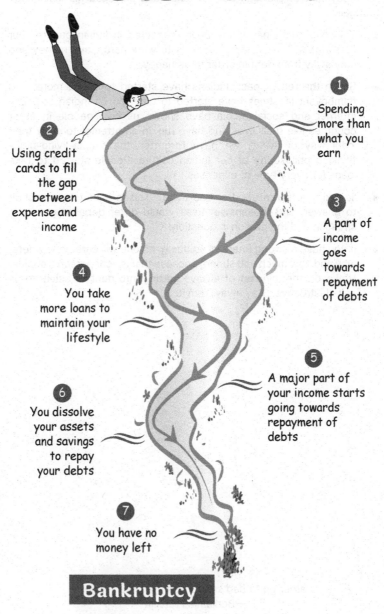

1 Spending more than what you earn

2 Using credit cards to fill the gap between expense and income

3 A part of income goes towards repayment of debts

4 You take more loans to maintain your lifestyle

5 A major part of your income starts going towards repayment of debts

6 You dissolve your assets and savings to repay your debts

7 You have no money left

Bankruptcy

Are You Already Bankrupt?

If a major part of your monthly income goes towards paying your debts, then you are in a grave situation. Here are a few indicators to help you understand if you are bankrupt or moving into the vicious circle of bankruptcy:

- Your income is far behind your essential expenses and ever-mounting pile of interest and debt repayments. No savings are possible.

- Bills are never paid on time since you do not have the money for them.

- You get frequent calls from loan recovery agents, landlords and utility bill recovery teams. You then resort to frequent changing of phone numbers to hide from these callers.

- You need to ask your friends and family for financial help on a regular basis; they then start avoiding you.

- You even stop making a list of your outstanding payments.

- A major part of your expenses are made using credit cards since there is nothing in your bank account.

- You withdraw money using your credit card, and you enter a deeper pit when you are charged interest of 36–42 per cent per annum.

- You cope up by paying just the minimum amount due on your credit card every month.

- You might even miss the credit card payment due date and be charged late fees, as you don't have even the amount to pay the minimum amount due.

- You keep taking loans to pay your previous loans. Under the pretext of a home loan top-up, you take one to pay off the dues on your credit card or the vehicle loan.

- You get into frequent arguments with the family or your partner and often lie to them. This leads to a polluting atmosphere in the family.

- Sometimes, you might also resort to addiction or black magic to relieve your stress and soon mess up the situation further. This might lead you towards depression.

> *'The goal isn't more money. The goal is living life on your terms.'*—Chris Brogan

- To take a loan is not always bad. But are you getting a loan to pay for your needs or just to display your flamboyance? Using your loans for the right purposes and repaying them in time is important.

- No bank can give you a loan without your will and consent.

- Getting a loan is your own decision. Take a conscious decision to take it, use the loan amount wisely towards building your wealth and not for making the bank richer. Don't become an unpaid bank employee who works by paying the bank lifelong interest.

- We will look at the reasons why we should aim to become loan-free at the earliest.

Why Become Debt-Free at the Earliest?

> 'If you think nobody cares if you're alive, try missing a couple of car payments.'—Earl Wilson

1. To increase income

● The amount you spend towards paying your loan can be invested in various investment options to increase your income.

● Your monthly instalment consists of two elements—principal and interest. The longer the tenure over which you choose to repay your loan, the higher will be the interest element in the instalments.

● Example: If you take a home loan worth Rs 10 lakh at 10 per cent interest:

Repayment tenure	Monthly instalment	Total interest paid
20 years (240 months)	Rs 9650	Rs 13.16 lakh
5 years (60 months)	Rs 21,247	Rs 2.75 lakh

Additional interest paid for the extra fifteen years of repayment tenure: Rs 10.41 lakh

● You can save on interest by keeping the tenure to a minimum or by paying a higher amount towards paying off the principal whenever possible. Saving on the interest amount is equivalent to increasing your income.

● You will save on the monthly instalment amount once all outstandings are paid off. You can then use the amount saved towards other expenses, investments or to buy new assets.

● You should think of becoming debt-free, considering the return on investments and the power of compounding interest.

2. To become the true owner of your assets

● You are not the rightful owner of your home while you are repaying your home loan. The same is the case with car loans, where you don't own the car until the car loan is fully repaid.

● Say, you have taken a loan from the State Bank of India for a period of fifteen years. You should visualize the nameplate on your home as follows: 'Mrs Neha and Mr Vikram Deshmukh (Landlord: State Bank of India).'

'Debt gives you the ability to look like you're winning when you're not.'—Dave Ramsay

- The faster you repay your loans, the sooner you will be able to enjoy the ownership of your home, car or other assets. You might get this feeling while repaying your loans as to whether you are working for yourself or just to pay off your instalments against your loans.

3. **To increase your financial cover**

- The interest on loans will continue, irrespective of the weather, the season or your financial situation. You would have experienced this during the recent pandemic.

- The amount you need to repay your loans sets you drifting away from your long-term goals. The sum that can be set aside for emergency funds, children's higher education or retirement funds is spent on loans.

- You can invest towards various goals once you are debt-free and can experience financial security. That is why you must repay all your loans as soon as possible.

4. **To be safe from risks**

- Alongside loans, many types of risks also enter your life. If you become debt-ridden and have not saved anything for emergencies, you are just a step away from financial crises.

- Late payment of salaries by employers, insecurities in your employment, a major medical expense or similar situations can disrupt your instalment repayment cycle.

- Since problems never come alone, one problem tends to bring a few more problems along. You might get frequent calls and visits from the loan recovery department of your bank. In the worst case, the announcement of the auction of your personal property may be printed in the newspapers, leading to a loss of image for you.

- Once you are debt-free, you are also free from all the risks mentioned above. You are also better equipped to face any unseen emergencies.

5. **To spend on your favourite things without guilt**

- Your cash in hand is depleted by the loan instalments you have to pay, and you will feel restricted when you intend to buy your favourite things.

> *'Some people are just stuck in their ways and have been brainwashed into believing that credit cards and debt are an unavoidable part of life.'*—Dave Ramsay

- You might also get caught in an awkward situation. Example: You use all your savings to get your favourite mobile phone. Now, you have to take a loan to buy the next thing you want.

- Not being able to spend on your favourite things, taking loans to cover those expenses and not being left with any money to spend—this vicious loop can go on for a while. That is why you should avoid unnecessary expenses or postpone a few as much as possible.

- Once you are left with additional money after you have saved, you do not feel guilty about spending it.

6. To choose early retirement

- The amount you saved from becoming debt-free before the earliest period can help you create a fund for your retirement.

- All the running around that you did to earn money throughout your life is of no use unless you can enjoy your wealth and are satisfied with it.

7. To obtain a good credit score

- Taking multiple loans depletes your credit score, and banks will charge a higher rate of interest on the subsequent loans you take.

- Those who have a good credit score can get loans at a lower rate of interest. These days, even employers check employees' credit scores; hence a good score can increase your chances of getting a good job too.

8. To get good job opportunities

- Emerson said, 'A man in debt is so far a slave.' A person in debt is a type of slave.

- You do not easily look for another job when you have monthly instalments to pay and are badly in need of the monthly salary. The moment your employer finds out about this, he may even delay your increments.

- The constant stress of loan repayment may have a negative impact on your mindset and reduce your productivity, leading to losses in business or stagnancy in employment.

> 'Modern man drives a mortgaged car over a bond-financed highway on credit-card gas.'—Earl Wilson

- A debt-free person will never work for someone at low wages. If one is debt-free, one could opt for high-opportunity, high-salary jobs rather than low-potential, low-salary jobs.

Psychological Benefits of Being Debt-Free

9. Opportunity to work without stress

- You always feel pressured when you are debt-ridden. What if I lose my job? You always have this thought at the back of your mind. You may also feel guilty even while making the smallest of expenses.

10. Great Mental Health

- Not just mental stress, but the burden of loans may also lead to mental health issues such as sadness and depression. As against this, you will feel very relieved and be in a state of positive mental health when you are debt-free.

- You feel light when you are debt-free, and the feeling of being stuck does not exist any more. You can sleep peacefully. Also, you can now think actively about your family, friends, hobbies, likes and dislikes, and live a happy and satisfied life.

11. Growth in Self-Confidence

- You think lowly about yourself when you're debt-ridden, and this affects your self-confidence. People with a lot of debts to pay off try to show a virtually perfect world to their networks and try to hide their real financial situation.

- Constantly spending on expensive homes, premium cars and branded clothes adds to our total loans. Conversely, your self-confidence magically grows by leaps and bounds once you are debt-free.

- Your life is in your control. The feeling of not being a slave to any bank, job or business helps increase one's self-confidence.

12. Freedom from Health Issues

- To feel constantly pressured about finances reduces your attention span and self-control. People ridden with debt usually take shortcuts to cure their health problems instead of looking to solve their health issues for good.

'Creditors have better memories than debtors.'—Benjamin Franklin

- Financial stress can cause physical problems too. Debt-ridden people do not look in the best of shape, and their stress can lead to heart problems, diabetes, ulcers, allergies and the like.

- A debt-free person is free from worries too and can have sound mental and physical health.

13. Better relations

- Sadness, depression, stress and worries that come along with debt also bring along unwanted guests such as fear and anger. These negative emotions may cause rifts in relations at home and at the workplace.

- The constant worry about paying EMIs may also become a reason for unwanted arguments with partners or colleagues.

- Comparing your financial situation with that of your friends will lead to jealousy. A debt-ridden person is always ready to blame others and disturb his own mental peace. Example: A person would blame his boss for paying less wages.

- Once debt-free, you are happier and work towards strengthening your relations with others. Your sad mindset vanishes all of a sudden.

14. A happy married life

- Debts can create problems between life partners. Your better half should fully know about your debts and the percentage of income that goes towards the repayment of various loans.

- You may buy a big home or a car and get home interiors done to make your partner happy, even when it is not in your budget.

- Later, when tension rises in the relationship due to your stretched finances, you might blame your partner and kids for the situation. They may then retaliate by saying that if you had discussed the real financial situation back then with them, they would have never asked for the lifestyle upgrades done on borrowed funds.

- Everyone in the family should be part of discussions related to the solution of financial problems. Healthy discussion brings transparency to the family. A debt-free family is always happier and more satisfied than a debt-ridden one.

> 'A person either disciplines his finances or his finances disciplines him.'—Orrin Woodward

15. You Become Better Parents

● The journey towards becoming free from debt helps you save too. As parents want their children to get the best education, you can invest that saved amount to cover your children's higher-education expenses.

● Parents intend to get their kids admitted to sports coaching, such as for badminton, chess or swimming. But how would you spend on these if you are neck deep in debt? A debt-free person can spend towards the holistic development of his or her children.

● Also, in the process, your children get to learn a lot from your financially responsible behaviour.

16. You Can Help Others

● It is only when you are debt-free that you can financially help your friends, relatives and others in need.

● Your journey of becoming debt-free becomes an inspirational success story for many others who are on that path.

Apart from the benefits mentioned above, there are many more that result from becoming debt-free. People who are debt-ridden are bad at implementing their financial plan. We will look at the process of becoming loan-free in the next chapter.

How to Free Yourself from Debt

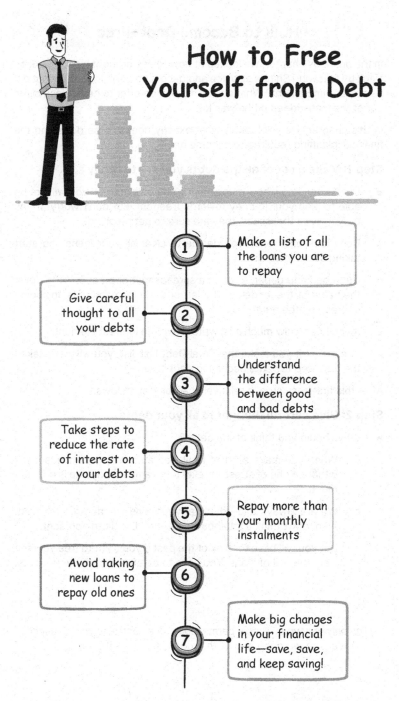

1. Make a list of all the loans you are to repay

2. Give careful thought to all your debts

3. Understand the difference between good and bad debts

4. Take steps to reduce the rate of interest on your debts

5. Repay more than your monthly instalments

6. Avoid taking new loans to repay old ones

7. Make big changes in your financial life—save, save, and keep saving!

How to Become Debt-Free

In the previous chapter, we looked at how Nilesh brought his life back on track by following Shinde's advice and becoming debt-free. But what did he actually implement? What advice did Shinde offer to help Nilesh climb out of the loan-ridden pit he was in?

In this chapter, we will look at what exactly needs to be done and the financial planning required to become debt-free.

Step 1: Make a list of all the debts you are to repay

- Unless you know how much money you owe in total, you will not be able to plan your journey towards freedom. But don't worry! If you bravely face the issues, they are sure to get resolved.

- Don't look back once you decide to clear all your loans and start taking steps towards it.

- Get a pen and paper, or open a spreadsheet or an app. Write down the name of the lender on the left and the loan amounts, including interest, on the right.

- If you know how much it is, write down the interest element.

- The moment you make the 'Total Debt List' list, you will have taken the first step towards becoming debt-free.

After this first easy step, a relatively harder step follows.

Step 2: Give careful thought to all your debts

- Why should you think of the debts?

  o When you make a list of total loan amounts, your mindset will either be one of stress or relief if the amount payable is not very much.

  o We are always told—don't let your mind wander into the past. Also, don't think a lot about the future. Live in the present.

  o But you will have to think of the past if you want to free yourself from the evil of loans. You have to carefully ponder your debts.

'The only way you will ever permanently take control of your financial life is to dig deep and fix the root problem.'—Suze Orman

Step 3: Look at your good debts and bad debts

o   There are two types of debt (loans)—good and bad, as we saw in the previous chapter.

o   The debts that help you grow your wealth, such as the home loan, education loan and business loan, are good debts.

o   Loans taken to cover unnecessary expenses incurred towards showing off to the world, such as for furniture, expensive electronic items and foreign trips, are bad debts.

● **If you have taken good debts**

o   Do not worry if the loans you have taken fall in the good debts category. Be confident that the loans are helping you grow or will help you in the future.

o   Example: Buying a home is both a personal and social milestone. You will be able to repay the entire loan within fifteen to twenty years if you pay your instalments regularly. The value of the property increases by then and brings financial stability. The fact that we own a home helps boost our morale and pushes us to do even better. The only expectation is that you keep paying the instalments against your loan regularly.

● **If you have taken bad debts**

o   Our social media and WhatsApp messages are flooded with positive quotes. If you have taken bad loans, it is time to remind yourself of all those messages and put them into action.

o   Why did we take bad loans? Think about this, and decide that you will never make the same mistake again.

o   If you are really serious about becoming debt-free, write down this line, 'I will never make the same mistake of taking a bad loan', on top of your list of loans.

o   Smart people do not commit the same mistake twice. If you have read this book up to this point, it means you are genuinely looking forward to becoming debt-free. Congratulations!

'Fun can be bought with money, but happiness cannot.'—Dave Ramsay

o   Your loved ones might, at times, make you take loans. However, people who truly love you will always support you. So, do what you feel is right!

Step 4: Take steps to reduce your rate of interest

● When you go through the list of all the loans you have made in the first step, you will identify the loans with higher rates of interest. Your goal should be to clear the high-interest loans at the earliest.

● If you have taken a home loan five years ago at a 12 per cent per annum rate of interest, you can request the lender to reduce it to the prevalent 6.5–8 per cent per annum rate of interest. If your bank does not respond to your request, you can look for other banks that might.

● If the interest rate on credit card outstandings is 36–42 per cent per annum, do you think other companies will charge less? What would the charges be if your loan is foreclosed? You can get answers to these questions by speaking to the customer care department of the credit card-issuing banks.

● Keep the following aspects in mind while planning the rate of interest:

o   Your bank will not let you go to a different bank owing to your long-standing relationship with them

o   Your repayment history

o   Your CIBIL score

o   Offers from competitor banks

o   The bank's trust in your profile and the possibility of your requiring more loans in the future

● What should you be aware of? Unless you are certain that a particular bank's loan offer is the cheapest option for you, don't waste your time communicating with them. Also, avoid being overinquisitive. Don't get overburdened by information overload in evaluating various banks.

You will not need to do a lot of hard work in the next step. You would just need to become frugal.

> 'Stay optimistic about your future even when others aren't.'—Grant Cardone

Step 5: Repay more than your monthly instalments

- An instalment is made up of two elements—principal and interest. The higher the principal that you repay, the less interest you have to pay on the balance. This is no rocket science but a rather simple mathematical concept to understand.

- Putting your extra funds to good use:

  o Some look at the monthly instalments they pay as a formality. They do not pay even a rupee extra towards clearing their loans, even when they have a huge amount of money lying idle in their savings account.

  o Some put any additional money they have into term deposits. The banks offer about 5 per cent in interest as returns on your deposits and charge 7–10 per cent when you borrow from them. This means you are losing money here, even when you have the required funds. If you have additional funds sitting idle in your savings account, you should use them for reducing your outstanding loan amount.

  o We are conditioned to pay different types of instalments. That you have four different instalments to pay against loans is not something to boast about.

  o The more instalments you pay, the further away you are from financial freedom.

Mayur took a loan of Rs 50 lakh at an interest rate of 10 per cent per annum. Based on the repayment tenure, he has the following options:

Option	Tenure	EMI	Total interest	Share of interest in total payable amount
1	120 months = 10 years	Rs 66,075	Rs 29.29 lakh	59 per cent
2	180 months = 15 years	Rs 53,730	Rs 46.71 lakh	93 per cent
3	240 months = 20 years	Rs 48,251	Rs 65.80 lakh	132 per cent
4	300 months = 25 years	Rs 45,435	Rs 86.31 lakh	173 per cent

The interest element increased with the rise in tenure for Mayur. It is worth noticing that the rate of interest in all the options is fixed at 10 per cent. The difference in the instalment amounts to be paid is only because of changes in the tenure.

- EMI is different in each case due to changing interest amounts.

- EMI is high when the repayment is done in a shorter tenure.

- As against this, EMI is low when the tenure is high and the principal repaid every month is lower too.

- The interest is calculated on the balance amount of the loan. Therefore, when you repay more than the stipulated amount, you will have to pay less interest since the tenure will also come down.

- What did Mayur do? He curtailed his expenses and paid whatever extra he could get towards his loan and began his journey to becoming debt-free.

Before moving to the next step, begin with implementing whatever you have learnt. Imagine that you have repaid all your loans and the bank has sent you a loan closure letter. You are no longer worried about having EMIs to pay and have already started planning to invest the amount you will now save every month. If you feel so much better from just the thought of becoming debt-free, think how beautiful your life would be if, in reality, you were debt-free!

Step 6: Avoid taking new loans to repay old ones

- We have to clear all our loans and avoid taking new ones to become loan-free.

- You have Rs 500 in one pocket and Rs 1000 in another. If you keep the entire Rs 1500 in one pocket, does that increase the money you have? No. Similarly, if you take a loan to repay another, your situation is not going to improve.

- Switching loans is beneficial only when you have an interest rate advantage. Example: If your current loan is at an interest of 15 per cent per annum and the new loan is at 12 per cent per annum, you would benefit from switching your loan.

- If you take a new loan with a higher tenure just because you are finding it difficult to make ends meet while paying off your loan instalments, you are actually looking at a temporary fix. The solution to this is either to increase your income or to reduce your expenses.

> 'It takes twenty years to build a reputation and five minutes to ruin it. If you think about that, you'll do things differently.'—Warren Buffett

- Example:

    o   Vandana is barely able to pay her monthly car loan instalment of Rs 25,000.

    o   She still has to pay twenty-four instalments towards the loan.

    o   The bank is offering her an increased tenure, of up to forty-eight instalments, and an additional Rs 2 lakh as a top-up on her existing loan.

    o   What should Vandana do if the bank is keeping the EMI constant at Rs 25,000 per month?

    o   First of all, she must consider whether she really needs the additional amount.

    o   If not, she should avoid taking the top-up to save on additional interest. She should then curtail some of her other expenses and repay the balance of the loan in twenty-four or fewer instalments.

When you climb these steps, you will be able to see the finish line—meaning, a debt-free life. But don't give up before you reach there.

Step 7: Make big changes in your financial life—save, save and keep saving!

Remember—when you repay a loan, you have an additional amount available to repay other loans.

If you are paying an additional amount towards the repayment of a loan, the interest charged on the balance will also be lower.

You should be on a mission to become debt-free. Take the following actions towards it:

- **Make a personal financial budget:**

    o   Calculate your net worth. It is the difference between your assets and liabilities.

    o   All your financial decisions should be directed towards increasing your net worth—either by increasing your assets or by decreasing your liabilities.

'The longer you're not taking action, the more money you're losing.'—Carrie Wilkerson

o   The first step in finance management is the preparation of a budget. Plan it and avoid unnecessary expenses. Saving one rupee is like earning ten.

o   Find out where you are spending more by auditing your expenses regularly.

o   Maintain a diary or prepare your income and expenses statement and update it on a daily basis. Make it a habit and ask your family to follow it too.

o   Prepare a financial calendar and enter your investments, loan repayments and other such details in it.

● **Save money—financial planning of purchases and expenses:**

o   The importance of saving is mentioned on page 93.

o   Make a habit of saying 'No' to yourself. Many a time, you spend a lot under pressure from your friends and relatives. A single 'No' from you can save you a lot of money. Get rid of the mindset of spending just because others are spending too.

o   Become bigger in stature, not just for others, but for your own self too.

> 'If money is your hope for independence, you will never have it. The only real security that a man will have in this world is a reserve of knowledge, experience and ability.'—Henry Ford

How to repay a twenty-five-year loan in ten years

The additional amount paid towards the repayment of the loan, in excess of the EMIs, reduces the tenure.

Pay as per the original plan

Pay an additional amount equal to one EMI every year

Increase your monthly repayment by 5 per cent

Increase your monthly repayments by 10 per cent

Loan will be repaid in 9 years and 11 months.

Loan will be repaid in 12 years and 11 months.

Loan will be repaid in 19 years and 1 month.

Loan will be repaid in 25 years.

To download the early repayment calculator spreadsheet, please visit https://arthasakshar.com/book.

Home Loan—Is Early Repayment Better or Dragged on as a Long-Term Investment?

If you have additional savings, should you use it to repay the home loan before the stipulated time or invest it somewhere? There is no perfect answer to this. We looked at how to become debt-free in the last chapter. But you need to think differently in the case of home loans.

The government is always looking for ways to promote ownership of homes by people. This also helps in promoting employment through the construction activities this entails and gets the economy moving. Governments build policies and infrastructure to enable easy home loans. Although the home loan is one of the most commonly availed-of loans, it operates in a different way from other loans.

Benefits of a Home Loan:

1. **Low rate of interest:** The cheapest of the loans we can get is the home loan. In 2023, home loans are available at an interest rate of 7–9 per cent per annum. Other loans are expensive, compared to this.

2. **Benefits of government initiatives:** If the loan amount is small, the qualifying borrowers can avail of a tax deduction under PMAY (Pradhan Mantri Awas Yojana), helping them to further save money.

3. **Tax deductions:** The following deductions are available for financial year 2023–24. The taxpayer has to opt for the old tax regime to avail these deductions.

    a. **Interest on home loans:**

        ■   If the property is constructed or purchased through a home loan, the interest portion can be deducted from the income received in the form of rent. To avail this benefit, the home should be fully constructed and the owner should have taken possession of the home.

        ■   If the borrower owns two properties and neither is given out on rent, interest paid on such self-occupied property can be claimed as deduction.

> *'No wealth can ever make a bad man at peace with himself.'*—Plato

■ If the property has been constructed or purchased through a home loan, up to Rs 2 lakh paid towards interest can be availed of as a deduction.

b. **Principal in loan repayment**

■ Sections 80C, 80CCC and 80CCD(1) allow the borrower to claim a deduction of up to Rs 1.5 lakh against a home loan. This includes the total of the principal on the home loan, life insurance premium, Provident Fund contribution, Public Provident Fund contribution, investments in Sukanya Samruddhi Yojana, National Savings Certificate, school fees, college fees, pension schemes, etc.

Check Whether Pre-payment of Your Home Loan Will Benefit You

1. Inflation and repayment of home loan

● The home loan is usually to be repaid over fifteen to twenty-five years. The EMI is decided at the time of disbursal of the loan.

● But the instalments are later adjusted against inflation and the value starts decreasing. Example: If one is paying Rs 50,000 as EMI in 2023, the instalment will still be Rs 50,000 in 2041. However, the value of Rs 50,000 may be Rs 25,000 (as per 2023 terms) in 2041 due to inflation. The borrowers can benefit from this.

2. From the point of view of income tax

● Many people think repayment of a home loan before the agreed tenure also means the inability to claim income tax deductions in the years saved. This thought process makes them take on the burden of repayment for years together.

● People don't fully understand the tax savings that are due to home loans. In a nutshell, a home loan can help save only a limited amount in tax.

'Stores are never nice to people. They're nice to credit cards.'—J.F. Lawton

- **Repayment of principal**

  o You can claim a deduction of a maximum of Rs 1.5 lakh as repayment of the principal, even if you have paid more than that. The taxpayer has to opt for the old tax regime to avail these deductions.

  o The total permissible amount of Rs 1.5 lakh can easily be exhausted if you have invested in other options deductible under sections 80C, 80CCC and 80CCD(1), even without taking the principal repayment into consideration.

- **Deduction of Interest**

  o If you have not rented out the home, you can claim a maximum of Rs 2 lakh per financial year even if you are repaying more than that, as per the provision of the Income Tax Act.

  o In the preliminary years, the interest element in the instalment is much higher than the principal element. That is why the amount paid towards interest is much more than Rs 2 lakh if you have taken a loan of a high amount.

Knowing the total amount of the loan, the tax slab you fall under and the proportion of interest and principal in your instalment will help you decide whether you should repay your home loan in advance or not.

3. **Low rate of interest on home loans and high returns on investments**

- Assume that you are repaying your home loan at an interest rate of 6.5 per cent interest per annum. You have money left after paying for all expenses, saving for emergencies and clearing all instalments.

- You would use that amount towards repayment of your loan or invest that in a long-term high-return investment.

- If you consider returns on investments in equity-oriented mutual funds over the past thirty years, they have always surpassed the amount you would have saved by repaying the loan at the rate of 6.5 per cent per annum.

'I never want money to dictate what I can and can't do in life.'—Jessica Moorhouse

- If you create a term deposit out of the amount that can be used to repay the loan, it will not be beneficial to you as the returns you will get after tax will be less than the interest you pay on the loan.

- If you are able to pay the home loan instalments with ease, you do not need to hurry to repay the entire loan. Utilizing that money to invest wisely can help you get better returns over a period of time.

4. If you want to fulfil your goal of becoming debt-free

- Pay as much as possible towards the loan and reduce the loan amount principal.

- If you are paying home loan instalments on two properties, it is wise to try and clear as much of the first loan as possible so that you can upgrade at the earliest.

- If you have cleared the loan on your first home and are paying instalments for your second home, then you should try to become debt-free at the earliest. Please consider the points discussed above, especially the difference between the appreciation of your house property value and the interest cost you pay every year on your home loan.

All the best for becoming debt-free!

सुखमापतितं सेव्यं दुःखमापतितं तथा |
चक्रवत्परिवर्तन्ते दुःखानि च सुखानि च ||

—सुभाषित

(*Enjoy positive situations that you experience in life and accept the negative situations as well. Both positive and negative situations go in a circle. Follow your destiny with a smile without complaining about it.*)

• Part 5 •

Investments

Debt

Income

Investment

Saving

Budget

Planning

Money Works

Money Works

Introduction

The most important milestone in your journey of financial planning is the understanding of 'investment'.

It is the most ignored and misunderstood term. Investing your savings wisely can help to fulfil your various dreams, goals and needs.

Investment means setting aside your hard-earned money to create more wealth for you. Your money gets into the business of creating more money.

Many of us must be thinking—how do we invest money when we already find it hard to meet our daily needs? But let us look at this aspect from a different angle. We are able to meet our financial needs today since we are physically active. What about tomorrow, when we grow old? The question—What about tomorrow?—reinforces the importance of investment.

Our savings should be invested in such a way that the returns we get can help us fulfil our goals.

Remember this!

- Investing and saving are two different concepts.

- The risks involved in investing depend upon your financial capacity.

- Investment does not consist of any magical elements that will make you rich overnight.

- Investment, just like other financial plans, is for everyone.

- Inflation increases the cost of daily necessities every day. The number of needs you can fulfil with Rs 100 today is much higher than what it can be tomorrow. Your fixed income will not be sufficient to match inflation tomorrow.

'It is better to have a permanent income than to be fascinating.'—Oscar Wilde

The Six Steps to Financial Freedom

The returns from your investments will sufficiently meet your financial needs while still leaving you with a surplus.

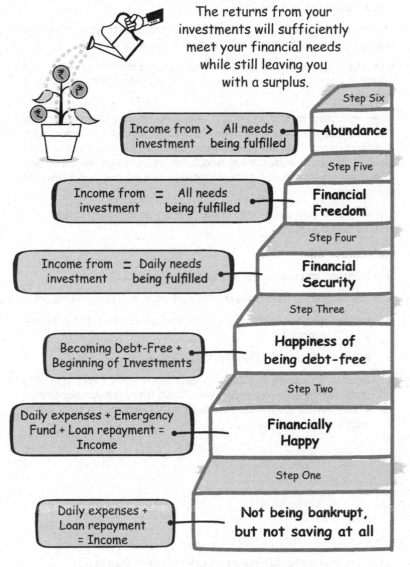

Step Six

Income from investment > All needs being fulfilled — **Abundance**

Step Five

Income from investment = All needs being fulfilled — **Financial Freedom**

Step Four

Income from investment = Daily needs being fulfilled — **Financial Security**

Step Three

Becoming Debt-Free + Beginning of Investments — **Happiness of being debt-free**

Step Two

Daily expenses + Emergency Fund + Loan repayment = Income — **Financially Happy**

Step One

Daily expenses + Loan repayment = Income — **Not being bankrupt, but not saving at all**

Investing helps to fulfil your aspirations and dreams!

Difference between savings and investments

	Savings	Investments
What kind of needs does it fulfil?	Urgent expenses, emergency needs and contingency funds	Fulfilling long-term goals, wealth creation, achieving financial freedom
Where does it begin?	You start saving when your income is more than your expenses	Investment starts once you have saved money
Mindset	'Saver's mindset' is important to start saving	Once you achieve your goal of savings, you can begin investing with confidence
Direction	Usually, it is not directed in a particular way	Direction is important while investing
Example	Bank savings account, recurring account, term deposit, amount saved in lockers at home	Immovable property, gold, shares, mutual funds, etc.
Risk of loss	Less/nominal	Moderate or high, depending on the type of investment
Returns	Small/nominal	Moderate or high, depending on the type of investment
Liquidity (availability of money from the instrument)	The amount in savings accounts can be used whenever needed	It can take time for the funds to be made available

'Spending is quick; earning is slow.'—Russian proverb

How Does Inflation Eat Up Your Investment?

'Inflation explosion!'

'Inflation has messed up financial plans.'

'Government has failed to control inflation.'

We are bombarded with news such as these. We generally know what inflation means, but we should understand how inflation affects our investments and therefore, our financial future too.

While we are always blasting the government for rising inflation, we should introspect and think of what solutions we can implement on the personal front to cope with it. 'Accept the inevitable'—just like this quote, we have to accept the reality and make our investment decisions likewise.

Inflation Is the Constant Rise in the Cost of Goods and Services

● The amount you need to pay for buying a product is not enough to pay for the same product in a few years. Inflation makes the same product cost more as compared to the present day. Inflation is counted in terms of percentage which is known as the rate of inflation.

● The worst aspect of inflation is the compounding effect of rising costs.

Example 1:

o You purchased a product for Rs 1000 last year. If you consider the rate of inflation at 5 per cent, the same product would cost Rs 1050 now.

o If the inflation rate remains 5 per cent the next year too, the same product would cost Rs 1103, as the base rate for calculation is not Rs 1000 but Rs 1050.

o After ten years of inflation at 5 per cent, the cost of this item would rise to Rs 1629.

Example 2:

o Suppose the price of 1 litre of milk in the year 2010 was Rs 15 and that price has increased to around Rs 70 in the year 2023.

● One has to shell out more money for all goods and services with growth in the economy, as demand for goods and services will rise. To meet the demand, manufacturers have to ensure supply, which if less will result in a price rise.

● Prices keep increasing as there is a constant rise in demand in a booming economy.

● However, inflation cannot be termed as bad in every instance. A rising economy is characterized by stable prices and a controlled rate of inflation. In a developed economy, the earnings and disposable income of the citizens are high and inflation is not as high as it is in developing economies.

● In India, the Central government and Reserve Bank of India are responsible for keeping a watch on the rate of inflation.

'You must gain control over your money or the lack of it will forever control you.'—Dave Ramsey

Inflation, Savings and Investments

● Your current income may cover or exceed your expenses. You may be able to save some money. But it is important to find out whether your savings will be sufficient to cover your long-term goals and the rising rate of inflation.

● Long-term goals would include a comfortable retirement, children's higher education and their marriage. You need to start planning, saving and investing right now for these needs.

● **Savings:** A few options can give returns that may match the rate of inflation—they could be term deposits, National Savings Certificate, Post Office deposits and recurring deposits.

● **Investments:** You should think of investments that will give you a higher rate of return than the rate of inflation. Example: Shares, mutual funds and immovable property.

● Example: Akshay saved Rs 1 lakh in hard cash and kept it in a locker. One must appreciate Akshay for saving this money and for not having touched it for two years. But the number of products he can buy using that amount will be less than what he could two years before. We invest in savings deposits that offer a return of 4 per cent return or keep our money in a current account, which will offer nil returns when the rate of inflation is 4–5 per cent.

● The value of Rs 1 lakh in 1984 is just Rs 7451 at 2020 rates. Savings alone are not enough; one must invest in options that offer high returns to battle inflation.[1]

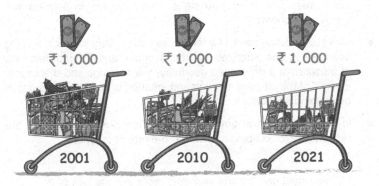

● Inflation nibbles away at your hard-earned money on a constant basis.

● Example: Achyut has saved Rs 1 lakh in a savings account that offered an interest rate of 4 per cent. After a year, his savings increased to Rs 1,04,000 (Rs 1,00,000 principal + Rs 4000 interest). Achyut falls in the 20 per cent income tax bracket. He will have to pay tax of Rs 800 on the interest earned, which means his income from interest after tax will be Rs 3200 (interest of Rs 4000 – tax of Rs 800), and the effective rate of interest will be just 3.2 per cent (interest income of Rs 3200/principal of Rs 1,00,000).

● This 3.2 per cent rate of interest on savings is not enough to cover the rate of inflation if we assume it to be 4 per cent.

● If your age is thirty-five, you should think of what the rate of inflation will be in the decades leading up to the time you are sixty, and you must invest accordingly.

When can you start investing?

● The answer is easy—when you have a surplus amount after saving for your emergency funds, you should start investing without any delay.

● When we think of investment, only long-term investments get highlighted. Many of us are confused between savings and investments. Savings are not investments.

● We know the meaning of the saying, 'What you sow is what you reap.' Investment is just like sowing—meaning, you will reap well if you sow right. Likewise, sowing at the right time and under the right circumstances can allow you to reap a good rate of returns.

● Do not lose heart if you started investing late in life. You can still benefit from the magic of compounding over many years in future.

Compound Interest—the Eighth Wonder of the World

'Compound interest is the eighth wonder of the world. He who understands it, earns it . . . he who doesn't . . . pays it.' —Albert Einstein

We have become used to hearing the term 'investment'. People around the globe invest money. Based on their income and savings, some may invest just Rs 50 a month and some others Rs 5 lakh a month.

But most of us face financial instabilities owing to rising costs and financial emergencies. And people always complain of not being able to save enough and having to live a life of meagre means. By the time we realize we're going wrong in our financial planning, we may have reached the far end of our lives.

That is why, if you want to plan your finances well, you have to understand the importance of compound interest.

The Magic of Compound Interest

- People think of the lottery, betting and gambling when they think of *growing their investments multi-fold.* But we overlook a legal and sure way of financial growth—investing at compounding interest.

- We learn both simple and compound interest during our school days but forget all about the latter when we grow up. But understanding it is very beneficial, especially for investors.

What is Compound Interest?

- Investment involves a base principal amount, and the interest is calculated on that amount.

- In the next round of interest calculation, you not only earn on the base principal amount but also on the interest earned. This cycle continues till such time as the amount stays invested.

- This way, your principal amount keeps increasing every year. As such, you earn higher interest too.

'There are people who have money, and there are people who are rich.'—Coco Chanel

The Difference between Simple and Compound Interest

- If your friend invests a certain amount at simple interest and you invest the same amount at compound interest, the returns you will both get at the end of the same tenure will be massively different.

- The reason is, the interest is calculated on the base principal amount year after year. But when we talk about compound interest, the principal increases every year and the interest is earned on that increased amount.

- This difference can be understood with the table given below:

Year/ Investment	Based on simple interest	Based on compound interest
1	Principal 100 + Interest 10 per cent = 110	Principal 100 + Interest 10 per cent = 110
2	Principal 100 + Interest 10 per cent = 110	Principal 110 + Interest 10 per cent = 121
3	Principal 100 + Interest 10 per cent = 110	Principal 121 + Interest 10 per cent = 133
4	Principal 100 + Interest 10 per cent = 110	Principal 133 + Interest 10 per cent = 146
5	Principal 100 + Interest 10 per cent = 110	Principal 146 + Interest 10 per cent = 160
	Total = 550	**Total = 670**

'In the long run, it's not just how much money you make that will determine your future prosperity. It's how much of that money you put to work by saving it and investing it.'—Peter Lynch

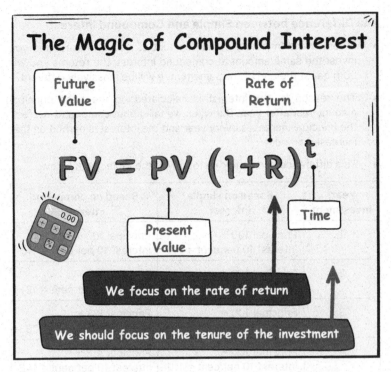

- Just as when you invest, how long you stay invested lets the compound interest unfold its magic. The secret to getting rid of all financial worries is long-term investment. Let us understand the importance of the time for which you are invested when it comes to compound interest.

- The popular American president Benjamin Franklin had gifted £1000, or around $4500, to the cities of Boston and Philadelphia when he died in 1790. He had set conditions as to when the gift could be used. Franklin was well aware of how compounding worked. The gifts were to be encashed on a specified date and the compound interest would show its magic by that time.

- After 100 years, 75 per cent of the total amount was to be used for public welfare, while the balance 25 per cent was to be kept deposited for another 100 years.

- After 200 years, i.e., in the year 1991, both cities received a hefty sum of $6.5 million each.

- This example of the benefits of compounding reasserts the importance of 'time' in investment. In the words of Benjamin Franklin, 'Money makes money. And the money that money makes, makes money.'

- Time is an important element in investment. Along with the principal amount you begin with, the consistency and discipline you exercise in your investment journey are equally important.

Importance of Time

- Rahul and Amit are good friends. Both started working at twenty-five. With the first salary, Rahul started investing Rs 10,000 in a plan that gives 10 per cent returns.

- Amit liked to live a flamboyant lifestyle and never thought of investing until he turned forty. As he turned forty-one, he started to invest Rs 18,000 per month in an investment plan that gave 10 per cent returns.

- When both retired at age sixty, the principal each had totally invested amounted to Rs 43,20,000.

- Even if their principal was the same, since Rahul had started investing at the age of twenty-five, his investment corpus amounted to Rs 4.24 crore, whereas Amit's was valued at Rs 1.38 crore. Since Rahul had started investing earlier, his investments had grown to triple of Amit's.

- Rahul gave thirty-six years for compounding of the returns. Although he was investing only Rs 10,000 every month, he continued doing that for thirty-six years, and the magic of compounding did the rest.

- On the other hand, Amit had invested for just fifteen years. Although he was investing more every month than Rahul, his funds were Rs 2.86 crore less than Rahul's.

- Amit lost a huge opportunity to earn a big amount of money by starting late. Let's plot their investment journeys in a table.

> 'If you understand compound interest, you basically understand the universe.'—Robert Breault

The success story of Rahul, who started investing early

	Rahul	Amit
Age at which investing began	25 years	41 years
Investment every month	Rs 10,000	Rs 18,000
Retirement age	60 years	60 years
Tenure of investment	432 months	240 months
Rate of interest	10 per cent	10 per cent
Total principal investment	Rs 43,20,000	Rs 43,20,000
Returns at the age of retirement	Rs 4,24,18,176	Rs 1,37,82,544

To see the calculations for the example given above, download the spreadsheet: https://arthasakshar.com/book

'Formal education will make you a living; self-education will make you a fortune.'—Jim Rohn

You have Rs 5 lakh to invest. Let us look at the difference in returns based on the tenure.

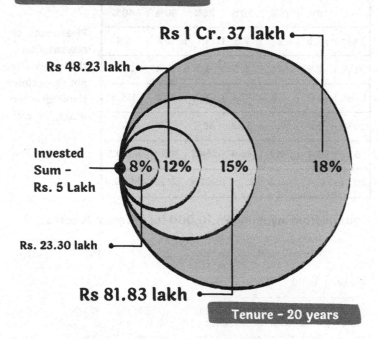

Magic of Compound Interest

Rs 1 Cr. 37 lakh

Rs 48.23 lakh

Invested Sum – Rs. 5 Lakh

8% 12% 15% 18%

Rs. 23.30 lakh

Rs 81.83 lakh

Tenure – 20 years

Magic of Compound Interest

Invested Sum	-	Rs. 5 Lakh
Tenure	-	20 years
Returns at 8%	-	Rs. 23.30 lakh
Returns at 12%	-	Rs 48.23 lakh
Returns at 15%	-	Rs 81.83 lakh
Returns at 18%	-	Rs 1 Crore 37 lakh

To see the calculations for the example given above, download the spreadsheet: https://arthasakshar.com/book

'The strongest force in the universe is compound interest.'—Albert Einstein

Why is a longer tenure important to benefit from compound interest?

Different returns on investing Re 1 for different tenures

	10%	15%	20%	25%	30%	40%
5 yr.	1.6	2	2.5	3.1	3.7	5.4
10 yr.	2.6	4	6.2	9.3	13.8	28.9
15 yr.	4.2	8.1	15.4	28.4	51.2	155.6
20 yr.	6.7	16.4	38.3	86.7	190	836.7
25 yr.	10.8	32.9	95.4	264.7	705.6	4499.9
30 yr.	17.4	66.2	237.4	807.8	2620	24201.4

Please note, the returns after thirty years are not three times those after ten years, but rather **87 times!**

Returns from investing Rs 10,000 for different tenures

	10%	15%	20%	25%	30%	40%
3 yr.	13,310	15,209	17,280	19,531	21,970	27,440
5 yr.	16,105	20,114	24,883	30,518	37,129	53,782
10 yr.	25,937	40,456	61,917	93,132	1,37,858	2,89,255
15 yr.	41,772	81,371	154,070	2,84,217	5,11,859	15,55,681
20 yr.	67,275	1,63,665	383,376	8,67,362	19,00,496	83,66,826
25 yr.	1,08,347	3,29,190	953,962	26,46,978	70,56,410	4,49,98,796
30 yr.	1,74,494	6,62,118	23,73,763	80,77,936	2,61,99,956	24,20,14,324

> 'When it comes to compounding, don't trust your intuition—you have no idea how powerful it is!'—Manoj Arora

Investing with Compound Interest

- Earning income on income means investing at a compound interest. A government scheme such as the Public Provident Fund (PPF) offers an opportunity to earn returns by the compound interest method.

- Investing in well-performing shares or mutual funds for the long term helps one benefit from compounding interest.

Disadvantages of Compound Interest

The compound interest concept values both time and money. It is both advantageous and disadvantageous. It can therefore be our best friend or our worst enemy.

Compound Interest and Debt

- We have already looked at the positives of compound interest. It is beneficial to multiply our wealth through investments. But do not overlook the negatives of compounding. When it comes to loans, compounding interest can be dangerous.

- Extension of loans based on compound interest has led to torture for poor and marginalized farmers for many years in our country. Evil-intentioned moneylenders have used it as a tool in lending to the poor.

- Since many farmers need funds for farming or their children's marriage, they have no resort but these moneylenders to borrow money from. And they have no understanding that the loans they get are based on compound interest.

- They then get caught in a vicious cycle of debt, and end up spending their whole lives repaying their loans, which they pass on to the next generation too. Burdened by their debts, many resort to taking their own lives. This evil practice still continues in isolated parts of the country and also among the marginalized, poor and needy people living in the cities of India.

- Being educated does not mean we will be free from compound interest payments. We should be cautious while taking a loan from a bank, a non-banking financial institution or a microfinance institution. You should look carefully at the way interest is charged on the loan. Otherwise, you will be counted as an 'educated Illiterate'.

> 'Risk comes from not knowing what you're doing.'—Warren Buffett

Loan on Compound Interest

- You will have a hard time repaying a loan that is taken on compound interest. It could be dangerous if we delay or are undisciplined about its repayment.

- Credit card spends are such a type of loan. You should duly pay the complete amount due to avoid paying high interest in proportion to the amount you have borrowed. Sometimes, the interest paid is more than the amount paid towards purchasing a product by using a credit card.

- Today, fintech start-ups and non-banking financial institutions offer loans at the click of a button. Although loan processing is fast and the amount you get can help you satisfy your financial need at that moment, you will have to repay at a rate of interest that is compounded.

The Following Aspects Need to Be Considered to Avoid This:

- Study the repayment plan and the calculations by which the interest payable has been arrived at.

- Never miss your monthly instalment. Pay an additional amount towards principal repayment if possible to reduce the impact of compounding.

- It is better to pay off small loans such as credit card bills as early as possible.

> 'Good and evil increase at compound interest. That's why the little decisions we make every day are of infinite importance.'—C.S. Lewis

Fundamental Rules of Investment

How much should I save? How much should I invest? How much of it goes towards equity investment? The answers to these questions will differ from person to person. However, a few fundamental rules are common to all.

1. Save at least 10 per cent of your income

- Rule—You should set aside at least 10 per cent of your income as savings.

- Is it possible to save 10 per cent of your income every month? This firstly depends on your designation and salary. To set aside 10 per cent of one's income as savings might seem impossible for people in the bigger cities where expenses are higher but salaries may be low. Also, if you are the sole earning member of the family, setting aside 10 per cent as savings seems difficult.

- At such times, your savings should gradually increase, in proportion to your earnings.

2. Emergency fund: Savings covering three to six months' expenses

- We have learnt about emergency funds in a previous chapter. Turn to page 99 to revisit emergency funds.

3. What should the proportion of loans to your income be?

- A thumb rule is that not more than 35–40 per cent of your income must be allotted for loan repayments. If this threshold is being crossed, you will always face a scarcity of funds.

- Since we are talking about 35–40 per cent of income as the upper threshold for loan repayments, it is better if your monthly instalments amount to less than this. Let us look at a few reasons:

- Your monthly financial planning will go haywire if a major portion of your income goes towards repaying loans on the one hand, and your income decreases or expenses increase on the other.

'How many millionaires do you know who have become wealthy by investing in savings accounts? I rest my case.'—Robert G. Allen

- Also, this is discouraging as you might wonder whether you are working for yourself or for your lending bank when you set aside a high proportion of your income towards loan repayment.

- Even banks do not offer new loans easily to people who pay more than 35–40 of their income as EMI.

4. How much to invest in shares?

- Rule: The formula for calculation of how much you must invest in shares is [100 (-) your age].

- This means your age deducted from 100 should be the percentage of your income invested in shares. Example: A person aged thirty years may invest 70 per cent of his income in shares.

- Investing in shares means high risk and high returns! With growing age, your appetite for risk starts shrinking. Every person reacts differently to risk. A few might be aggressive while others are conservative about earning high returns. Use this rule to stay safe from the ups and downs of the share market.

5. How much to invest in options that offer fixed returns?

- Rule: The proportion of investment in fixed return-offering options such as term deposits and bonds should be a percentage whose figure is equal to your age.

- The famous American investor John Bogle said, 'My favourite thumb rule is if your age is twenty years, invest 20 per cent in government bonds, if seventy, invest 70 per cent.'

- The reason behind this is that the principal amount invested should be safe even if the interest earned is comparatively less.

6. How much should your net worth be?

This rule talks about what the ideal value of your net worth should be.

- Rule: Expected net worth = 10 per cent X your age X income before tax

- Example: The expected net worth of a person aged forty years with an annual income of Rs 5 lakh = 10 per cent X 40 X 5,00,000 = 20,00,000

- This rule became popular with the launch of Thomas Stanley's book *The Millionaire Next Door*.

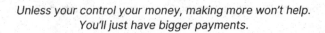

Unless your control your money, making more won't help.
You'll just have bigger payments.

- However, this formula can be applied only to those who have just started to earn or have faced a severe financial issue.

7. How much should your retirement fund amount to?

- Many people feel they don't need to save anything for their post-retirement life. They strongly believe that their children will look after them.

- However, it is becoming increasingly difficult to cover all of one's needs and desires in today's overcompetitive world. You should trust your children for sure, but you should not become a financial burden on them.

- One has to look after one's partner's health and spend towards one's own healthcare with growing age. You should have your own retirement fund for all this.

- Advancements in science have increased life expectancy. Also, the cost of goods and services is continuously on the rise as a result of inflation. Therefore, you need to make provisions for the costs you will incur in the future.

- You can calculate the amount to be saved for your retirement fund in two ways:

  o   Twenty-five times the expected yearly expenses

      ■   Rule: Retirement fund = Expected annual expenses X 25

      ■   Example: If your annual expenses amount to Rs 3 lakh (Rs 25,000 X 12 months), then your retirement fund should be Rs 75 lakh (3,00,000 X 25).

  o   Twenty times your yearly income

      ■   Rule: Retirement fund = Total yearly income X 20

      ■   Example: If your income before tax is Rs 6 lakh per year, then you need to save Rs 1.2 crore as your retirement fund (6,00,000 X 20).

- You can also choose the goal of saving thirty times your income as a retirement fund for a financially secure retirement or *'Atmanirbhar Retirement'*.

'Opportunity is missed by most people because it is dressed in overalls and looks like work.'—Thomas Edison

8. The Rule of 72

The Rule of 72 shows in how many years your investment will double

| 72 | ÷ | Rate of interest | = | Number of years it will take to double the investment |

──────── **Example 1** ────────

| 72 | ÷ | 6% interest | = | 12 years |

Saurabh used to save Rs 1 lakh as term deposit in a bank at 6 per cent rate of interest. His investment will become Rs 2 lakh in twelve years.

──────── **Example 2** ────────

| 72 | ÷ | 14.4% interest | = | 5 years |

To double his investment in the share market within five years, Parag will have to invest in options that give a minimum of 14.4 per cent returns every year.

> *'Fortune sides with him who dares.'*—Virgil

- Your money will double in 72 years at a 1 per cent rate of interest (72/1 = 72)

- Your money will double in 24 years at a 3 per cent rate of interest (72/3 = 24)

- Your money will double in 12 years at a 6 per cent rate of interest (72/6 = 12)

- Your money will double in 6 years at a 12 per cent rate of interest (72/12 = 6)

● Why 72? The answer to this lies in the formula for compound interest. The difference between 72 and 100 can be filled with compounding. Even if this is a theoretical calculation, you can still look at it as a guiding principle.

  ○ **From the income point of view:** When a bank offers a 4 per cent rate of return on our savings, it will take about eighteen years for the amount to double. That is why you should look at other options that offer higher rates of return.

  ○ **From the expense point of view:** Let's look at how banks earn interest on loans. The interest levied on credit cards is minimum 24 per cent. If you divide 72 by 24, the answer is three years. This means, if you don't repay your credit card outstandings, your loan will double in about four years. Look at options where you can replace your high-interest loans with lower-interest loans.

● If you develop the habit of considering the rule of 72 while making financial decisions when it comes to investments and loans, you will always have an upper hand.

'The rich invest in time, the poor invest in money.'—Warren Buffett

How to Invest at Different Stages of Your Life

When someone asks, 'What is the right time to start investing?', the answer is, 'The earlier the better!' There is no age restriction when it comes to investing. But it is important to know where and at what stage of life you should invest. Let us look at an example.

Neel was very happy while showing his savings on a mobile screen to his father, a finance expert who had recently retired from a bank with a huge pension. Neel's father was proud of him, considering the flamboyant attitude of his son's generation towards savings. He felt this was the right time to speak to Neel about investments.

Neel's father said, 'You are saving well, Neel, but it will not be sufficient in a few years. So, if you start investing right now, you will get good returns.' Neel replied, 'I have just started saving money and will start investing after a few years.' His father said, 'You may start investing whenever you want, but understand what kind of investment will be suitable at what age.' Neel was all ears.

Investment at Different Stages of Life

Young people

- This segment has many investment options. Young women have just started to work or have been employed only for a few years and don't have many financial responsibilities.

- First of all, if you have recently started to earn, open a bank account and make provisions for your salary to be credited there.

- Let the balance, after all your expenses, lie in the savings account. Save at least three to six months' expenses in that account as your emergency fund. Once you have done this, you can then start thinking about investing the surplus.

- More than thinking about what to invest in, starting to invest at the earliest is important.

- There are a few mutual fund schemes if you are looking for tax-saving options. Although retirement is far away, it is better to start

'Rule number one: Don't lose money. Rule number two: Don't forget rule number one.'—Warren Buffett

planning for retirement right now, considering the volatility of the job market, both in the government and private sectors.

- Invest some amount in PPF every month to take the benefit of the compound interest you will get on it and the tax-saving aspect. This will take care of your long-term investment.

- Also start investing in shares, bonds and mutual funds. It is important to track, deposit in and withdraw money from these instruments on a regular basis.

- Take advice from experts, as you must build a hefty retirement corpus. Start investing slowly and gradually towards that.

Middle-aged adults

- This is a stable class of people. They have a few financial responsibilities too.

- They have to consider their children's education and their marriage expenses while making investment decisions.

- First of all, high-risk investments such as shares and equity mutual funds need to be looked at carefully at the time of investing in them.

- It is always advisable to take a second opinion. You can always consult a financial adviser before making any decision. That way you can be aware of the risks involved and invest wisely.

- Make provision for your children's education and marriage expenses.

- You might have to face some unexpected problems. Review your insurance policy to match your needs and lifestyle.

About-to-retire adults

- If you started investing when you were young, you would have achieved a highly stable life at this stage.

- Those who made provisions for their children's education and marriage expenses would be living a stress-free life at this stage. But if you have loans on immovable property, try to clear them before your retirement.

- Invest in shares and mutual funds with caution to reduce your financial risk. Invest in options that allow you to continue with

'When I was young, I thought that money was the most important thing in life; now that I am old, I know that it is.'—Oscar Wilde

your current lifestyle and will also offer you financial stability after retirement.

- You can benefit from the additional returns offered on some deposits once you cross a certain age and retire. Example: Senior Citizen Savings Fund, Post Office income schemes, etc.

- Many financial schemes offer lump-sum payouts. You can invest in them to get money after retirement. However, it is crucial to plan your finances once you get a huge corpus in hand.

- Many a time, people have vested interests in advising senior citizens as to how to use their money. In such a scenario, it is important to not be overemotional and to plan in such a way that the money is sufficient for your daily needs and takes care of your partner's needs after your demise.

'I think we went far enough.' said Neel's father.

'Yes. In fact, I understand where to invest money at what stage. I also understand the importance of starting to invest from a young age,' said Neel.

Investing from a young age is indeed beneficial!

- But if you have delayed your decision to begin investing, remember that it is better late than to be sorry.

When, Where and How to Invest

'I don't understand much about savings or investments.'

'I cannot decide where to invest since I am not educated enough.'

'I don't find the time to think about investments.'

People who have excuses citing one or the other reason for their inaction on the investment front are actually devaluing their own money.

One of the biggest names in the world of investment, Warren Buffett, once said, 'Price is what you pay; value is what you get.' This means, more than how much you invest, what you get as returns is more important.

> 'To be yourself in a world that is constantly trying to make you something else is the greatest accomplishment.'
> —Ralph Waldo Emerson

Types of investments: Primarily, there are two types of investments.

1. **Short-term investments:**

   These are temporary investments done for a tenure of three months to a year.

   They can easily be converted into liquid money.

2. **Long-term investments:**

   They are done for a tenure of more than one year and can give good returns on investment.

   There are various ways in which to invest in long-term instruments. However, we might get confused since we are constantly bombarded with multiple options by banks and mutual fund companies and are too lazy to sit and plan our finances. The following table will help you clear your confusion about risk and returns.

Risk

High risk Low nominal returns No one will choose this option	High risk High returns Shares, mutual funds, property
Low risk Low returns Post Office Deposits Bank Term Deposits Bonds Debt Mutual Funds	Low risk High returns This option does not exist

Returns

'*Wealth is the ability to fully experience life.*'—Henry David Thoreau

- Long-term investments that are high-risk, high-reward can help in building your wealth over a period of time.

- Investments with low risk and low returns help in building a small level of stable wealth over a period of time.

Types of Investments and Income Thereof

Type of investment	Income
Term deposit, recurring deposit	Pre-decided rate of interest
Shares	Dividends earned, profit from sale of shares
Mutual funds	Dividends and profits on sale of mutual fund units
Immovable property	Profit from rent and price appreciation

Investment Options

Option	Tenure	Rate of returns before tax (per cent)	Security	Returns	Volatility	Liquidity
Bank term deposits	7 days to 10 years	5 to 9	High	Low to High	Low	High
Bonds	1 month to 1 year	6 to 10.5	High	Medium to High	Medium	Medium

'Try to save something while your salary is small; it's impossible to save after you begin to earn more.'—Jack Benny

Gold	1 month to 1 year	8 to 10	High	Medium	Medium	Medium
Real estate	A few months to many years	1 to 20	Medium	Medium to High	Medium	Low
PPF	3 years to 15 years	6 to 10	High	Medium	Low	Medium
Shares	A few minutes to many years	10 to 20	Low	Medium to High	High	Low to Medium
Mutual funds	1 day to a few years	8 to 15	Medium	Medium to High	Medium	High

Many options for investment are available today

A few of them have been in use for many years now. These options are safe, easy to understand and invest in, and involve low risk. The returns, however, are comparatively limited too. These options are generally used by everyone. A few examples of such options are given below:

1. Fixed deposits

● Fixed deposits offered by banks are the most common investment option.

● The rate of return is fixed at the time you open a deposit. The interest income depends on how long you invest your money in it.

● Almost all banks offer similar rates of return on similar deposits.

● These investments have a tenure starting from seven days and can stretch up to ten years. You need to decide on the tenure based on your needs.

● From a 9 per cent rate of return that was offered a few years ago, the rate of interest is currently 5–7 per cent. Most banks offer an additional 0.5 per cent rate of interest to senior citizens.

● There are various types of fixed deposits, based on where you deposit your money.

o   Fixed deposits with banks

o   Fixed deposits with cooperative credit societies

o   Fixed deposits with companies

o   Fixed deposits with non-banking financial institutions

- All deposits made in banks up to Rs 5 lakh are covered by insurance.

- Many companies grow their capital by way of collecting money through fixed deposits. The rate of interest depends upon their position in the market and is usually higher than what is offered by banks on their fixed deposits.

- It is better to study the background and performance of a company before investing in its term deposits. Sometimes, we forget to check the facts because of our greed to earn higher interest and lose even our principal in the process.

- TDS is charged on interest earned when it crosses a certain threshold.

- If the total interest earned is less than the threshold allowed by income tax authorities, you can submit form 15G/15H to avoid TDS.

- Important:

  1. We think of deposits as an investment alternative, but they are categorized as savings products and not as investment products, considering the returns thereof.

  2. Study the interest earned after tax. Example: You can earn an interest of Rs 12,000 at 6 per cent per annum on a deposit of Rs 2 lakh. If you are in the 20 per cent tax bracket, your interest after tax will be Rs 9600 after deducting 20 per cent, i.e., Rs 2400, as tax. The real interest rate then is 4.8 per cent and not 6 per cent. If you fall in the 30 per cent tax bracket, your rate of return after tax will be just 4.2 per cent.

  3. The rate of return after tax is often less than the rate of inflation. If your interest after tax is just 4.8 per cent while the rate of inflation is about 6 per cent, then you are lagging by 1.2 percentage points.

> 'Financial freedom is available to those who learn about it and work for it.'—Robert T. Kiyosaki

4. Fixed deposits are best suited for those who have small-to-medium-term goals, want to secure their principal amount and expect a regular income.

2. Recurring deposits

- Recurring deposits, commonly known as RDs, were the favourite investment option in the 1990s.

- People who wanted to achieve short-term goals invested in recurring deposits.

- The interest, although low, is fixed at the time of opening the deposit.

- This alternative is popular among those who want to start small and develop the habit of saving regularly. Banks and Post Offices offer this deposit even today.

3. Public Provident Fund

- Commonly known as PPF, this type of investment has been popular for decades.

- Interest earned by way of compounding, tax deduction and fixed returns are considered important reasons for investing in PPF.

- Investment amount: A minimum of Rs 500 and a maximum of Rs 1.5 lakh can be deposited in a PPF account each financial year.

- The Central government announces revised rates every three months.

- The amount has to be deposited for a tenure of fifteen years. The account is closed on completion of the tenure. Even if you keep investing after the completion of the tenure, you are not entitled to earn any interest.

- You can request for an extension of the tenure by way of a formal application.

- Income tax exemption: Investment in PPF is exempted by way of EEE (exempt-exempt-exempt). This means the principal amount, the interest earned and the total corpus available for redemption after completion of the tenure are all exempted from tax.

- Loan against PPF: A person investing in PPF can avail of a pre-approved loan after completing three years of holding the fund. You can get a loan against your PPF amount between the third and fifth year of opening the account.

● The rate of interest earned on PPF:

Including the additional cess applicable according to the tax slab	31.20 per cent	20.80 per cent
Investment in PPF	Rs 1,50,000	Rs 1,50,000
Interest earned at 7.1 per cent	Rs 10,650	Rs 10,650
Tax savings on interest	Rs 3,325	Rs 2,215
Total benefit	Rs 13,975	Rs 12,865
Actual return on PPF	Rs 9.32 per cent	Rs 8.58 per cent

You would realize from the table given above that you can earn a decent amount when you invest Rs 1.5 lakh every year in PPF.

4. Post Office Savings Scheme

● In the earlier days, not all villages and smaller towns had bank branches. That is why the locals turned to Post Office saving schemes.

● Post offices offer various investment alternatives, such as savings accounts, five-year recurring deposits, PPF accounts, National Savings Scheme, Kiran Vikas Scheme, term deposits and senior citizens' savings schemes.

● Although the returns on investment are low, the risk is also low, since these schemes are backed by the government. Some of the alternatives also offer tax deductions.

5. National Pension System (NPS)

● Many of us desire a government job even today. The reason is the pension offered post-retirement. Unlike developed nations, we do not have state-provided retirement benefits for citizens. Considering these issues, the government of India came up with the National Pension System to encourage people to save towards their retirement.

'I think everybody should get rich and famous and do everything they ever dreamed of so they can see that it's not the answer.'—Jim Carrey

- The Pension Fund Regulatory and Development Authority of India (PFRDA) was formed to oversee pension-related matters in both the government and private sectors. The NPS was formed under the PFRDA.

- Employees contribute a part of their salary towards NPS every month.

- NPS is a predefined contributory scheme, where your contribution is invested in equity, bonds, government securities and alternative investment funds, based on your preferences. NPS subscribers can opt for active or auto choice for asset allocation. In the active option, the subscriber decides how much money gets invested in each asset class, whereas in the automatic option, asset allocation gets determined based on the subscriber's age.

- There are two distinct accounts under the NPS: Tier I and Tier II. The Tier I account is the mandatory account and when opening an NPS account, it is automatically functional. You cannot withdraw your contributions till you reach the age of sixty. The Tier II account has no restrictions and you can withdraw money any time you want.

- Investors who have completed a tenure of three years are allowed to withdraw partial amounts of their deposits (including employer's contribution) for a valid reason (marriage, construction of house, medical or education expenses). This helps investors to cover major unforeseen expenses.

- PFRDA manages all matters of the NPS. It has appointed professional fund management organizations, including ICICI Prudential, SBI, LIC, HDFC, Kotak, etc., to manage the pension fund. These organizations are different from the ones that manage mutual funds from the same financial houses. Depositors can choose from any of these pension fund managers when they begin to invest.

- The NPS offers income tax benefits both at the time of making contributions and at the time of withdrawal on maturity. Apart from this, investment done towards NPS can get an additional deduction of Rs 50,000 under section 80CCD (1B) of the Income Tax Act when the old tax regime is opted for. This contribution is beneficial for people with high incomes.

> *'Money can't buy happiness, but it will certainly get you a better class of memories.'*—Ronald Reagan

- Operating charges of managing NPS are low as compared to other investment options. NPS contributions would grow and accumulate over the years. The more you invest in NPS, the higher your accumulated amount. The power of monthly compounding makes NPS one of the most attractive and popular retirement-corpus-building products.

6. Gold, Silver and Precious Metals

- Among the first and most popular investments are gold, silver, other precious metals and diamonds.

- In the earlier days, people had limited alternatives to invest in. Whatever people saved after their expenses was used towards personal interests. Any money left was then used to buy precious metals or immovable property.

- The royal families would wear gold to show the world how rich they were. Since the kings controlled their kingdoms by virtue of their wealth and property, they would often resort to ordering thrones made of gold or building grand royal palaces.

- Just like the royals, their ministers, the rich merchants and landlords of the kingdom also were mesmerized by such bling. Eventually, even the common people started following this trend and began investing in whatever was possible on their part to acquire these items.

- That others should get to see what we earn is a general mindset we all carry. Your ownership of a parcel of land might not be known to people unless you mention it to them, but we have the habit of talking about how rich we are whenever possible.

- Wearing a lot of gold jewellery is a common way to show off our wealth—it is worn in a particular way so that our gold chain is visible under our shirt, the rings are clearly seen on each finger or the gold watch is prominently displayed on the wrist. All this is done to show off. However, what we do with our wealth is our individual choice.

- Only two classes existed in ancient times—the rich and the poor. The latter found it hard to make ends meet, so they always stayed away from purchasing gold and other precious items.

'If speaking is silver, then listening is gold.'—Turkish proverb

- Although social priorities have changed with the rise of the middle class, gold never lost its shine. In wealth creation, the importance shifted to buying one's own home and vehicle, educating the children, buying retirement funds, etc. While all this was happening, gold was still given high priority, especially for marriage purposes.

- India opened its doors to the world economy in 1991 and the middle class started to earn money. Jewellery showrooms started their operations in small towns. The new-age middle-class customer was persuaded to buy gold by means of using various marketing techniques.

- This middle class could enjoy money for the first time and India has become the largest importer of gold in the world in the past thirty years.

Benefits of Buying Gold

1. Liquidity

- You can liquidate gold at any jeweller's shop. You can also raise funds in case of an emergency by selling gold. This flexibility is not available in the case of immovable properties.

- Small items of gold purchased on special occasions have helped many during difficult times.

- Gold loans are available at a low rate of interest and in quick time. NBFCs such as Manappuram Gold Finance and Muthoot Finance have processed gold loans worth crores of rupees to date and have built a one-of-its-kind gold-loan franchise business.

2. Nothing can shine like gold

- The emotional connect that gold has exceeds that of any other type of investment.

- People use all their life savings and turn them into gold during once-in-a-lifetime occasions such as weddings.

- We cannot imagine someone wearing their shares or mutual fund units at a wedding.

- Once you have covered all your expenses, the satisfaction you get from buying gold cannot be expressed in words.

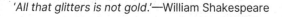

'All that glitters is not gold.'—William Shakespeare

3. Security

Gold has always seen an upward trend in the long run, which means the value of gold will always keep increasing.

Important

- If you purchased 10 gm of gold at Rs 25,000 per 10 gm in 2012 and the rate of gold in 2022 is Rs 50,000 per 10 gm, it might feel like a 100 per cent return on investment. But there is a catch. This 100 per cent return is spread over ten years, which means the annual rate of return is just 7.17 per cent.

- Compared with the rate of inflation, this rate of return is low; lower than from other investment alternatives.

Drawbacks of Buying Gold

1. **No fixed returns:** Banks offer interest on deposits, immovable properties fetch rent, shares get dividends—but gold brings no fixed returns. The only returns are what people get when they sell gold after a price rise. On the contrary, looking after physical gold can mean expenses.

2. **Rate of return:** You do not liquidate gold even during its bull run, in the hope that its value will keep rising. However, historically, as compared with other investment alternatives, the returns from gold are much less.

3. **Need for security:** There is always the fear of theft or of losing precious gold or jewellery. That is why people opt for a bank locker, which has a cost in the form of locker rent.

4. **Quality:** Tanishq is one of the largest jewellery brands in India. They sell jewellery made by Titan, which is owned by the Tata Group. The way they won customer trust in India is interesting:

   - Although we know the fact that all that glitters is not gold, people were blindly trusting traditional jewellers and buying gold from them. Tanishq installed carat meters in their showrooms, and people were shocked when they got their gold checked! The gold they had purchased thinking it was of 24-carat purity was actually of a lesser quality or purity.

> 'We must learn who is gold, and who is simply gold-plated.'—Unknown

- Although, with the introduction of hallmarking of gold, the fear of being cheated for quality has reduced, buyers are still confused about how it works.

5. **Additional expenses:**

   - Making charges and labour charges are added to the cost of gold when you buy it in the form of jewellery. A charge is levied when you sell jewellery, and the jewellers pay you the amount only after deducting this charge. The amount paid as GST on the purchase of gold cannot be redeemed.

   - The following options are available if you do not want to take the risk of securing physical gold but also want to make profits from the rising cost of gold.

     - **Gold bonds:** The major banks in India offer gold bonds, based on the prevalent price of gold in the market, at a 2.5 per cent interest rate.

     - **Gold ETFs:** Gold exchange traded funds are commodity funds that are considered a substitute for physical gold. These funds perform just like individual stocks, their movement subject to ups and downs in the price of gold.

Important

- The same set of financial rules do not apply to everyone. Once you have covered your basic needs and saved for your future, there is nothing wrong with spending on gold, whatever the amount. Money spent towards other luxuries is an expense, but that spent on buying gold is considered an investment.

- If buying gold or other precious metals and stones motivates you to increase your productivity and strengthens your relationship with your partner, you should definitely go ahead with it.

- Spending and investing are two different concepts. Mixing the two may lead to mental and financial problems. That is why you should study the subject and invest in jewellery only if it ranks high on your priority list.

> 'Gold is the money of kings; silver is the money of gentlemen; barter is the money of peasants; but debt is the money of slaves.'—Norm Franz

Real Estate = Real Property

Investment in immovable properties has been practised since time immemorial. Many people turn towards investment when they save money. Gold, movable and immovable assets have a physical existence, and they are considered to be wealth that can be experienced in person.

In the earlier days, landlords formed a majority of the rich class. The one who held the most land attracted the most wealth and power. With the objective of distributing land and reducing disparities among the people, Prime Minister Indira Gandhi passed a law to bring land ceiling reforms into force, mandating that no person in India could own more than 25 acres of land.

Looking at the price rise in the housing sector, people shifted their investment focus from traditional options to the housing sector. Also, urbanization leads to the rapid expansion of cities. A lot of people migrated to the cities in search of better opportunities. They needed places to stay and started renting homes, which gave rise to a new asset class for investors.

The universal law of demand is—the price rises when demand exceeds supply. New land cannot be created since it cannot be manufactured in factories. The CEO of SpaceX, Elon Musk, intends to build homes on Mars, just like Amazon's Jeff Bezos, who is trying to achieve a similar feat through his company Blue Origin. Although this looks like a distant dream today, the price of land here on earth is going to increase, without a doubt.

Options for Investing in Real Estate

- Owing to its massive growth, the real estate sector is now looked upon as one of the most sought-after investment alternatives. In the earlier days, real estate purchase was limited to agricultural land, and homes were limited to dwellings meant for self-use. But in the modern era, real estate is looked at not just as an emotional possession but as a business proposition too.

- Real estate has been the most popular investment alternative in the past two decades. However, since the rate of returns on investment in the bigger cities is gradually falling, people are now looking at newer alternatives.

'Buy land, they're not making it any more.'—Mark Twain

- Real estate includes agricultural land, non-agricultural (NA) plots of land, business properties and residential properties like bungalows, row houses and farmhouses.

Real Estate Investment Options

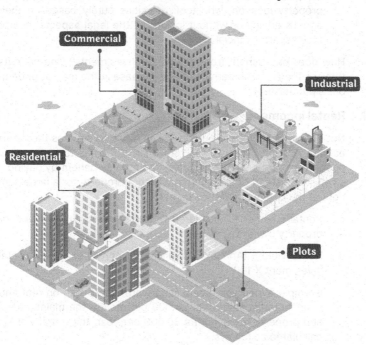

- Cities offer good education facilities, jobs and business opportunities. Economic disparities in the smaller towns and villages send income seekers to the cities. This urbanization proves to be a boom factor for the real estate business.

- Land parcels near the cities were divided into smaller parts. With the rise in population, smaller towns started expanding. These land parcels were bought with the objective of selling them in the future at a high profit. As demand exceeded the supply of plots of land, a price rise followed, and the cycle continued.

> 'Landlords grow rich in their sleep without working.'
> —John Stuart Mill

o   The people who invested in legally sanctioned, future-ready, well-timed and rightly priced real estate benefited from their decision to buy land parcels.

o   Others who invested by taking huge loans just to reap the benefits of rising real estate prices without studying the property location, who took decisions purely based on their agent's advice or without looking at the legal aspects, had to face severe financial losses.

● How does one benefit from real estate investments? One benefits through the rent one earns and any increase in the market price of one's purchase.

1. Rental income

Not everyone can afford a house or an office as soon as they start earning. Property owners can rent their properties to such needy people and earn a monthly income. The tenants benefit by paying a small sum instead of investing in buying a property for a large sum right at the beginning of their careers.

o   Rental income is considered to be returns on investment for property owners.

o   Rental yield = (Annual rental income - Annual expense) / Total investment X 100

o   Example: When you give a shop worth Rs 25 lakh on rent and your rental income is Rs 20,000 per month, the maintenance and property tax being Rs 30,000 per year, the rental yield is calculated as follows:

	Based on the tax slab of the investor	20.80 per cent	31.20 per cent
a	Annual Rental Income	2,40,000	2,40,000
b	Annual expenses: Property Tax + Maintenance charges	30,000	30,000
c	Gross Rental Income (a-b)	2,10,000	2,10,000

'The best investment on earth is earth.'—Louis Glickman

d	Taxable income (30 per cent standard deduction) i.e. (70 per cent X c)	1,47,000	1,47,000
e	Income tax	30,576	45,864
f	Rental income after tax (c-e)	1,79,424	1,64,136
g	Investment in property/ Market value of the property	25,00,000	25,00,000
h	Rental Yield Rate (f/g*100)	7.18 per cent	6.57 per cent

- The rental yield helps you compare real estate investments with other types of investment, such as mutual funds.

- More than the amount of rent, it is important to find out if the rental yield exceeds the returns you would get from other types of investments.

- You are fortunate if a tenant, who pays rent on time and is not a menace to the neighbours, agrees to an increase in the rent every year and uses the property without damaging it.

- Many people take loans and invest in real estate with the thought of earning rental income and benefiting from the rising market value of the property. It is expected that the EMI being paid for the property will be covered by the rental income. However, some find paying the instalments difficult if the property is not rented throughout the year. The only solution is to take the least possible loan while investing in real estate.

- A few homeowners had to forgo or reduce rents during the Covid-19 pandemic to retain their tenants.

- In the current times of 'work-from-home', there is no guarantee that you will always find an ideal tenant despite your owning a good property.

2. Increase in market value over time

- The value of a property increases in proportion to the demand-supply ratio. The size of the apartment, location, neighbourhood, its

> *Money speaks only one language: If you save me today;*
> *I will save you tomorrow.*

vicinity to schools, hospitals, markets, bus and railway stations and the airport, also play a role in deciding the market value.

- 'A woman was duped by buying property on the Moon!'—you might have read such news. People are desperate to own a flat, a plot or farmland. However, you may get cheated if you are not well-informed about the property you are buying.

- It is important to get all the legal checks done before investing in any property. People find it difficult to find the time for this and to go through the complicated procedures to check various facts such as land ownership, rules of the local governing body, rules about NA plots and fresh case laws issued by the honourable courts. It is always advisable to consult a legal practitioner before dealing with any property-related matter.

- A great many of us are faced with this doubt: Should I buy or rent a home? We will look for answers to this in the next chapter.

Should You Buy or Rent a Home?

Suresh and Ramesh are twins and were always seen together doing similar work. Both were happy as they had got jobs in the same organization. Their salaries were in the same range too.

- A few years later, both thought of buying homes. For the first time, they had different financial opinions. Suresh decided to move into a rented apartment since he didn't want to invest a lot at the beginning of his career. But his twin brother, Ramesh, had contrasting thoughts. He was influenced by what his forefathers had taught him and had always thought of buying a home. Ramesh decided to get a loan to buy his dream home, while Suresh started living in a rented home.

- Their thought process took them along different routes.

- Suresh decided to invest the money he saved by opting to stay in a rented home, while Ramesh scripted a different story by investing in a new home with the help of a home loan.

'The best time to buy a house is always five years ago.'—Ray Brown

- According to Ramesh, the amount spent on buying a home would have been almost equal to or less than the amount spent on rent.

- Even if at first the rent might have appeared to be less than the EMI taken by someone, it will keep increasing with time whereas the EMI will remain the same throughout the tenure of the loan, unless part of the loan amount is prepaid or the rate of interest increases significantly. In short, rent will increase over a period of time while EMI will remain the same. That is the reason why Ramesh decided to opt for buying a home on EMI.

Financial Planning

- Since Ramesh had just begun to work, he felt the burden of paying the home loan instalments. But being young, he did not have any other financial commitments and curtailed his unnecessary expenses, diverting his savings into repayment of the loan.

- Frequent eating out at restaurants and an extravagant lifestyle were avoided to control expenses. Ramesh could repay his loan by saving money in this way. This helped him develop good financial habits.

- Ramesh, who was an immature, flamboyant party animal, suddenly transformed into a mature person. He planned his finances in advance to take care of the EMIs he had to pay.

- Suresh, on the other hand, continued his lifestyle and invested in long-term investments such as PPF and mutual fund SIPs. Both were long-term investments and did not require frequent financial planning.

Investments and Immovable Property

- Ramesh got a salary increment a few years later, leading to a reduction in his monthly financial burden. He had put his hardships behind him and was growing financially. On the other hand, the price of his property had appreciated, strengthening his personal assets. He was in a position to sell his property at a profit in a few years' time.

- In a way, his investments were now reaping returns.

> *'Focus on where you want to go, not on what you fear.'*—Tony Robbins

- Even Suresh was happy since his salary had risen too. However, his rent was also rising every year. The rent he had paid was an expense. But he had been wise to invest his savings in fixed deposits, mutual funds, shares and PPF. That would grow his wealth.

- He had gradually understood the importance of savings.

Psychological Satisfaction

- A homeowner gets social recognition in Indian society. The same happened with Ramesh. This also helped him to get married early.

- Suresh had to negotiate his rent with the homeowner every year and get his contract registered. He had to shift his home if the negotiations were not fruitful or he if he got into an argument with the landlord. All this led to psychological stress.

Both Suresh and Ramesh were happy about their own decisions because they were well-planned and neatly executed. Nothing can be 100 per cent correct or wrong. Every coin has two sides. The conclusion is, whether you act like Ramesh or Suresh, depends on your own understanding and financial attitude.

Do not compare buying a first home to other types of investments. It helps one to become stable in life. But what about your second home? Is that to be looked at as an investment? You can decide that on the basis of the following example.

Benefits of Owning a Home

Financial Benefits

- Easily available home loan at a low rate of interest

- Repayment helps to invest and compulsorily save

- Tax savings

- Benefits from a price rise in the future

- Owning a home helps in securing the homeowner from inflation

Psychological Benefits

- Self-esteem

- A place for your family's safety

- You can design your home as per your choice

- Your children can have a better future as they have the security of inheriting the home

- Social status

'No one's ever achieved financial fitness with a January resolution that's abandoned by February.'—Suze Orman

Should you **buy** or **rent** a Home?

Why should you start investing early?

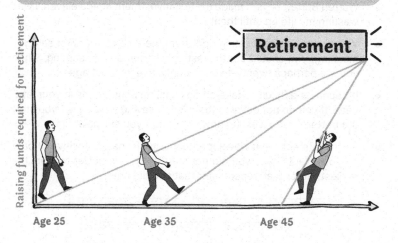

Make your financial future happy

- **Age 25** You can reap the benefits of compounding if you start early. You can achieve your financial goals and build your retirement funds easily when you start investing early.

- **Age 35** You will have to invest a higher sum towards your retirement funds.

- **Age 45** You have very few years left to retire and will have to save a large sum towards retirement.

Generally, in Indian society, it is held that for every Rs 100 earned, Rs 25 should be expenses, Rs 25 is to be donated, Rs 25 saved for children and the balance Rs 25 invested. In short, 25 per cent of your earnings should be allocated to investments as a way to secure your future.

The majority of us do not start investing early or realize the importance of starting early. However, an early start is always beneficial.

> 'You can be young without money, but you can't be old without it.'—Tennessee Williams

How Early Is Early?

- Warren Buffett says, 'I made my first investment at age eleven. I was wasting my life up until then.'

- You should begin investing right from the time of your first salary—meaning, you should start investing when you start earning, when you are perhaps twenty-two to twenty-five years of age.

- It becomes difficult to take on financial responsibilities in your later years if you do not develop the habit of saving. The earlier you start the better. Start investing now. Trust that you still have time.

- An investment habit developed early in life has a positive impact on your life. In case you did not start early, it is better to start the earliest rather than repent later that you did not.

गतवयसामपि पुंसां येषामर्था भवन्ति ते तरुणाः |
अर्थे तु ये हीना वृद्धास्ते यौवनेऽपि स्युः ||

– सुभाषित

(*You are young if you have money in your old age.
Conversely, a financially weak person ages in his youth.*)

'It is very simple to be happy, but it is very difficult to be simple.'—Rabindranath Tagore

Don't Invest Just to Save Tax!

Tax saving is as important as returns on investment. The amount saved as deduction on taxes gets more importance than actual returns on investment at times. The most frequently used statement by companies trying to sell tax-saving products is 'Invest to save. You will save thousands in taxes while investing.' Many companies in the financial sector promote insurance or other such schemes during the months of December-January as tax-saving instruments.

Main Objectives of Investing

- The main objective of investing is to create provisions for a financially secure future. That doesn't mean you ignore tax saving at all.

- Although saving taxes is important, that cannot be the prime motive for making an investment.

- Investing in alternatives that offer a low rate of return just to save taxes may lead to financial losses.

- You can invest up to Rs 1,50,000 to save tax under section 80C as per the Income Tax Act. As an employee, you have additional tax savings from EPF contributions. Also, for those who have a home loan, the principal repayment is considered a deduction.

- Other alternatives, such as PPF, NSC, bank term deposits of more than five years and Equity Linked Savings Schemes (ELSS) also contribute to saving tax under section 80C. Public Provident Fund offers a higher rate of return as compared to term deposits, and the interest earned from it is also tax-free. The only issue is the lock-in period of fifteen years.

- You should not invest just to save taxes. Investment and tax-saving are two different destinations and the routes to reach there often seem to be confused with each other.

- Although investment in equity mutual funds is often long-term, it can be used to cover emergency financial needs as well. Similarly, you can achieve your yearly tax-saving goals by reinvesting the same money after the lock-in period in these equity schemes. This means you do not need to keep investing more and more every year to save on taxes. You can use those savings to invest in other alternatives.

> 'Nothing is certain except for death and taxes.'
> —Benjamin Franklin

Situation 1

Akshar had recently started working on a good salary. After a few days, he received a call from a relationship manager at the bank where he held his salary account. Since he had found a job immediately after completing his education, he felt he was on top of the world. But just earning a good salary does not mean you understand everything about finance. After a discussion with the bank executive, he assumed he took the right decision in investing in a high-premium insurance policy on the premise of tax saving, as advised by the executive.

Situation 2

Ishita ran her own beauty parlour. She had a habit of investing in term deposits, PPF, ELSS, etc. at the last minute in the month of March in a do-it-yourself (DIY) style.

Ishita was proud of her habit of reading tax-saving information online. During the pandemic, her parlour was closed for nearly four months. In her hour of need, she realized that none of her investments could be liquidated, and that was a loss of sorts.

What if You Invest Only Keeping Tax Savings in Mind?

1.   Delay in achieving financial goals

Most of the tax-saving investment options are long-term investments. They have a pre-decided lock-in period, which means the amount invested cannot be liquidated before a stipulated period.

Alternative	Maturity tenure	Option to liquidate before maturity
PPF	Fifteen years	Some amount can be withdrawn
National Savings Certificate	Five years	No option to withdraw
Tax-saving bank term deposits	Five years	No option to withdraw

> 'Both poverty and riches are the offspring of thought.'
> —Napoleon Hill

ELSS	Three years	No option to withdraw for three years
Life Insurance	Based on the policy—ten to twenty-five years	Policy can be surrendered after three years but the surrender value is less than the premium paid.

This table highlights that many of us cannot afford to keep investing for the long term. We give up after the bubble of initial excitement bursts and lose a lot of money in doing this.

- **Important:** You will have to decide whether to invest in tax-saving alternatives or to pay tax and enjoy the rest of the money or invest it based on your short-term, mid-term and long-term financial goals.

2. Insufficient insurance cover for self and family

- Every insurance policy is a long-term agreement with the insurance company, which stands cancelled when we stop paying the insurance premiums before the stipulated deadline.

- Both getting a policy to save taxes but which does not provide sufficient cover and terminating premium payments mid-way are wrong.

- **Important**—While selecting an insurance policy, note the coverage needed for you and your family. You need to buy a policy that you can afford.

3. Unnecessary investments

- When you take a home loan, you will be eligible for deduction under section 80C of the Income Tax Act:

  o Principal repayment up to Rs 1.5 lakh.

  o Interest payment up to Rs 2 lakh, as per section 24, can be claimed as a deduction from income while calculating income tax.

- You would invite financial trouble if you bought a bigger house than you can afford just to benefit from income tax deductions.

- Calculate the additional interest you would have to pay, the rising market value of the property and many other elements instead of just focusing on the tax-saving aspect while buying a property.

> *'I'd like to live as a poor man with lots of money.'*
> —Pablo Picasso

4. Investing more than what is required to save taxes

- The amount paid as provident fund deducted from one's salary, children's school fees and expenses towards health often gets ignored when tax planning is done in haste.

- Tax-saving instruments often lock your money in for a long period. In the name of tax savings, many of us lock in more than the required quantum of funds and cannot access our own money when it is required.

What Should You Do?

1. Remember—tax saving and investment are two different concepts.

2. Investing taking into consideration one's long-term objectives is important.

3. Buying insurance policies without studying them in detail just to save tax can lead to financial losses.

4. Many a time, paying taxes is a wise decision.

5. We have the habit of investing at the eleventh hour when the month of March is about to end. This can lead to investing in unnecessary alternatives just to save taxes. It is better to think of tax planning from the beginning of the financial year.

6. A large sum of your hard-earned money will be locked if you are investing big amounts just to save taxes.

- If you plan to buy a home during the year and your money is invested in tax-saving term deposits that have a lock-in period of five years, this money will not be available before the stipulated period. If you had paid taxes instead, the balance amount would have been available for the down payment for the home. Your tax planning should depend on your financial goals.

- Invest in NPS and PPF to reach your financial goals, such as the creation of a retirement fund and for tax saving at the same time.

- Young persons who are just starting their careers should pay special attention while tax planning. Many pay large sums towards PPF and insurance policies, and their savings are then insufficient to pay for buying a home. Taxes will in any case be saved when you pay EMIs on your housing loan. That is why it is better to choose investments such as ELSS. It is better to pay taxes on occasion, and the philosophy of saving money in order to achieve one's financial objectives is often beneficial.

'Wealth is the ability to fully experience life.'—Henry David Thoreau

• Part 6 •
Share Market
&
Mutual Funds

Money Works

Is Investing in Stocks the Most Beneficial Investment Option?

- When we think of the share market, we dream of high returns or huge losses! We also have certain preconceived notions about investing in it.

- We come across negative news such as, 'A crash in the share market has wiped out Rs 2 lakh crore of investor wealth', 'The share market nose-dives', 'Crude oil prices hit the roof', 'Fear looms over the share market', etc. Such news makes us believe that the share market is a place of uncertainty, meant only for the rich, or is too complicated for common people to understand.

- If the concept of investment seems complex or passive to you, then the share market is way out of reach for you. However, developing an interest in the share market will help you gain knowledge of it and make some money too.

- Shares have given much higher returns than other asset classes in the past few years.

- The Covid-19 pandemic has added to financial worries for people globally. Many experienced the financial crunch resulting from the pandemic. However, those who had been connected to the share market for a long period of time found that their financial position was comparatively stronger. Although many of us were surprised at this, we need to accept this as a fact. We should examine how this became possible and plan our investments likewise.

- Indian society harbours many a misconception about the share market, leading to only a fraction of people investing in it.

- Capital markets around the world grew by a staggering 31 per cent during the pandemic, and a bigger story is unfolding in the Indian stock market. The value of the Indian capital market had come down to Rs 101 lakh crore in March 2020 but sprang back to Rs 232 lakh crore in June 2021 and crossed the Rs 300 lakh crore mark for the first time on 5 July 2023.[1,2] You can imagine the returns earned by investors during that period.

- The value of the Indian stock market appreciated by Rs 121 lakh crore in a year, which means the investors who remained invested during that period became richer by that amount. In short, it is clear that you will not be able to financially prosper if you ignore this type of investment. That is why we are going to learn about investing in the share market in this chapter.

- Why must we sit on the fence when so many are investing in the share market? Shouldn't we earn from the share market? The answer is yes, we should earn from it, but only after learning about it.

- It is better to avoid the type of stock trading that has the highest risk involved—intra-day stock trading—as much as possible. We should invest for the long term in companies that we trust and whose nature of business we understand. If your risk appetite doesn't allow you even that, then the best way to gain from the stock market is to invest in mutual funds and let the fund manager do the job of managing your investments.

- Warren Buffett is a name known to everyone for the past two to three decades. For those who do not follow the finance world, he is a man in his nineties today, a billionaire known for his philanthropy too. Those who are familiar with him know him as the Oracle of Omaha. He built his wealth from the ground up and is literally earning billions of dollars based on his understanding of stocks and from investing in the right place and at the right time. Whenever asked about the secret of his success, he talks instantly about his mentor Benjamin Graham's concept of value investing.

- Whoever the investor might be, it is important for him or her to study a company before investing in its shares.

- Warren Buffett says, 'Invest in those companies whose shares you would never sell.' He earned his riches on the same philosophy. His greatness cannot be described in brief and the reader is advised to read about his principles and achievements.

- We will have to study the share market to understand the investment opportunities in it.

'The greatest sin is to think of yourself as weak.'
—Swami Vivekananda

Before investing in the Share Market

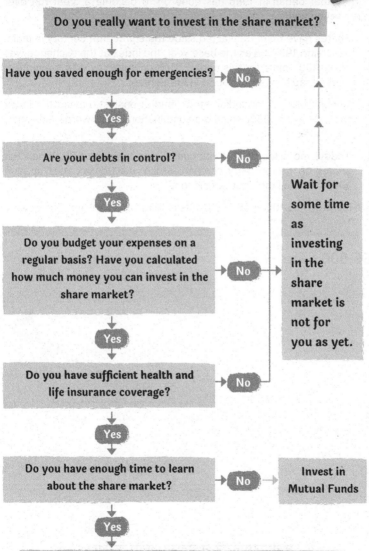

Do you really want to invest in the share market?

Have you saved enough for emergencies? → No

Yes

Are your debts in control? → No

Yes

Do you budget your expenses on a regular basis? Have you calculated how much money you can invest in the share market? → No

Yes

Do you have sufficient health and life insurance coverage? → No

Yes

Do you have enough time to learn about the share market? → No → Invest in Mutual Funds

Yes

Wait for some time as investing in the share market is not for you as yet.

Start investing in share markets with constant learning!

The Exciting Journey from 100 to 66,000 Points

The chief index of the Bombay Stock Exchange, the Sensex, crossed an all-time high of 66,000 points for the first time on 13 July 2023. The journey that began in 1986 has gone on to become a great run over thirty-seven years.

- Shares have been transacted since the eighteenth century in India. Assuming 1987–88 as the base year, the index at the exchange was set at 100 points for this period. Thirty companies with the highest market capital were included in the Sensex.

- Deepak Mohoni, an Indian stock market analyst, named the index the 'Sensex' in 1989, which is a combination of two words, 'sensitive' and 'index'.

- Today, more than 5000 companies are listed on BSE. When the shares of the top thirty companies rise, the Sensex goes up, and when they fall the Sensex falls too.

The journey from 100 to 66,000 points is filled with many ups and downs.

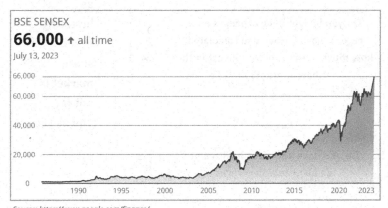

Source: https://www.google.com/finance/

न कालमतिवर्तन्ते महान्तः स्वेषु कर्मसु।
Great people never delay their duties.

Important milestones in the journey of Sensex

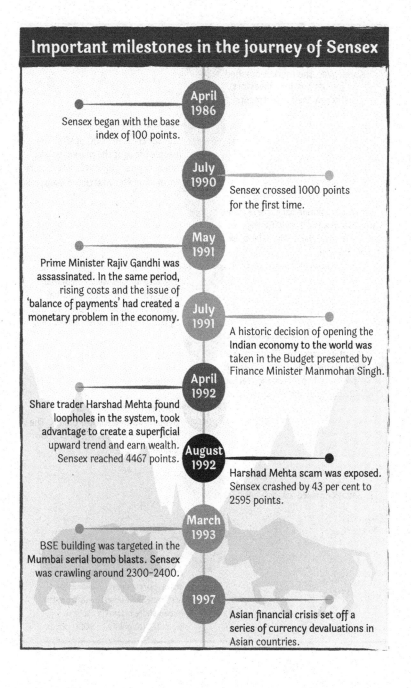

April 1986
Sensex began with the base index of 100 points.

July 1990
Sensex crossed 1000 points for the first time.

May 1991
Prime Minister Rajiv Gandhi was assassinated. In the same period, rising costs and the issue of 'balance of payments' had created a monetary problem in the economy.

July 1991
A historic decision of opening the Indian economy to the world was taken in the Budget presented by Finance Minister Manmohan Singh.

April 1992
Share trader Harshad Mehta found loopholes in the system, took advantage to create a superficial upward trend and earn wealth. Sensex reached 4467 points.

August 1992
Harshad Mehta scam was exposed. Sensex crashed by 43 per cent to 2595 points.

March 1993
BSE building was targeted in the Mumbai serial bomb blasts. Sensex was crawling around 2300-2400.

1997
Asian financial crisis set off a series of currency devaluations in Asian countries.

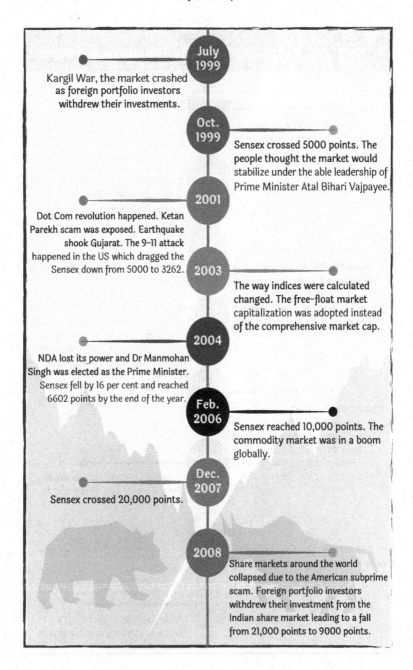

July 1999
Kargil War, the market crashed as foreign portfolio investors withdrew their investments.

Oct. 1999
Sensex crossed 5000 points. The people thought the market would stabilize under the able leadership of Prime Minister Atal Bihari Vajpayee.

2001
Dot Com revolution happened. Ketan Parekh scam was exposed. Earthquake shook Gujarat. The 9-11 attack happened in the US which dragged the Sensex down from 5000 to 3262.

2003
The way indices were calculated changed. The free-float market capitalization was adopted instead of the comprehensive market cap.

2004
NDA lost its power and Dr Manmohan Singh was elected as the Prime Minister. Sensex fell by 16 per cent and reached 6602 points by the end of the year.

Feb. 2006
Sensex reached 10,000 points. The commodity market was in a boom globally.

Dec. 2007
Sensex crossed 20,000 points.

2008
Share markets around the world collapsed due to the American subprime scam. Foreign portfolio investors withdrew their investment from the Indian share market leading to a fall from 21,000 points to 9000 points.

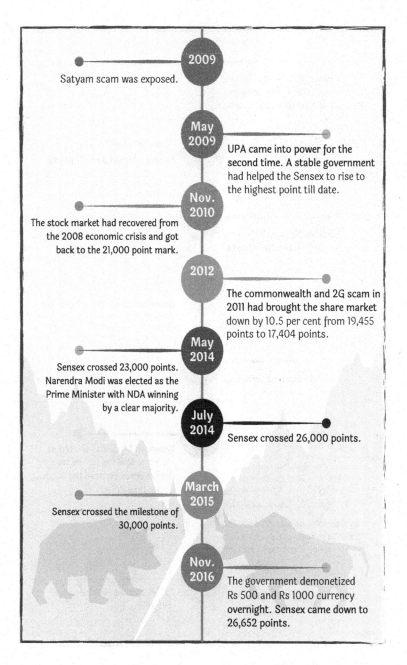

2009

Satyam scam was exposed.

May 2009

UPA came into power for the second time. A stable government had helped the Sensex to rise to the highest point till date.

Nov. 2010

The stock market had recovered from the 2008 economic crisis and got back to the 21,000 point mark.

2012

The commonwealth and 2G scam in 2011 had brought the share market down by 10.5 per cent from 19,455 points to 17,404 points.

May 2014

Sensex crossed 23,000 points. Narendra Modi was elected as the Prime Minister with NDA winning by a clear majority.

July 2014

Sensex crossed 26,000 points.

March 2015

Sensex crossed the milestone of 30,000 points.

Nov. 2016

The government demonetized Rs 500 and Rs 1000 currency overnight. Sensex came down to 26,652 points.

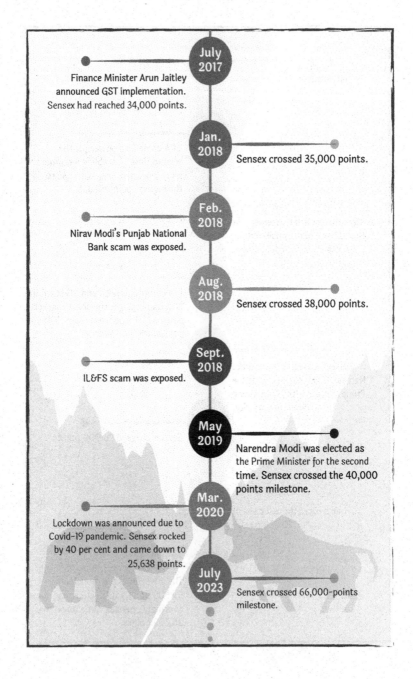

Finance Minister Arun Jaitley announced GST implementation. Sensex had reached 34,000 points.

July 2017

Jan. 2018

Sensex crossed 35,000 points.

Feb. 2018

Nirav Modi's Punjab National Bank scam was exposed.

Aug. 2018

Sensex crossed 38,000 points.

Sept. 2018

IL&FS scam was exposed.

May 2019

Narendra Modi was elected as the Prime Minister for the second time. Sensex crossed the 40,000 points milestone.

Mar. 2020

Lockdown was announced due to Covid-19 pandemic. Sensex rocked by 40 per cent and came down to 25,638 points.

July 2023

Sensex crossed 66,000-points milestone.

- The Sensex has scaled new heights from time to time over the decades despite going through rough patches and despite the many financial scams that have rocked the country. It has recorded growth of a whopping 660 times, rising from 100 in 1986 to 66,000 points.

- Shares that grow in multiples in value are called 'multibaggers', and the Indian share market has witnessed many a multibagger to date.

- Motilal Oswal Financial Services Ltd released a study in December 2020 tracking the top-performing companies between 1995 and 2020.[3] During this period, the Sensex had surged from 3200 points to 29,500 points, at a compounded annual growth rate (CAGR) of 9.2 per cent. Also, more than 100 companies had surpassed this CAGR of 9.2 per cent.

- Infosys was at the top of the list of the 100 fastest wealth-creating companies in India. During this period of twenty-five years from 1995 to 2020, Infosys was the frontrunner in this category.

  o Infosys is considered to be the leader in the information technology industry in India. The second largest company in India after TCS, Infosys's CAGR during the twenty-five-year period was 30 per cent.

  o Identifying opportunities in the IT sector, Narayan Murthy started this company with the help of six friends and a capital of Rs 1 lakh in the year 1981.

  o The company was valued at just Rs 53 crore when Infosys launched their IPO in the year 1993. In 1995, their market value was Rs 300 crore which had grown to Rs 2.73 lakh crore by December 2020 and to Rs 5.30 lakh crore by June 2023.

  o The company, which employs more than 3.43 lakh employees, announced an income of Rs 1.47 lakh crore and a profit after tax of Rs 24,108 crore in the financial year ending March 2023. People who invested in the shares offered by Infosys in 1995 have earned returns amounting to 688 times their original investment till 2020.

- In the last twenty-five years, many companies have given investors returns that were 100 times their original investment. The list

> *'If you don't know who you are, the stock market is an expensive place to find out.'*—Adam Smith

includes Bajaj Finance, Eicher Motors, Vinati Organics, Atul Ltd, MRF Tyres, Kotak Mahindra Bank, Coromandel International, Voltas and Avanti Feeds.

- Let us look at how the magic of compounding works with the example of pharmaceutical major Divis Laboratories Ltd (Divis Labs):

  o Hyderabad-based Divis Labs launched their initial public offering in the year 2003.

  o The offer was priced at Rs 140 per share.

  o Cost of 100 shares (100 × 140) = Rs 14,000.

  o In 2007, shareholders got 500 shares for every 100 shares held after a share split.

  o A 1:1 bonus was declared in the years 2009 and 2015. That is why 500 shares held in the year 2007 became 1000 and then 2000 later.

  o The market value of a share also reduces when share splits and bonuses are announced.

  o The share price hit Rs 3543 on 22 June 2023.

  o The value of 100 Divis shares held from the year 2003 to June 2023 (2000 X Rs 3543) = Rs 70,86,000.

  o The returns are 506 times, at a CAGR of 36.53 per cent. These returns were 767 times, at a CAGR of 44.64 per cent when the shares hit an all-time high of Rs 5371 on October 2021.

- If you search for 'multibagger stocks', you will come across several such examples. The investors who studied the market and identified those opportunities earned a fortune.[1]

- Just looking at high returns is one side of the coin. There are many companies whose shares hit a negative value too.

- This list includes popular names such as Reliance Power, PC Jewellers, Videocon Industries and Coffee Day Enterprises. You can search for such examples by looking for 'value destroyer stocks'.

- As the economy has a positive forecast, many large-scale companies are going to grow more than before. Many investors are shifting

> 'The intelligent investor is a realist who sells to optimists and buys from pessimists.'—Ben Graham

their attention to the share market due to this. Whether you will be a part of it will depend on your personal choice and your risk appetite.

What Did We Learn?

- The Indian economy has shown positive growth despite facing all kinds of problems over the past four decades.

  o   Natural calamities: Floods, earthquakes, cyclones, heavy rainfall, climate change, the Covid-19 pandemic, etc.

  o   Political problems: Assassination of country's leaders, uncertain Opposition parties in the coalition governments, uncertainty in government policies.

  o   Border tensions and terror attacks: The Kargil War in 1998, the 26/11 terrorist attack, and many other terrorist attacks.

  o   Financial problems: Scams, uncertain policies, biased government policies favouring certain industrial houses, etc.

  o   Global incidents: The 9/11 terrorist attacks in the US, war between nations, biased policies set by developed nations, rising prices of crude oil, Russia–Ukraine war, etc.

- Many good and bad incidents have happened in the share market in the past few years.

- We usually think about tomorrow or the near future when making any decision. However, we should think long-term when making our financial decisions.

- Investing in the right shares helps us create wealth over the long term. Always remember what Warren Buffett said, 'Buy it thinking you will hold it forever.'

'If you wish to get rich, save what you get. A fool can earn money; but it takes a wise man to save and dispose of it to his own advantage.'—Brigham Young

History of the Stock Market

Cicero was a well-known statesman in ancient Rome. In the first century BC, historians found references to Cicero complaining about the price of rising shares. There are references to Romans, back then, being involved in share trading.[4]

Thereafter, there are no references to shares for many centuries until the fourteenth century, when some references emerge from Italy. There was no central rule in Italy at that time. Various smaller kingdoms ruled the various regions of the land. Florence, Milan, Naples and Rome were some of the few prosperous city-states known to be important financial centres of the world.[4]

● The banking system happens to have originated in the same era. The Medici family had a banking business. They were well-connected to many royal families in Europe. One of their family members was also named the Pope.

● You can sense the influence of banking over all sectors.

● Some banks had started to sell the loans they had given to their customers. They could sell high-risk, high-interest loans to money lenders and other banks back then.

● City states would sell their bonds when they were short of capital.

● The common man became part of the transactions between the city states and the money lenders. The administrators of Venice were at the forefront of this business. They would make a list of the current loans on boards and meet potential customers. Italian companies were also the first to issue shares. Companies in England and other European nations followed in the sixteenth century with the concept of 'Joint stock company', i.e. one whose stock is owned jointly by shareholders. These companies became important for colonization by Europeans.

The World's First Share Market

● The first share market was set up in 1531 in Antwerp, Belgium. Both traders and landlords would meet trading companies, brokers and investors in the share market.

● Promissory notes and bonds were prominently dealt with in the share market. The traders would get into various kinds of partnerships,

'Most people think buying is investing, but they're wrong; [it] doesn't make you an investor any more than buying groceries makes you a chef.'—Gary Keller

and profits were distributed based on them. However, dealings in individual shares had not started yet.

The Beginning of the East India Company Era

● At the beginning of the seventeenth century, the Indian Subcontinent was known as East India in Europe. Trade relations between the two regions date back to 2600 BC, meaning around 5000 years ago.

● However, by the seventeenth century, European traders were making more profits than their East Indian counterparts.

● You must be thinking: where did the Indians go wrong, or what could have been done back then? Some of the reasons for this were the lack of a central, powerful ruler here, no ambition on the part of the subcontinental traders to cross the seas, internal clashes between kingdoms, and financial and political instability.

● The sixteenth century was a milestone in modern history. The Renaissance led to immense economic progress on the European continent. Modernization, rise in population, progress in the banking sector, new trade routes and new ways to manufacture goods had brought about this progress. New-age capitalism was born out of it.

European traders imported cotton, silk, spices and salt from the Indian Subcontinent and earned large profits by selling them. The higher the profits, the higher the risk! The traders were always worried about what nature had in store for them—inconsistent weather, cyclones and the raging sea. Likewise, they also had to face the threats of piracy, attacks and theft.

● A trader or a small trading organization could not bear such financial losses.

● The sea traders would get investors to fund their voyages and pay them huge returns from their profits. On the other hand, an unsuccessful voyage would mean losses for them.

● The East India Company was the most advanced form of trading organization at the time. It was recognized as one of the world's first mega-corporations.

● Even the investors became wise over a period of time. Instead of investing their capital in a single voyage, they started investing in multiple voyages to hedge their risk. These limited partnerships were valid only for the tenure of a single voyage and the company

> *'It doesn't take money to start a business. It takes a businessman to start a business.'*—Agent Steven

ceased to exist on completion of the voyage. A new company would be formed for the making of a new contract for a new journey.

- The Dutch, French and British governments chartered the trading companies to use the name 'East India Company' at the beginning of the sixteenth century. The British East India Company was formed on 31 December 1600, and the Dutch East India Company on 20 March 1602.

- The Dutch East India Company's capital was 65 lakh guilders, meaning 64 tonnes of gold. The shares allotted to investors were listed on the Amsterdam Stock Exchange, which was a revolutionary event at that time. The company built their empire over the next 200 years, and investors earned huge profits.

- The East India Companies brought about a sea change in the world of investing. They would pay a share of their profit as dividends. Over a period of time, dividends were paid after a stipulated period instead of after every voyage. This led to the companies being kept in existence.

- The people who bought shares were referred to as investors. They could sell their part of the ownership to others. This helped to ease the capital-raising process.

- The growing East India Companies started buying better resources, and their power of charter allowed them to kill any local competition and establish their monopoly.

- A sure way of earning profits had been established by means of this route.

- Although shareholders could sell their shares in these companies to others, the stock exchange had not begun functioning fully. They had to look for a share trader. Shares of the East India Company were in paper format.

- Most of the share traders in England used to sit in a coffee shop in London transacting the sale and purchase of shares. The bonds and shares used to be listed on the walls of the coffee shop.

- To bring in ease of transacting, a stock exchange was established.

- In 1875, the Bombay Stock Exchange was formed, making it the first share market in Asia. However, share transactions had been taking place in India since 1850.

> 'Compound interest on debt was the banker's greatest invention, to capture, and enslave, a productive society.'—Albert Einstein

- The share traders would sit under a banyan tree in the building opposite Mumbai Town Hall to transact. The Bombay Stock Exchange is considered to be among the ten largest share markets in the world.

- A few Indian corporate houses have been doing business for the last 200 years. Although the share market might seem like a new concept for many people, a few organizations made their shareholders richer many years ago too.

Year of establishment	Corporate House
1736	Wadia Group, Britannia Industries, Bombay Dyeing
1806	SBI
1820	RPG Group
1857	Aditya Birla Group
1865	Shapoorji Pallonji
1866	Nestlé
1868	Tata Group
1884	Dabur
1888	Kirloskar Brothers
1897	Godrej Group
1903	Taj Hotels
1910	ITC Ltd

Although investments in shares and the functioning of share markets may seem alien to you, well-informed investors have been making a fortune for years in developed nations using them. Experts predict that the golden period of India's economy is about to start. This could be your golden phase too. Will you be part of this history too?

> 'You get recessions, you have stock market declines. If you don't understand that's going to happen, then you're not ready, you won't do well in the markets.'—Peter Lynch

What Are Shares? The Basics

- Capital is the most important element with which to begin any kind of business!

- In a proprietary business, all capital is raised from just one person. Two or more partners raise capital in a partnership firm, whereas shareholders help to raise capital in a company. Shares do not denote virtual wealth; they have a legal and monetary existence. Shares mean part ownership of the company.

- The companies whose shares can be purchased and sold in the share market are known as listed companies.

- Companies need to raise additional capital to expand their business or pay their dues. Other reasons for which they may raise capital include:

  o Capital expenses: for creation of capital assets such as land to operate business from, construction of a factory, purchase of machinery, etc.

  o Working capital: for purchase of raw materials, products, payment of wages, making sales, offering a credit period to customers, etc.

- Companies receive shareholders' money as capital and offer them shares in return. This way, everyone can participate in and own a part of a company by means of shareholding, as the process is public.

- The following are the types of company owners in India:

  o Promoters: those who run the company and list the company's shares in the share market to raise capital. They look into the day-to-day operations of the company and are accountable for the smooth running of the company's business.

  o Indian shareholders

  o Foreign portfolio shareholders

  o Private equity funds

'Think big, think fast, think ahead. Ideas are no one's monopoly.'—Dhirubhai Ambani

- Ways to raise capital from the capital markets: Initial Public Offering (IPO), Rights Issue, Qualified Institutional Placement (QIP), bonds follow-on offer, etc.

- Shareholders transact using various financial instruments, including shares, bonds, derivatives, etc., and the share market acts as a mediator for these transactions.

- The Securities and Exchange Board of India (SEBI) is the regulatory authority for the Indian capital market on behalf of the government of India. It formulates the rules and regulations for companies to list their shares on the BSE and the National Stock Exchange (NSE), the manner in which transactions should take place, the rules for stockbrokers involved in various transactions, etc.

- The following stock exchanges are active in the Indian share market:

    o   Bombay Stock Exchange (BSE)—primary index: Sensex

    o   National Stock Exchange (NSE)—primary index: Nifty

    o   Both are SEBI-authorized stock exchanges based in Mumbai, and lakhs of investors transact on them on a daily basis

- BSE: The Native Share and Stock Broker Association was formed in 1875 and was converted into the BSE we know today. In 1986, the Sensex was introduced as the equity index representing thirty trading companies in India. Online trading began in 1995. Today, the BSE is known as one of the prominent stock exchanges in the world.

- NSE: The National Stock Exchange was formed in 1992. The NSE is accredited to bring stock exchanges in electronic form to India ahead of the BSE. The index, the Nifty-Fifty, started in 1996 and consists of the top fifty shares on the NSE.

- Stockbrokers: The middlemen involved in the purchase and sale of shares are called stockbrokers. They have to be members of a stock exchange to carry on their business. HDFC Securities, Kotak Securities and Angel Broking are examples of broking companies.

- Investors and share traders: Investors buy shares for the long term with the intent of earning dividends from them and increasing their wealth as and when the price of their shares rises. Share traders like

> 'Investing is the intersection of economics and psychology.'
> —Seth Klarman

to make profits in the short term by continuous sale and purchase of shares. They make money on short-term opportunities.

How Does the Share Market Work?

- Listed companies, stockbrokers, traders and investors buy and sell shares through the stock exchanges.

- Companies enter the primary market by making Initial Public Offerings (IPO). These companies raise capital by selling their shares in order to expand their businesses. These shares are then available in the secondary market. The investors who buy these shares become part owners of the company.

- The business of selling and purchasing shares is termed 'trading'. The price of shares fluctuates with their sale and purchase, just as with any other product. It is determined by the rise or fall in the demand for it. As demand for a share increases, its price also increases.

- The profit after tax earned in the year by a company is distributed among shareholders as dividends. If a company wants capital to expand its business, the profit is invested back into the business instead of being paid as dividends to the shareholders.

- When companies make profits and their business sees positive growth, both their share price and the demand for their shares increase. You can buy or sell the same shares as many times as you please so long as they are listed on the exchange.

- Share prices increase in the capital market based on future predictions for the companies they represent. Share prices are directly proportional to a company's progress, meaning, they rise with growth in the company and decline with losses in the company.

'The money you have is equal to the courage you exhibit.'
—Grant Cardone

Profits Earned from the Share Market

Growth in capital

Rise in the price of shares

Example: In 2001, the price per share of Shree Cements was Rs 30. As of 30 June 2023, the same share was priced at Rs 23,887.

Dividend income

A part of the profit is distributed in the investors in the form of dividends

Example: In the financial year 2022–23, ITC Ltd paid 15.50 per share as dividend to its shareholders.

- Today, thousands of mega-companies such as Reliance Industries, Infosys, TCS, HDFC, State Bank, Wipro and Mahindra have expanded their businesses by raising capital from the stock markets and have directly and indirectly created millions of jobs.

- Companies such as Hindalco Industries, ITC, Mahindra and Mahindra, Reliance Industries, Tata Steel and Nestlé, have held their positions in the Sensex since 1986.

- Likewise, ACC, Grasim Industries and Bombay Dyeing have been part of the Sensex since 1986 and are now part of BSE 100 too.

'Business is money game with few rules and a lot of risk!'
—Bill Gates

A Few Notable Companies Listed on the Stock Exchange

4 Wheeler Automobiles	MARUTI SUZUKI	 TATA MOTORS	Mahindra	ASHOK LEYLAND
2 Wheelers	Hero	BAJAJ	TVS	EICHER
Tyres Manufacturers		CEAT	apollo TYRES	BKT
Automobile Industries	EXIDE INDUSTRIES LIMITED	motherson sumi systems limited	UNO MINDA	BOSCH
Government Banks	SBI	Punjab National Bank	IDBI BANK	Bank of Baroda
Private Banks	HDFC BANK We understand your world	ICICI Bank	kotak Kotak Mahindra Bank	IndusInd Bank
Paints	asianpaints	Berger	KANSAI NEROLAC PAINTS LIMITED	INDIGO Be surprised!
Chemicals	DEEPAK NITRITE	Pidilite	GAIL	TATA CHEMICALS	AARTI INDUSTRIES LIMITED
Information Technology	tcs TATA CONSULTANCY SERVICES	Infosys	HCL	wipro	Mindtree	PERSISTENT
NBFC	BAJAJ FINSERV	SBI card 	Muthoot Finance	MANAPPURAM FINANCE LIMITED

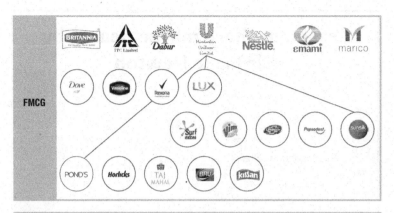

FMCG	
Telecom	
Retailers	
Insurance	
Pharmaceuticals	
Business Corporations	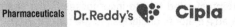 
Media	
Real Estate	

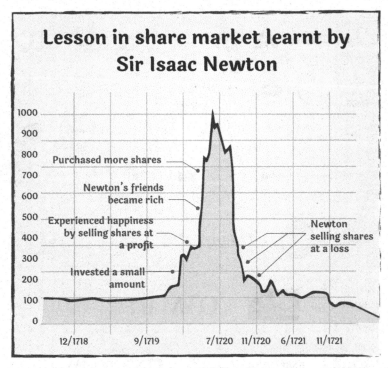

Sources : Marc Faber, Jeremy Grantham, Sir Isaac Newton

- World-renowned physicist Sir Isaac Newton discovered the laws of motion. He is considered to be one of the greatest scientists of all time. But even the brightest mind had to incur losses in the share market. In 1720, he faced a major financial loss to the tune of 20,000 GBP (British pound sterling), which would amount to crores of Indian rupees today.[5]

- He was so deeply hurt by the incident that no one was allowed to utter the words 'South Sea' in his presence.

- In the eighteenth century, the company South Sea was known for giving good returns to its investors. Newton held a few shares of the company. Apart from this, he also held government bonds, low-return insurance policies and a few other investments in his portfolio.

- The shares of South Sea company grew eight times in value over a period of six months. Newton sold his shares and earned a profit. At that time, the share price was 300 GBP a piece.

- In 1713, South Sea company was assigned the task of transporting African slaves to the southern coasts of America. It enjoyed a lot of perks and also dominated the South American seas with the help of the British government.

- The founders of the company had planted many fake news stories about the glorious future South Sea company would enjoy in the years to come. The number of newspapers published in London was on the rise during the same period. The newspapers talked about how South Sea had helped many people to become rich.

- They created a rosy picture of the company and everyone believed that South Sea company was about to transport all the gold and the wealth from South America to England. Everyone, from the poor to the rich, was trying to buy South Sea shares in every possible way. The share price was constantly increasing since demand was on the rise.

- Newton felt that he had sold his shares at a very low price and had faced severe losses. The virtual profit that his friends had made by holding on to their shares made Newton unhappy. He liquidated all his other investments and put everything into buying South Sea shares again. The share price had reached 700 GBP by then.

- In a few days, the share price climbed to 900 GBP. People in England were running after South Sea company shares.

- However, the reality was strikingly different as South Sea had no major opportunity or project in hand.

- The founders and their close aides began to sell their shares. The share price began to fall since the founders were liquidating their shares; the general investors thought the company either held no future or that its share price had reached its peak.

- Newton did not think of saving even his principal amount while South Sea shares were on their decline. Finally, he sold his shares at a price of 300 GBP a piece, leading to a financial loss of more than 20,000 GBP for himself.

- His quote became famous when, fed up with the share market, he said, 'I can calculate the movement of the stars, but not the madness of men.'

- South Sea continued to operate even after this turmoil but its investors could never recover from the artificial price-hike bubble

'If investing is entertaining, if you're having fun, you're probably not making any money. Good investing is boring.'—George Soros

they had got caught in. The British Parliament brought about many amendments to their laws to make sure investors never had to face such losses again.

What Did We Learn?

Newton was considered to be the brightest mind of his generation. When such an intelligent person could not resist the temptation of following the herd, only to realize later the blunder he had committed, people like us need to take extra care before investing.

- Just because the price of its shares is increasing does not mean that a company is doing great.

- Not all investors study the companies they invest in.

- You cannot avoid making silly mistakes in one field just because you are an expert in another.

- Don't invest in stocks just because someone told you to do so.

- More than theoretical knowledge, you need to have practical understanding, do some self-study and develop the ability to take timely decisions in the share market.

> 'Investing is not a game where the guy with the 160 IQ beats the guy with the 130 IQ. Once you have ordinary intelligence, what you need is the temperament to control the urges that get other people into trouble in investing.'—Warren Buffett

Misconceptions about the Share Market

Many of us are scared at the very mention of the share market. There are examples of people losing everything in the share market, and also of those who had nothing but could build a fortune through it. Emotions such as excitement, attraction, fear and curiosity come alive with the very mention of the share market. There is no magic in your money vanishing or doubling in a second. Yet, there are many misconceptions about the share market in society. We will look at a few of them here.

Misconception 1: Investing in the share market is like gambling

Is investing in stocks similar to betting? The answer is both Yes and No.

- Gambling means entering into a financial transaction without any self-study or thought given to what may happen in the future.

- It is often done just on the basis of someone's recommendation, with half-knowledge on the part of the gambler. And on the basis of luck!

- There are many forms of gambling, such as betting or the lottery, where you become rich if luck favours you.

- You have to go by blind faith since the outcome could be anything.

When does investing in the share market become a gamble?

- If you are investing in the share market on the basis of blind faith and relying on just luck, it is no better than gambling.

- It is a gamble when you invest without adequate knowledge or by falling for tall claims, or if you chase impossible dreams of becoming rich overnight. You leave your investment to chance in this kind of transaction.

- Some people invest in, say, company X after reading material from unverified sources, asking for recommendations from self-proclaimed experts, watching videos recommending the company or overhearing discussions on how the shares of company X are

> '*Far more money has been lost by investors preparing for corrections, or trying to anticipate corrections, than has been lost in corrections themselves.*'—Peter Lynch

going to grow multi-fold. It would be considered a gamble if you invested in company X without verifying the facts and doing some study on your own.

When would an investment not be considered a gamble?

- You should study the following information about company X before investing:

    o   What is the exact nature of its business?

    o   Does the industry to which the company belongs have a great future?

    o   Are the founders and the top management trustworthy?

    o   Are the shares available at the right price currently?

    o   Is the company heading towards bankruptcy?

    o   What are the sales and profits recorded over the past five years?

    o   Can the applicable rules and regulations for the industry change all of a sudden, leading to a negative impact on profits for the company?

- Investing in the share market calls for a continuous learning process. The way a tree planted today will bear fruit in a few years, you can benefit in the long term from investing in the share market.

- Taking risks and playing blind is different from this. Sir Benjamin Graham made this apt comment about blind investing: 'Never fool yourself by thinking you are investing while you are betting.'

Misconception 2: All news about the share market is true

- Many of us think the share market is where it rains money. But how do we start believing all this? The following are a few sources from where these notions emerge:

News:

    o   'Investors earned millions from shares of ABC company'; 'Shares of EFG company grew 10 times'.

'In investing, what is comfortable is rarely profitable.'
—Robert Arnott

o   You get attracted to mass media such as newspapers, websites, blogs, channels, etc., and believe what they say.

o   We don't get interested in what they say unless it is something shocking, unprecedented or exciting. That is why they build their news around huge profits or huge losses made in the share market.

o   Many share market experts appear on television channels to predict which shares will rise or fall. If you buy or sell shares on their advice and face a financial loss, they don't lose a single rupee.

o   Watching financial news constantly and frequently checking various financial apps on your mobile is injurious to your financial health.

Share market classes, stockbroker advertisements, webinars, etc.

o   Training is important in learning and developing any new skill. There are various mediums through which one can learn about the share market, such as live classes, digital classrooms, books, YouTube videos, newspapers, magazines, etc. A few well-experienced and honest trainers share their financial wisdom without making a loud noise about it. But such gems are rare to find.

o   No one will be excited upon reading an advertisement which says, 'Investing in the share market is a boring job where you have to study every day and yet there is no assurance of high returns.'

o   Some stockbrokers make tall claims such as 'Earn five times your investment if you invest with us', or 'Only we have found hidden gems for you'.

o   There is a saying in Hindi—*Jo bikta hain woh sahi hain!* (Whatever sells is right!) Many fake influencers make tall claims based on this belief and you start believing that you will earn high returns from the share market by adopting this mindset.

o   Right now, we are unaware of what predictions may have been made in the past. It is better to keep away from being constantly

'It is remarkable how much long-term advantage people like us have gotten by trying to be consistently not stupid, instead of trying to be very intelligent.'—Charlie Munger

bombarded by such news and focus on getting the right information on select shares.

Misconception 3: The share market can help you get rich quickly

o   We have all read inspiring tales of people who have made a fortune in the share market, and we feel that we should give it a try too.

o   If you expect your investment to grow in multiples immediately after you have made it, please note that the share market is not a Kamdhenu (wish-granting cow) or a kalpavriksha (wish-granting tree) to grant you your wish immediately.

o   Be cautious if someone tells you how to quickly earn a lot of money on the share market.

o   Shares of various companies are purchased and sold in the share market. The demand for the shares of a company and their price rise when a lot of people feel the company is going to earn good profits. On the contrary, if people think a company is going to face hard times due to competition in the future, changes in technology, or negative news or predictions, its share price and demand for its shares are going to fall.

o   Finally, share prices are dependent on the profits earned by companies. The market does not favour companies that record occasional profits. Companies must make consistent profits and be persistent in their efforts to do so. However, in the age of cut-throat competition, it is an uphill task for a company to show steady growth.

o   If you have been patient and persistent with your investments in the right shares, you will definitely earn good money.

o   Legendary investor Warren Buffett earned 99.5 per cent of his wealth after the age of fifty-two.

> 'It's far better to buy a wonderful company at a fair price than a fair company at a wonderful price.'—Warren Buffett

Misconception 4: High risk = high returns

o   Usually, risk arises when you are not sure of what you are doing. But if you have the right knowledge and training, you can earn good profits while keeping the risk at a minimum.

o   There is a higher risk element in high-return investments, but that does not imply that high risk = high return.

o   It is a wise decision to invest when the share market is down. Instead of feeling low about it, look at it as an opportunity to invest.

o   When and where to invest should be decided after studying the target companies or by taking advice from experts. There are many stories of people who wanted to quickly earn money and lost everything in their pursuit of it. That is why it is better to learn and get full information about your target companies before investing.

o   You may make some errors while investing. Hence, it is important to keep yourself updated about the share market. Some companies might look good from the outside but could be hollow from within. That is why making informed decisions is very important.

Misconception 5: You need a lot of money to invest in the share market

o   This is a popular misconception that gains strength since many of us do not know what the share market is and how it operates.

o   You can give yourself the opportunity to understand the share market once you are beyond the mindset of 'money attracts money'.

o   You do not need lakhs of rupees to begin investing. You may begin with a few hundred rupees too, provided you have researched the stocks you want to invest in.

o   Warren Buffett began his investment journey at the age of eleven with just a few dollars. Even investors such as Rakesh Jhunjhunwala and Vijay Kedia did not have huge capital when they started, yet they earned billions from the stock market.

o   You can learn from your initial mistakes and the loss does not feel a lot when you begin investing small amounts.

Misconception 6: It is too difficult to learn about the share market and it is better to rely on experts for advice

o   You don't need a high IQ to invest in the share market. According to Peter Lynch, who has authored multiple books on the share market, someone who understands grade-five mathematics can understand how the share market works.

o   You don't need to be an expert to be an investor in the share market. But consistent learning and the will to implement what you have learnt would be important.

o   A formal degree or a high IQ is not necessary for an investor to buy and sell shares.

o   Both Sir Isaac Newton and Albert Einstein suffered losses in the share market in the years 1720 and 1929, respectively. If IQ was a prime necessity for investing, these stalwarts would not have faced financial losses on the stock market.

o   Our success is dependent on how good we are at controlling our emotions. Exercising patience while looking for the right opportunity helps too. Many investors have lost their money by yielding to fear or greed.

o   The investors who dream of becoming rich in a short span of time fall prey to greed. This way of investing without understanding the risks involved often leads to losses.

Misconception 7: Investing on your own is difficult

o   No work is easy or difficult. The definition of easy or difficult differs from person to person, which is why investing seems either easy or difficult to people.

o   You do not need stockbrokers or godfathers to invest in the share market. A bit of patience, common sense and in-depth understanding of the stocks and the markets are all that is required!

o   With the newer technologies, investing on one's own is easily possible and can also lead to one earning great profits.

Misconception 8: Investing is easy. Buy shares at a lower price and sell at a higher price

o   People who have never invested in the share market or have no information whatsoever about it carry this misconception the most.

> 'Nobody can predict interest rates, the future direction of the economy or the stock market. Dismiss all such forecasts and concentrate on what's actually happening to the companies in which you've invested.'—Peter Lynch

o   Even experts can go wrong in predicting which shares will rise and which will fall.

o   Both your research and predictions can go wrong. Just because you invested in a particular share or because you have a gut feeling about it does not mean the price of the share will rise.

o   It is important to analyse the current performance of stocks using your experience, research and updated knowledge of the market.

The skills required to Invest in the Share Market

Fundamental Analysis

Technical Analysis

Understanding of Financial Documents

Self-control in the matter of Emotions

Basic knowledge of Accounting

Basic knowledge of Income Tax

Knowledge of the Economy

Curiosity

The habit of Self-evaluation

Long-term Vision

Knowledge of different Industries

Learning to picking the Right Information

Misconception 9: Only young people should invest in the share market

o 'I am forty and am past the age for investing in the share market.' If you have a similar thought, you are completely wrong.

o Remember, the biggest risk in front of you is not taking any risks. If you keep investing in traditional alternatives, you will find it difficult to win the race against constantly rising inflation.

o If you have amassed a good amount of experience by the time you turn thirty-five, you may restrict your investment in shares, but bypassing it completely is not recommended. If you are fairly settled in life, it's possible that your risk appetite may have grown too. That is why you can start taking baby steps and begin investing in the share market.

Misconception 10: Mutual funds are a good investment

o Those investors who cannot invest and re-evaluate their investments in stocks on a regular basis could take the mutual funds route.

o Also, it is believed that mutual fund managers are well-experienced and that mutual funds are safe for that reason.

o Mutual funds that consistently beat the benchmark index are considered to be doing good. However, as per historical data, the majority of mutual funds fail to do so.

o Investing in the right mutual fund is a good alternative to investing in shares, and it is always beneficial to consult an investment adviser if you don't have time to learn about it.

Misconception 11: Investment in the same shares over generations means it is a family tradition

o The share market is not something like running an ancestral family grocery store where picking the same shares to invest in is followed by successive generations.

> **❝**
>
> *'Failure or success do not happen by accident, they are the compound interest of action or inaction.'*—Ifeanyi Enoch Onuoha
>
> **❞**

o   Investing in the same shares that seniors in the family favour is the wrong way to invest. The way the Sensex operated twenty-five years ago was very different from the way it does today. Stocks such as Century and Arvind were considered to be blue-chip stocks at one time, whereas TCS and Bharti Airtel did not even exist at one time.

o   Don't fall in love with a particular company. Your goal should be to earn profits on your investments. Here, business matters more than emotion.

Misconception 12: IPOs are a quick way to get rich

o   Companies list their shares on the stock exchanges so that investors can buy them for investment and sell them.

o   These companies list their shares with two objectives in mind. One is to raise capital for business operations and the other is to earn profits for the company's founders, the initial investors and private equity organizations. This is known as an 'offer for sale'. In the offer-for-sale option, the money raised goes to the investors instead of to the company.

o   Once an IPO is announced, the news is bombarded to people through various mediums of mass communication, and the people are persuaded to apply for shares in the IPO.

o   The company DMart (Avenue Supermarts Ltd) launched its IPO in 2018. The shares were oversubscribed by 200 times at the time of the launch. The issue price at the time was Rs 300 and the shares were listed at Rs 600. Those who immediately sold their shares earned double their money. In the next three years, the price of the shares went up by twelve times.

o   You would be tempted to invest in other IPOs by reading DMart's success story. But hold on, not all companies are like DMart. Very few companies can hold on to the listed share price. Their share prices start declining if they do not show favourable financial results.

> 'Individuals who cannot master their emotions are ill-suited to profit from the investment process.'—Benjamin Graham

o   Every company tries to raise capital by offering shares through their IPO. Companies put in a lot of effort to reach the committed profit level because stock prices are slaves of companies' profits and cash flows.

We looked at the misconceptions people have about the share market. We will study the golden rules for success in the share market in the next chapter.

> *'Opportunities come infrequently. When it rains gold, put out the bucket, not the thimble.'*—Warren Buffett (thimble: a small metal cap to protect a finger when sewing)

Golden Rules for Success in the Share Market

Investments made in the share market can help investors achieve their financial dreams. Although there is no set formula for success, following a few rules is worth a try. Implementing these can help you become successful in the share market. It is important to follow certain rules and maintain discipline in order to earn good returns.

1. **Accept the fact that the share market will carry certain risks**

- Risk is part of life. Always living in a secure environment instead of accepting this fact is to exist in a state disconnected from reality.

- Everyone wants to earn long-term gains from their investment in shares without facing uncertainties or going through the turmoil of the share market.

- Many of us might wonder: why is it so difficult to earn profits if the popular stock market rule is to buy at a low price and sell at a high price?

- For how long can we wait for the share price to fall so that we can buy stocks at the right time or how long shall we allow the stock price to rise before we sell? Is it possible to always identify the right time at which to buy or sell? Many experts have tried to find answers to this question and have come up with the following observations through their collective understanding:

  o 'The idea that a bell rings to signal when investors should get into or out of the market is simply not credible. After nearly fifty years in this business, I do not know of anybody who has done it successfully and consistently. I don't even know anybody who knows anybody who has done it successfully and consistently.'—John C. Bogle

  o 'When it comes to so-called market timing there are only two sorts of people: those who can't do it, and those who know they can't do it.'—British investor Terry Smith

  o 'The only value of stock forecasters is to make fortune-tellers look good.'—Warren Buffett

  o 'I can't time stocks. I don't know anybody else who can either.'—Warren Buffett

  o 'We wish we had perfect market timing (as well as the ability to fly). The reality is that no one does or ever will.'—Seth Klarman

- What can you conclude from the above quotes? No one can predict what ups and downs are in store for the investor in the share market.

- People whose investments have increased multi-fold must have faced a lot of setbacks in their investment journey. However, we often overlook them. At a low phase, they must have surely been tempted to sell all their shares and buy them back when the market fell further. But most of us have never been able to time this to perfection. That is why a successful investor remains calm even in a volatile market.

2. Avoid daydreaming

- There is nothing wrong with expecting high returns from your investments, but you may face trouble if your financial goals are based on unrealistic assumptions. In short, avoid daydreaming and live in the present moment. Emotions have no place in the share market.

- You get profits when the market rises and incur losses when it crashes—that is the nature of the stock market. Remember, the market does not take your emotional or financial condition into consideration in its day-to-day operations.

- One of the greatest investors of recent times, Warren Buffett, has earned average returns of 19 per cent annually. If someone is claiming to get higher returns for you, be cautious in taking any decision based on his or her advice.

3. Ignore meaningless and unnecessary advice

- We give more and undue importance to the advice given by friends, colleagues and people around us than to finance professionals.

- Learn to ignore meaningless or baseless advice. A huge amount of free advice is floated on television and the Internet. Investors may not benefit from every bit of advice that comes this way. We tend to get confused with information overload and may make wrong financial decisions in the process.

- The key to becoming a successful investor is to be alert every time. Don't trust tips that guarantee huge returns in quick time.

> 'Investing in stocks is an art, not a science, and people who've been trained to rigidly quantify everything have a big disadvantage.'—Peter Lynch

- Try to self-learn as much as possible before investing. Find out about the genuineness of the promotional mailers, newsletters and other information you receive before taking any action based on them.

- Many scammers disguise themselves as renowned companies and send short codes through SMS. It is also important for novice investors to stay away from penny stocks unless they are prepared to bear financial losses.

4. Always think long-term

- Once we buy a property, we don't check its market value every day. This is for many reasons. One is that property prices don't fluctuate on a daily basis, and the other is that we don't consciously check for the current price until the time we actually want to sell the property.

- We are sure that the price of the property will rise in the long term. However, people forget to apply the same rule in the share market.

- Historically, returns from the stock market are higher than from any other investments in the long term. If the goal of your investment is short-term, do not invest in the share market. Think of alternatives such as term deposits or liquid funds.

- Share markets do not perform at their best in the short term, and this may lead to investors losing their money.

- However, the share market is a great alternative if your financial objectives are for the long term. You can spread the risk by holding on to your shares for a long period of time.

5. Take informed decisions

- It is important to study the companies and the market situation every time you intend to buy shares. This cannot be avoided.

- The number of learning avenues available today is way more than what was available to our previous generations. However, it is not possible to study and learn new things unless you have a curious mind and have convinced yourself that the knowledge you hold is insufficient or needs regular updation.

> 'The best stocks will always seem overpriced to a majority of investors.'—Gerald Loeb

How to Gain Knowledge of the Share Market

1. Information made available to the public by all listed companies

● The information on the 'investors' tab on the websites of listed companies will provide:

  o   Annual reports

  o   Investor presentations

  o   Quarterly results

  o   Conference calls with analysts

  -   Transcripts, etc.

● You can get access to a data treasure if you go through the annual reports of the past few years.

2. Books

● Books based on the share market

  o   *The Intelligent Investor* by Benjamin Graham

  o   *One up on Wall Street, Beating the Street* by Peter Lynch

  o   *Common Stocks, Uncommon Profits* by Philip Fisher

  o   *Coffee Can Investing, Unusual Billionaires* by Saurabh Mukherjea

  o   *Masterclass with Super Investors* by Vishal Mittal and Saurabh Basrar

● Books that highlight success stories of companies, their management and the founders

  o   *HDFC Bank 2 0: From Dawn to Digital* by Tamal Bandyopadhyay

  o   *The CEO Factory* (Hindustan Unilever) by Sudhir Sitapati

  o   *Titan: Inside India's Most Successful Consumer Brand* by Vinay Kamath

● These are just a few examples of books on this huge subject. There are thousands of books written on the share market. You will not

> *'The stock market is designed to transfer money from the active to the patient.'*—Warren Buffett

finish reading them even if you devote your whole life to them. You should choose your own path to understand the basics of share markets.

3. Websites

Websites such as Moneycontrol.com, arthasakshar.com, screener. in, trendlyne, etc.

4. Newspapers and magazines

The *Economic Times, Business Standard, Financial Express, Mint, Outlook Money, Money Today*, etc.

5. Share-research reports, industry reports

- Brokers release their analytical studies on their websites. You can, for example, read about Aurobindo Pharma in many different broker reports to understand the company from various angles.

- Rating companies such as CRISIL and CARE release their ratings of companies regularly. You can also get the latest information from reports published by consulting firms such as KPMG and E&Y, such as on the automobile industry or the IT industry.

6. Blogs

Safalniveshak.com, alphaideas.in, drvijaymalik.com are known for their well-researched information.

7. YouTube videos

Many YouTubers are popular for sharing well-researched video content on the share market.

8. Social media

- Twitter handles known to share verified and well-researched updates.

- WhatsApp and Telegram groups that share basic information such as analysis of financial results and annual reports. (Kindly note, you have to avoid the groups where stock tips are shared; they do not come under this list).

> 'If stock market experts were so expert, they would be buying stock, not selling advice.'—Norman Ralph Augustine

All the sources mentioned above are just examples. You can search for newer sources based on your preferences. If you are associated with the automobile industry, you would have information from users about which vehicles are currently in demand, spare parts that are high quality, market sentiment, company policies, etc. You have to apply field knowledge too in the investing process.

Similarly, people working in healthcare would know about pharmaceutical companies, those in IT would know about the IT industry, agro-business employees would know about agro-chemicals, fertilizers, tractors, etc. In short, you would have a good amount of information about one or more fields, depending on the industry you are associated with.

The big question is: How do you extract the right information at the right time and put it to good use in today's age of information overload?

6. Choose the right companies to invest in

Warren Buffett's long-term business partner Charlie Munger says, 'No wise pilot, no matter how great his talent and experience, fails to use his checklist.'

You need to study a lot to find companies that give good returns. When you use a checklist, you automatically discard badly performing companies. The following points can be added to your checklist while deciding which companies to invest in:

- What is the nature of the company's business? What products and services are sold by the company? What does the company produce?

- Who is in the top management of the company? Who are the founder, chairman, CEO, and what are their educational qualifications, experience and track record? How many shares does the promoter group hold?

- Is the company consistently making profits or suffering losses? What does the pattern of quarterly results indicate?

- What is the company's competitive advantage? Does the company own renowned brands and have the financial strength and ability to manufacture at low costs? Does the company

> 'Time is the friend of the wonderful company, the enemy of the mediocre.'—Warren Buffett

possess the required permissions from the government to run the business? Example: telecom, electricity generation and mining cannot be done without a government licence.

- How was the financial performance of the company in the previous year? What do the numbers indicate about sales, net profit, profit after tax and free cash flow?

- Is the company's return on capital employed and return on equity more than 10 per cent to 15 per cent of the previous year's in the past five years?

- Is the balance sheet looking strong? What is the ratio of capital raised from shareholders to the loan taken from banks? Does the company have enough liquidity and investments?

- How much money does the company need to repay its loans in the short term and how much in the long term? Is the repayment being done on time? Is the company making enough profits to repay its loans? Have the founders pledged their shares as a mortgage for loans?

- Have the founders and management been named in any scams? Is the market share of the company growing or declining? Have the shareholders been cheated ever by the company?

- Who are the major competitors and who currently leads in terms of market share in the industry? What is the effect of the global competition on the company?

- What is the difference between the company's market value and the intrinsic value of its shares? Are its shares expensive or cheap? What is the margin of safety, if it exists?

- How do the goods and services of the company compare with that of its competitors? We think mainly of Colgate when toothpaste is talked about and Maggi in the case of instant noodles. Maruti Suzuki holds a market share of around 40 per cent in the automobile sector.

- When the founders and the top managers sell their shares, that shows they do not trust the company any more or that they need funds for their other businesses. On the contrary, when they are seen buying their own shares even at a higher price, that shows their confidence in their own company.

Investment in the share market is a subject of immense study. You may add your own points to the list given above and choose the right company to invest in to grow your wealth.

7. Money is to be earned and not to be lost

● The primary objective of any investment is to earn good returns. Wise investors never let their money go down the drain.

● Investment is not like betting. People in betting are not bound by any rules, whereas investors need to be more disciplined. They invest based on their study of companies and their experience.

● Recovering money from shares using what you are left with after you have made losses in the share market is a very difficult task.

Sr. no.	Invested amount (Rs)	Loss (per cent)	Loss in amount (Rs)	Balance	Returns required to make up the loss (per cent)
	A	B	C = A x B	D = A - C	E = C/D x 100
1	100	10	10	90	11 per cent
2	100	20	20	80	25 per cent
3	100	50	50	50	100 per cent
4	100	90	90	10	900 per cent

8. Be disciplined while investing

● There are a few rules for investing. The ones who follow them earn good returns.

● The weak horse also does win occasionally in a race. Similarly, a weak company's share might perform well for a short period and the performing company's share might dip. That is why patience is important for an investor.

'Investors should purchase stocks like they purchase groceries, not like they purchase perfume.'—Benjamin Graham

Mindset of new investors while buying shares

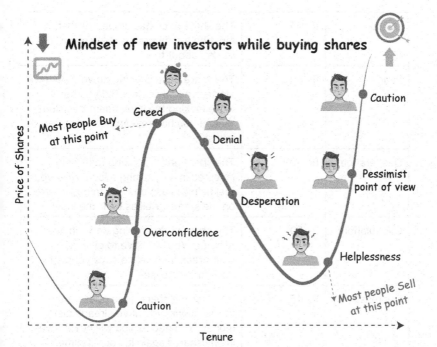

While the share price is on the rise	Per share price (Rs)	Thoughts, and actions taken
Optimism	Rs 50	You read somewhere that the price of a share is increasing.
Excitement	Rs 75	You feel that you should invest in the share once the price dips a bit.
Thrill	Rs 100	You buy the shares because the price seems to be rising constantly.
Euphoria	Rs 125	The share price has gone up after you invested. You decide to invest more by taking a loan
When the share price starts to dip		
Anxiety	Rs 115	The share price has dipped a bit. Nothing to worry about but, what if it goes down even further?

Denial	Rs 95	The share price has dipped further. It must be a temporary slide. You will not be sad about this.
Fear	Rs 80	The share price is going down. You have started to feel scared. Did you hurry while making the investment decision? What if you had researched more before investing?
Desperation	Rs 60	The share price is sliding fast. You invested in it by taking a loan. Now you feel helpless as you have to pay interest on the loan as well as bear the loss.
Capitulation	Rs 50	The share price is going down instead of rising. You will have to give up on your dream and sell to save yourself from further losses.
Depression	Rs 45	Whether the share price goes up or further down, you have already lost money. You decide you will never invest in any shares again in your lifetime.
When the share prices again begin to rise		
Hope	Rs 75	The share price has begun to rise again. You should not have sold it at a low price.
Relief	Rs 100	The share price is rising. Should you re-invest? But your previous experience has not been positive. You were right that the share price would rise one day (here, you conveniently forget the financial loss).
Optimism	Rs 125	You will not repeat the same mistakes. You are much more positive this time. (Even then, you buy the same share again at the current price).

9. **A company cannot guarantee a repeat of its past success in the future**

- A company's public reports, such as annual reports, highlight its past performance. They do not guarantee future success.

- Factors such as a strong management, a new line of products and services, research and development work, government policies and the country's economic condition and progress have a role to play in a company's performance.

- Assume that you hold shares of a pharmaceutical company engaged in exporting medicines to the US and earning huge profits for many years. One day, the Food and Drug Administration (FDA) of the US bans a drug exported by the company because of a change in the country's policies or a competitor brand comes up with a more effective drug at a lower price. In such a scenario, the share value of the company might dip. How the company fights back at such a time defines the course of the business.

- 'If past history was all that is needed to play the game of money, the richest people would be librarians,' says Warren Buffett.

10. Don't keep a constant eye on the share market

- Various mobile apps can send you share market updates through notifications. Also, there are scores of WhatsApp groups, Telegram channels, email newsletters, television news reports and analyses and YouTube videos constantly bombarding people with information on share market movements and recommendations.

- Since you can only focus on one thing at a time, you should be focused on your work as your priority. The money earned from this should be saved and wisely invested, based on your risk appetite.

- Investment in the share market and your primary source of income are two different aspects. Focusing on the ups and downs of shares can easily distract you and hamper your earnings from your primary work.

- Events at both the national and global levels impact the market. But thinking of the market continuously once you have invested, or being too excited or depressed about developments in it, should be avoided.

- Don't try to control factors that are beyond your control. Let your investment in the share market be a long-term one. Remember, the night will always be followed by a fresh day!

11. Not all shares that dip rise again

- Never forget this age-old wisdom: 'Do not try to catch a falling knife!'

> 'Whenever a bright person, a really bright person, who has a lot of money goes broke, it's because of leverage.'—Warren Buffett

- You will be making a loss if you are innocent enough to think that buying shares which have dipped by 50 per cent or 80 per cent will rise to all-time highs.

- Let us look at the example of YES Bank Ltd.

- In the chart shown above, we will see how the share price, which was Rs 275 on 29 March 2019, began to fall:

  o 17 May 2019: Rs 134

  o 19 July 2019: Rs 83

  o 30 August 2019: Rs 60

  o 11 October 2019: Rs 39

  o 6 March 2020: Rs 16

  o 31 July 2020: Rs 12

- Everyone who purchased shares at any of the stages above must have made a loss.

- You should rethink a share if it is constantly taking a hit because of continuous selling; this could be because the company's profitability is in question, or perhaps its very existence.

- On a similar note, many retail investors bring a loss upon themselves by investing in companies such as DHFL, Reliance Power and

> '*The four most dangerous words in investing are: "This time it's different."*'—Sir John Templeton

Jaypee Infratech. These companies decimated hundreds of crores of investors' money.

12. Create a balanced portfolio

- Knowing that loss is inevitable in the journey of investing in the share market is important. Even experienced and popular investors have faced financial losses in their investment journey. The difference is that they never gave up and left the market but always came back stronger.

- It is important to diversify your portfolio.

- While investing, you should always try and achieve the risk-to-reward ratio. This is a measurement used to compare a stock's potential profit or reward against its potential loss or risk.

- Don't invest 100 per cent of your savings in the stock market, even when you get good returns.

13. Don't buy shares using borrowed funds

- You can invest only when you are saving regularly. Investing in shares is a long-term process and you need substantial savings for that.

- Many of us think that not buying a share at a particular juncture would be a big lost opportunity to make great profits. Even if we don't have the money to invest, we might take a loan to buy shares.

- The potential investment opportunity never comes to life; in fact, the price of the shares you buy may dip while you keep paying interest on the loan taken. Here, you are making twin losses.

- Opportunities are always available in the share market. You should develop the mindset of letting go of an opportunity if you don't have enough to invest at that point, and invest when you have saved for it.

> 'Never invest in stocks with borrowed money or a faint heart. Both are fatal.'—Manoj Arora

The Difference between Share Trading and Investment in Shares

1. The number of demat accounts surged to 11 crore in January 2023, compared to 8.4 crore in the year-ago period, indicating growth of 31 per cent. Many Indian investors look at the share market as an easy way of making money.

2. Just primary knowledge of the share market and lack of experience may not help investors to earn money through the share market.

3. Social media platforms such as YouTube, Facebook and Twitter carry ads based on your preferences. If you regularly browse for share market-related content, you will see the following types of ads:

    A. Broker ads

        1. A man talks about the profits he earned from the share market by trading on his mobile screen. You are then told to open an account with the broker who is advertising if you want to earn huge money in a short span of time.

        2. A man wearing branded clothes, owner of a huge house and expensive cars and well-travelled internationally, tells a friend how he has achieved all this. You are then asked to open an account with a particular broking house if you too want a similar lifestyle.

    B. WhatsApp groups, Telegram channels

        ● Screenshots showing how a person earns thousands of rupees as daily profits are shared in groups or carried as status messages. Group members are asked to follow tips shared daily so they may make similar profits. This is followed by a link using which you can subscribe to paid services.

    C. Ads for share trading classes

        1. Learning from online or offline channels could be the best way to gain knowledge about the share market. You can

'Markets can remain irrational longer than you can remain solvent.'—John Maynard Keynes

verify the credentials of the trainers and their classes by going through reviews of them.

2. You need to do a comprehensive study of the stocks you wish to invest in before putting in your money. Don't buy shares just because someone suggested so.

D. Who will not mind earning a lot of money with the least amount of effort? Advertisers show you exciting things to catch your attention. Many people who watch these ads begin to daydream about the returns they would earn from investing in the share market.

E. 'All that glitters is not gold' is 100 per cent true in the case of intra-day trading. Your hard-earned money should become your financial strength by way of investments. If you are thinking about using it for intra-day trading, hold on!

F. What is intra-day trading? It is the buying and selling of shares on the same day to earn profits. This also includes selling at a loss to avoid further loss. This includes shorting shares too. Assuming that the price of certain shares will fall, you sell those shares and buy them later at a lower price. This is what shorting means.

G. What is an investment? A property appreciates over time and its value increases. The property owner can also earn money from this investment over the course of time. Selling the property at a higher cost than its purchase cost is implied in the transaction. Home, land, gold and shares are some of the popular investment alternatives. Some properties are even held for decades as an investment.

'If you have trouble imagining a 20 per cent loss in the stock market, you shouldn't be in stocks.'—Sir John Bogle

Difference between Intra-Day Trading and Investing in Shares

Intra-day trading of shares	Investing in equity shares
Objective	
To earn quick profits.	To create a portfolio over the long term and to earn consistent returns to create wealth.
Basis of decision	
Technical analysis.	Value investing.
Research	
Understanding the current market situation is important for buying and selling shares on the same day. Market sentiment is more important than company performance.	Before investing, detailed information about the companies one is looking at, the nature of their business, financial performance and other primary information needs to be researched. Here, a company's performance is more important than market sentiment.
Benefits and Profits	
The difference between the buying and selling price is considered as the profit at the time of selling of shares.	The share value is based on the progress and the profit of the company.
Tenure	
Shares are sold and profits are booked as soon as the prices rise. Share traders buy shares and sell them as soon as the price increases and targets are achieved.	Things work exactly the opposite way. The share price goes on increasing in the case of a performing company and the investors become partners in the company's success.

Frequency of buying and selling	
Traders have to constantly buy and sell shares.	Comparatively, the frequency of buying and selling is far less. Once an investor has researched and invested in shares, he usually does not sell them easily.
Proportion of Loan	
Most traders opt for loans in terms of either cash or margin money, and repayment is necessary in both cases.	Long-term investors avoid taking loans. If they do, it is for only a very small and meagre proportion of their total portfolio.
What if the share price falls below the purchase price?	
Traders sell the shares they have bought even if they are in a loss and focus on the next trade.	Even if the share price falls, investors who have done good research buy more of the same shares or re-evaluate their investment decision. Shares are usually not sold at a loss.
Popular names	
George Soros, Jesse Livermore, Paul Jones.	Warren Buffett, Peter Lynch, Mohnish Pabrai.

'People calculate too much and think too little.'—Charlie Munger

Is Intra-Day Trading the Same as Gambling?

- Although intra-day trading and gambling have certain similarities, it would be wrong to think both are the same.

- Gambling comprises forecasting an event of the future, testing your luck despite knowing the risks and transacting in terms of money.

- Gambling has been part of human history down the ages. In the Mahabharata, Yudhishthira had even staked his wife, Draupadi, in a game of dice. We keep hearing of the betting that happens in the game of cricket. Many Western countries have legalized betting. We can say the lottery business conducted in India is a form of gambling.

- Signs of a gambler:

  o A gambler is addicted to the adrenaline rush from gambling and can put a lot of money at stake to keep experiencing it.

  o A gambler believes he is not addicted to gambling but is doing something adventurous or for fun.

  o People in gambling may feel addicted, guilty and out of control, but they hardly take any steps to get out of it.

  o A gambler becomes irritated if someone tries to stop him from gambling.

  o A gambler is unsuccessful in his attempts to stop gambling.

  o He lies about his habit of gambling.

  o He avoids work and ignores family and career.

  o He gambles away the money set aside for certain expenses.

  o He takes huge risks in gambling.

  o He constantly borrows money to gamble with or takes new loans to pay off the old ones.

  o He gambles to earn back the money lost.

> *'There are old traders and there are bold traders, but there are very few old, bold traders.'*—Ed Seykota

- If the signs of gambling mentioned above are visible in your intra-day trading, it is fair to assume that you have crossed the line between trading and gambling.

- If a novice is trading after reading viral social media posts, tips and screenshots of profits earned from intra-day trading or fake news, it is as good as gambling. The reason is that the novice will lose his money to the experienced and established share traders. Please note—such traders would themselves be among the rarest of the rare.

- Historical examples:

  o A research report following a study on intra-day traders based in Taiwan during the fifteen years between 1992 and 2006 said that more than 75 per cent of the traders stopped their activity within two years after losing their money. Only 1 per cent actually earned profits—meaning 99 per cent suffered losses.[6]

  o In Brazil, during the years 2013 to 2015, out of the 300 traders dealing in equity derivatives, 97 per cent lost their money, according to a report published in June 2020. Just 1.1 per cent of the traders earned more than the minimum wage set by the Brazilian government.[7]

  o A study released by the Securities and Exchange Board of India (SEBI) in January 2023 revealed that 89 per cent of the individual traders (9 out of 10 individual traders) in the equity F&O (Futures and Options) segment incurred losses. The average loss was Rs 1.1 lakh in FY22.[8]

  o Among the active profit-making traders, it was discovered that the top 1 per cent of traders alone account for nearly 51 per cent of total net profit.

  o The findings from the study were based on data compiled from the top ten brokers in the country, accounting for 67 per cent of the overall individual client turnover in the equity F&O segment during FY 2021–22.

  o New traders join the business every day, lose their money and don't return to the share market any time soon.

> 'The hardest thing to judge is what level of risk is safe.'
> —George Soros

- Many traders, mobile apps and high-profile trading teachers are available in the market, offering tips for high-value share trading at minimal margins and brokerage.

- There is no limit to how much you can earn from the constant buying and selling of shares, but there is a limit to the money you have.

- In the pursuit of earning quick money, focusing on share trading instead of our jobs, professions or businesses is not always profitable.

- Many people have made profits from share trading, but they are very minuscule in numbers. Not everyone can win the lottery—similarly, not everyone can earn profits from share trading.

- There is a popular saying in the share market: Investment in the share market is like soap; the more you handle it, the smaller it gets.

- Long-term investments do not require hasty decision-making. They help in saving the principal and in keeping you mentally healthy.

- Your goal should be to invest in shares of great companies at the reasonably right time and for the long term. Warren Buffett's rule of '20-Slot' is useful here.

Warren Buffett's '20-Slot' rule

- In a lecture to USC Business School students, Warren Buffett's right-hand man, Charlie Munger, revealed a strategy that Buffett has used time and again to build success.

- Warren Buffet preaches that he could 'improve your ultimate financial welfare by giving you a ticket with only twenty slots in it so that you had twenty punches—representing all the investments that you got to make in a lifetime. And once you'd punched through the card, you couldn't make any more investments at all . . . Under those rules, you'd really think carefully about what you did and you'd be forced to load up on what you'd really thought about. So you'd do so much better.'

- Warren Buffett suggests that instead of risking your limited capital to earn from every opportunity, it is better to be focused and make informed decisions.

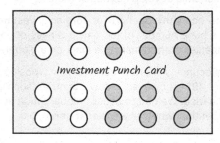

What Lies Ahead for the Stock Market in India?

The share market is dependent on the country's economy. We will try to understand the performance of the Indian share market.

1. India's Economic Progress in the Past Seventy Years

- Being a closed economy, the government policies in the early years following Independence disallowed foreign companies from setting up their businesses in India. The 'Permit Raj' had created roadblocks in India's economic development back then.

- In 1991, the economy opened for foreign investments and India witnessed a huge number of job and business opportunities. Also, Indian companies started making a mark on a global scale.

- The Indian economy started cementing its position in the world market after 1991; however, a few countries such as China were ahead in the race. We had to accept globalization and become part of the competition, whether we liked it or not.

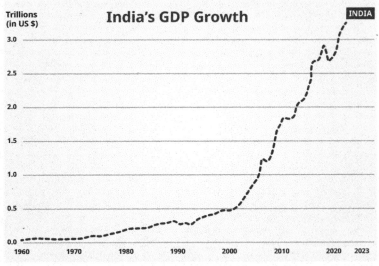

India's GDP Growth

GDP - Gross Domestic Product   Ref.: https://data.worldbank.org/country/india

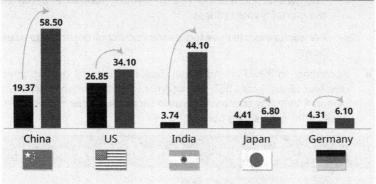

Largest Economies in the World by GDP in 2050 (US$ trillions)

■ 2023 ■ 2050

Source -
2023- World Economic Outlook Database, April 2023-International Monetary Fund. IMF.org.
2050 - 'The World in 2050' report published by PWC in February 2017

2. India's Demographic Dividend

When the working population, i.e., those aged between fifteen and sixty-five, exceeds the dependent population, i.e., children and senior citizens, a country begins to benefit from its demographic dividend.

- With a rise in the working population, production increases and the economy gets a boost. The population drives the economy and this is called the demographic dividend.

- India is a country of young people. According to a report by the United Nations Population Fund (UNFPA), India's working-age population, i.e., aged fifteen to sixty-four, is more than 67 per cent of the total population; those aged below fourteen years make up 27 per cent of the population, while those aged sixty-five and above account for 6 per cent of the population.

- The average age of the Indian population in 2022 was just twenty-eight, whereas it was thirty-seven in the US and China, forty-five in Europe and forty-nine in Japan.

- A country that enters the demographic dividend stage enjoys the following benefits:

o   Rise in per capita savings, giving a boost to the economy.

o   More employment opportunities.

o   The general and financial health of young people get better as the mortality rate reduces.

o   Per capita income rises too, as the number of dependents goes down.

● According to UNFPA, India can benefit from its demographic dividend till the year 2055—meaning at least thirty-two years from hereon.[10] Very few countries can be in such a beneficial demographic position for such a long period of time.

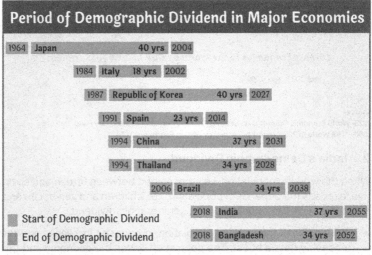

Ref. - United Nations Population Fund

● Japan benefited from a higher working population for more than forty years from 1964.

● China entered the demographic dividend phase in the year 1994, which gave a boost to its economy. China's economy has grown at an average of 8 per cent per annum.

● Just like Italy and Spain, countries such as Singapore, South Korea and Thailand have also benefited from the demographic dividend.

● A country will not benefit from its demographic dividend if it does not create a robust education and healthcare infrastructure keeping in mind the rising population. In the past few decades, a few Asian countries capitalized on this and witnessed a multi-fold increase in their GDPs. On the other hand, South American countries could manage to grow their GDP only by two times, as they did not plan social and economic policies well enough for their growing population.

- Even the UNFPA has made it clear that countries will not be able to benefit from the demographic dividend in the absence of quality education supported by skill development, healthcare and ample job opportunities.

- The possible effects of demographic dividend on economic progress:

  o A major boost to urbanization and industrialization in the upcoming years. Out of the total working population in the Asian continent, half of it would be in India alone.

  o According to the International Monetary Fund (IMF) World Economic Outlook database, India is projected to surpass Germany and Japan, becoming the world's third-largest economy by FY28. This advancement positions India right after the US and China, marking a significant milestone.

  o Per capita income would rise alongside the economy.

  o The number of spenders that belong to the middle class would rise too.

  o More than two-thirds of the savings in India are in the form of immovable property and gold. The scenario would change as people will take the share market route.

3. India's Growth Story

- The economy started to reorganize recently after a major push was given to digital transactions, the use of smartphones, the use of the Aadhaar card for banking, and by way of Jan Dhan Accounts for all.

- Many small investors entered the share market by way of mutual funds. The influx continues and will keep increasing. Many experts have forecast the breaching of the 1 lakh or 2 lakh mark by the Sensex. Although they are just predictions, they cannot be completely disregarded.

- The economy is getting organized at such a fast pace that it is heading towards new records unless some unseen force such as a pandemic disrupts its sprint. Those who can steer their way through the ups and downs of this run can earn a lot of money from it.

- Since India has had a stable government since 2014, the business outlook has been positive. The push received from infrastructure projects, mergers of various banks and companies, the ease of getting loans due to the rise in banking money, striking growth in the index that measures the ease of doing business, reduction in corporate tax (from 30 per cent to 22 per cent), improvement in the collection of indirect taxes by way of GST, and, finally, increased transparency in the economy, have led to growth and benefited the companies in the share market.

4. The Share Market and Your Investments

● The Sensex crossed the 66,000 mark for the first time in July 2023. Since 1979, the share market has grown by 66,000 per cent (from 100 to 66,000). Other types of investments cannot give such returns. But to earn it, the investors needed to have a strong belief that their investments would grow and overlook temporary fluctuations in the share market. Let us look at an example.

● In 2020, the share market hit rock bottom compared to the four years prior. The Sensex had been at 23,000 and the Nifty at 7000 in March 2016. They had climbed to 25,000 and 7700, respectively, by 2020. But in just a year and a half, the Sensex climbed by 134 per cent and the Nifty by 138 per cent. You can imagine the returns earned by investors who stayed invested in the share market through this period. Those who cannot handle the pressure of fluctuations should take the mutual fund route to benefit from shares.

● No one can stay invested forever in the market. Therefore, the one who liquidates her investments at the right time and earns good returns is called a wise investor.

● However, no one has been able to predict the right time for exit to date. That is why you should withdraw money from the share market when you hit a certain pre-decided rate of return or when you need funds.

● There is another easy way to achieve this. Instead of investing in a company that will give you good returns, investing in index funds can bring good returns in the decades to follow. But you would have to believe in the reasons mentioned above.

● The Indian economy and the share market are going to set new records owing to India's skilled human capital, its demographic dividend and advancements in information technology.

● India is the largest democracy in the world. Every government that came to power since 1991 has given major importance to financial growth. Whichever political party comes to power, creating employment opportunities with the aim of financial growth is going to be one of the most important policies to be implemented.

- India has multiple financial issues to solve in the long run and the policymakers are busy finding solutions to them too.

- The progress shown by companies decides the direction in which the share market is going to head. The market expands if the economy is progressing. A consensus among experts worldwide suggests that the Indian economy is set to soar to unprecedented heights in the forthcoming decades.

- Although the share market will grow in the long run, no one can predict the situation in the market the next day, the next week or the next month.

- Some experts predict the share market will witness a bull run hereon.

- It is important for you to be invested in shares or mutual funds to reap the benefits of the rising economy.

'Chase the vision, not the money; the money will end up following you.'—Tony Hsieh

What Are Mutual Funds?

- Investors need to do some in-depth study before deciding which companies to invest in and the right time to do it.

- For beginners, investment in mutual funds is the right medium with which to begin their investment journey.

- A mutual fund company:

  o   Has predefined and balanced investment objectives.

  o   It creates a large corpus by combining money from multiple investors.

  o   It invests this money, for which it has fund managers.

  o   The money is invested in various types of shares, bonds, and also in gold and other asset classes.

  o   It pays returns earned from these investments to its unit holders, i.e. mutual fund investors.

- The Securities and Exchange Board of India (SEBI) is the regulatory body that controls and moderates mutual fund companies in India.

- Business houses and companies that have good financial backing and proven track records can obtain a licence to set up mutual funds.

- SBI, HDFC, Aditya Birla and Sundaram are a few such examples.

- The Association of Mutual Funds in India (AMFI) is the association of SEBI-registered mutual funds in India, which includes all the registered asset management companies.

How Do Mutual Funds Operate?

- Investors deposit money at mutual fund companies.

- Mutual fund companies hire experts, analysts and fund managers to properly manage the funds created from pooling the money received from investors. Experts, including CAs, CFAs and management professionals from reputed B-schools, are also hired for their knowledge in order to reduce the risks and earn returns on the investments made.

- Mutual fund managers keep themselves updated on the market, analyse the trends and invest the funds.

- After deducting the company expenses, the returns earned from investments in asset classes such as equity shares, bonds, gold, etc., are shared among the investors.

- The returns, received in the form of dividends and capital appreciation, are paid to investors in proportion to their investment in the mutual fund.

- The unit holders are subject to market risks as they may make profits or face losses based on the performance of the fund.

- No mutual fund company guarantees dividend or capital appreciation owing to the market risks involved.

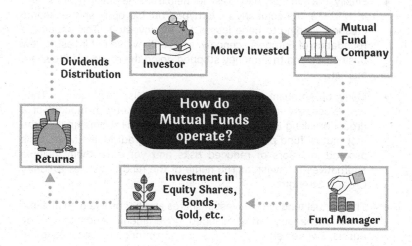

'If you have the stomach for stocks, but neither the time nor the inclination to do the homework, invest in equity mutual funds.'—Peter Lynch

History of Mutual Funds

- In the seventeenth and eighteenth centuries, Amsterdam was one of the financial centres of Europe. The local traders were involved in businesses that traded through the sea route.

- Abraham van Ketwich[11] was an owner of a sharebroking firm. Many of his clients had invested in shares of the East India Company.

- The British had colonized North America back then, and the English East India Company had taken huge loans for the same. A nationwide revolution took place in America and the English East India Company was not getting the expected returns out of its investments in America.

- Finally, the company had to ask for help from the British government. In 1772–73, the company's overhyped bubble burst and its shares crashed, leading to huge losses for the investors. This shook the foundation of Europe's economy, as people would not invest in new businesses and their money stopped doing the rounds of the share market.

- Many of Abraham van Ketwich's clients also lost money. They say, 'Necessity is the mother of invention.' Ketwich thought of a groundbreaking idea in that time of distress. He came up with the first mutual fund plan by the name of 'Eengradt Maakt Magt'. This assured investors of reduced risks and yet gave them multiple alternatives to invest in. The name of the fund translates to 'Unity Creates Strength'.

- This mutual fund could invest in shares and bonds listed on multiple stock exchanges. They included government bonds issued by Russia, Sweden and Denmark, loans given for plantations along the Caribbean coast, toll rights in Denmark and Spain, etc.

- It gained widespread popularity across the European continent and continued till 1825. Today, even after 250 years, the idea behind Eengradt Maakt Magt is still prevalent and is benefiting millions of investors around the globe.

> 'Intensity is the price of excellence.'—Warren Buffett

The Journey of Mutual Funds in India

Mutual funds were introduced in India in 1963 with the establishment of the Unit Trust of India (UTI). The government of India and the Reserve Bank had taken the initiative to set it up. The journey of mutual funds can be divided into four parts.

- During the period 1963 to 1987, only one mutual fund managed by UTI existed in the Indian market. Unit 64 was one of the most popular schemes back then. Towards the end of 1987, UTI was handling a portfolio of approximately Rs 6400 crore.

- Between 1988 and 1993, SBI, LIC and other public companies launched their mutual funds. By 1993, the total investment in mutual funds was valued at approximately Rs 47,000 crore.

- From 1993 to 2003, private companies started their mutual funds. As an industry, mutual funds were moving at a very slow pace owing to a lack of financial knowledge among the people during that period.

- The period after 2003 is important for mutual funds. UTI was split into two parts. From the older mutual fund schemes, one part was managed by an administrator and the other part was brought under the SEBI regulations, just like other mutual funds. Many foreign mutual funds also entered the Indian market. Some of them were successful in growing their business while others had to merge with or were acquired by other mutual fund companies.

- Over a span of fourteen years, from September 2009 to 31 May 2023, the Indian mutual fund industry has witnessed remarkable growth in terms of assets under management, expanding from Rs 7.50 lakh crore to Rs 43.20 lakh crore—a significant increase of approximately 5.75 times.[12] Government-backed mutual funds had started operating in 1986 and private companies had joined the party in 1993. As of today, more than forty mutual fund companies operate in the Indian market.

- As of 31 May 2023, the total count of investor folios has surged to 14.74 crore. Moreover, the inflows in the mutual fund industry, specifically through systematic investment plans (SIP), witnessed a

> 'If you will make the sacrifices now that most people aren't willing to make, later on you will be able to live as those folks will never be able to live.'—Dave Ramsay

substantial increase. In the fiscal year 2022–23, SIP inflows reached Rs 1.56 lakh crore, reflecting a remarkable growth of 62.5 per cent compared to the inflows of Rs 96,080 crore in FY20–21. (Ref: amfiindia.com)

- This upward trend in retail investor confidence reflects a growing trust and optimism in both the Indian stock markets and the mutual fund industry.

- Although mutual funds may seem a good way to achieve our current and future dreams while earning us good returns from the stock market and other investments, it is important to practise caution, as suggested by mutual funds in their own advertisements. It is important to assess our risk appetite and invest in mutual funds accordingly.[7]

Benefits of Investing in Mutual Funds

1. Professional fund management

- It is not easy to earn profits on a regular basis by investing in shares, gold or bonds.

- Do you find the time to learn about investments in your daily life? If the answer is yes, wouldn't you grow faster if you invested that time in your job or business?

- Investing in the right product at the right time calls for in-depth knowledge, technical know-how, expertise and ample time at one's disposal.

- Fund managers hold the tools, the ability, a team of experts, updated knowledge of the market and various types of information about fluctuations in the economy, changing government policies and matters that can affect a particular company.

- They also spend time on fundamental analyses and study financial viability.

- They put their experience to work and make informed decisions based on their wealth of knowledge.

- Once you have chosen a mutual fund that matches your financial goals, you can enjoy making profits through them while focusing on your work.

2. Diversification

- If you buy shares of a particular company and the share price of that company dips, you have to bear the losses. Mutual funds do not invest in shares of just one company.

- The shares of companies in the hotel industry had dipped during the Covid-19 pandemic. But those of the pharmaceutical and chemical industries had soared high. Since mutual funds invest in various industries, the fluctuations in the share market do not affect your investments much and the risk is relatively less.

> 'The principal role of the mutual fund is to serve its investors.'—John C. Bogle

- There are many types of mutual funds—viz., equity funds, debt funds, funds that invest in international companies, gold funds and real estate funds.

3. Liquidity

- Liquidity means the ease with which an asset can be converted into cash without affecting its market value.

- If you have invested in farmland and are in urgent need of money, it cannot be sold immediately as finding the right buyer, the legal formalities and the paperwork will take a lot of time to complete. The whole process might stretch from weeks to months.

- Most mutual fund schemes have an option for easy liquidation. Open-ended schemes allow easy exit at any point in time, and closed-ended schemes have a lock-in period but carry their own benefits. Like equity shares, the closed-ended funds also trade on stock exchanges. You may sell units of a closed-ended fund in the stock exchange at the existing market prices.

4. Transparent and professionally managed

- All transactions done in mutual funds are regulated by SEBI. It is mandatory for every mutual fund scheme to present its net asset value (NAV) on a daily basis and the details of its portfolio on a monthly basis to each of its investors.

- Various financial newspapers, websites and analysts keep a close watch on the performance of mutual funds.

5. Convenient and easily accessible

- It is easy to invest in and withdraw money from mutual funds; it can be done by filling out a physical form or through an online portal. Money can also be transferred from one fund to another. You have the option to withdraw only the amount you currently require.

- You can also buy and sell mutual funds within minutes online or via a phone call.

- Your investment in mutual funds can begin from as low as Rs 500.

> *'Knowledge speaks. Wisdom listens. Action wins.'*
> —Grant Cardone

6. Beneficial tax regime for investors

- You may need to pay a tax on the profit earned, based on the tenure and the amount earned.

- If you invest in a tax-saving scheme, you can avail of deduction up to Rs 1.5 lakh under section 80C of the Income Tax Act. These investments have a lock-in period of three years. You incur capital gains tax only when mutual fund units are sold. If you continue to stay invested, you will not have to pay capital gains tax on them.

- Short-term capital gains (STCG) tax is levied at a rate of 15 per cent (plus applicable surcharge and cess) on the transfer of listed equity-oriented mutual funds held for a period of less than twelve months.

- When you sell your mutual fund units after holding them for a period of at least twelve months, you are liable to pay long-term capital gains tax of 10 per cent (plus applicable surcharge and cess) with no indexation benefits.

- Your profits after tax are higher for mutual funds as compared to other investment alternatives.

Drawbacks of Mutual Funds

1. Management expenses

- The mutual fund companies deduct the cost of managing the fund from the money collected from investors. This cost would include the salaries of the fund managers, various experts, professionals, consultants, and the advertising and marketing costs, etc. These costs vary, depending on the mutual fund scheme in question.

- The expense ratio of an exchange traded fund (ETF) is low since the expenses are lower. The expense ratio is the annual cost paid to fund managers by holders of mutual funds or ETFs.

2. Exit load

- The investors have to bear the exit load if they wish to exit before the stipulated lock-in period.

'Mutual funds have historically offered safety and diversification. And they spare you the responsibility of picking individual stocks.'—Ron Chernow

- Therefore, it is always advisable to check the exit load before investing in any mutual fund scheme.

3. **Overdiversification can backfire**

- Mutual funds are preferred by those who do not want to invest in just one stock.

- However, investments in too many mutual fund schemes become difficult to manage later as the investor has to track multiple funds, and the profit earned from one can be nullified by the loss made in another. Make sure that diversification does not become di-worsification!

4. **Lock-in period**

- You cannot withdraw your money from schemes such as ELSS before the end of the lock-in period, which is usually three years.

Although mutual funds have a few drawbacks, they are beneficial for those who cannot find the time to research and invest in equities and yet want to earn from the stock market. Considering the pros and the cons, no alternative is as beneficial as mutual funds in the long term for common investors.

Star Fund Managers

- Fund managers who take the right decisions and help investors earn good returns are always in demand. They are widely followed and their interviews are closely tracked by everyone.

- John Bogle and Fidelity Group's Peter Lynch are regarded highly for popularizing mutual fund investments in the US. Books written by Peter Lynch have been bestsellers around the world. Peter Lynch, as the manager of the Magellan Fund at Fidelity Investments from 1977 to 1990, achieved an exceptional average annual return of 29.2 per cent. This consistent performance surpassed the S&P 500 stock market index by more than double, establishing the Magellan Fund as the top-performing mutual fund globally during that period.

Investment in Mutual Funds versus Direct Investment in Equity Shares

	Mutual fund	Direct investment in shares
1. **Management**	Managed by well-experienced, well-researched and expert fund managers.	Your investment decisions are entirely your responsibility.

	Mutual fund	**Direct investment in shares**
2. **Market research and regular updates**	It is okay even if the investor does not possess real-time updates and knowledge of the equity market, since fund managers have been appointed for this. However, it is important to learn about the fund house whose mutual funds you are planning to invest in.	Being updated and learning constantly is of prime importance in equity investing.
3. **Dividend, bonus shares and right to vote**	Since you purchase units of mutual funds, the company that runs the fund earns the dividend, bonus shares and the right to vote	Since you have directly invested in the equity of a company, you also earn the right to receive dividends, bonus shares and the right to vote.
4. **Risk**	Less risk: The market value of the mutual funds constantly fluctuates. The fund managers are engaged in earning the best possible returns for the fund. That is why the losses in the process are limited. In the case of direct investment in shares, the share price can fall to record lows, but in the case of mutual funds, fund managers invest only in specific companies. The investors are safeguarded from big losses since SEBI has strict rules and regulations for this.	High risk, compared to mutual funds. But although the risk is high in direct equity investments, the returns are higher too.

'Victory is always possible for the person who refuses to stop fighting.'—Napoleon Hill

	Mutual fund	Direct investment in shares
5. Demat account	A demat account is not necessary.	A demat account is mandatory.
6. Investment decision as regards purchase of shares	Once you invest in a mutual fund, you have no control over which shares the fund invests in.	Since you are directly investing in a particular share, you can choose your stock and timing according to your convenience and understanding.
7. Suitability for beginners	Often, beginners are intimidated by the fluctuations in the share market and end up making wrong decisions. Therefore, it is easier for them to start their investment journey with equity mutual funds in the form of SIPs (systematic investment plan), where a particular sum is invested every month.	Every investor has to study the market to understand which shares to buy or sell, at what price and when. You need ample time, a learning mentality and perseverance. You can begin with a small amount and work your way up.
8. Investment alternatives	You can invest in debt, gold and real estate, apart from other alternatives, through mutual funds.	Direct equity investment in the share market can only be done in listed companies.

'The only place where success comes before work is in the dictionary.'—Vidal Sassoon

	Mutual fund	Direct investment in shares
9. Ultimate use of investments and available options	Various alternatives are available, such as retirement funds, children's education funds, tax-saving funds, etc.	There is no specific option when it comes to the ultimate use of the money you make from investing in shares. It is up to you to decide what you would do with the money you earn from it.

Mutual Fund vs Term Deposit

	Mutual Fund	Term Deposit
1. Risk involved	Debt fund: Less risk. Equity fund: Medium to high risk.	Less risk. Investments in term deposits with nationalized and private banks are secured by way of insurance.
2. Guaranteed returns	No guaranteed returns, as returns are based on market conditions.	Guaranteed returns.
3. Countering inflation	Returns on equity mutual funds have generally been higher than the rate of inflation.	The returns after tax are often lower than the rate of inflation.

> 'Before you speak, listen. Before you write, think. Before you spend, earn. Before you invest, investigate. Before you criticize, wait. Before you pray, forgive. Before you quit, try. Before you retire, save. Before you die, give.'—William A. Ward

4. Liquidity	You can get money in one to two working days after liquidating units of mutual funds.	If the term deposit is liquidated before its maturity, 0.5 per cent to 1 per cent of the deposit may be charged and the balance is paid immediately.
5. Management expense	Management expenses are taken from investors' money.	No such expense is charged to investors.
6. Variety	Investing in mutual funds is equivalent to investing in gold, bonds, equity shares and such asset classes.	There is no variety in term deposits.

'To make the most of your money, I recommend sticking with mutual funds that don't charge a commission when you buy or sell.'—Suze Orman

Mutual Funds vs PPF

		Mutual Funds	PPF
1.	Investment limit	No limit.	A person can invest a maximum of Rs 1.5 lakh per annum.
2.	Tenure of investment	No specific tenure.	Fifteen years, which can be extended by five years by way of an application.
3.	Risk involved	Debt fund: Less risk. Equity fund: Medium to high risk.	No risk.
4.	Guaranteed returns	No guaranteed returns, as returns are based on market conditions.	Returns are guaranteed.
5.	Returns	Returns vary according to the nature of the fund. Equity mutual funds have given approximately 12 per cent to 18 per cent returns per annum, based on market conditions. Debt mutual funds have given approximately 7 per cent to 9 per cent returns.	The current rate is 7.1 per cent; the rate is updated every quarter by the government.
6.	Tax saving	Only investments in ELSS are exempt from tax. The investor has to pay taxes based on the dividend received and the type of mutual fund.	The invested amount is exempted under section 80C of the Income Tax Act. The interest and maturity amounts are also exempt from tax.

'Equity mutual funds are the perfect solution for people who want to own stocks without doing their own research.'—Peter Lynch

		Mutual Funds	**PPF**
7.	**Liquidity**	You can get money in one to two working days after liquidating units of mutual funds.	In some cases, a part of the invested sum can be withdrawn after seven years. After fifteen years, the entire sum with the interest earned is available.
8.	**Management expenses**	The management expenses are taken from investors' money.	No such expense in PPF.

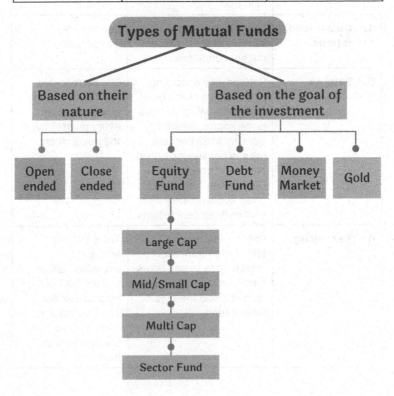

- **Based on their nature**
  - Open-ended
  - Closed-ended
- **Based on the goal of the investment**
  - Equity Fund
    - Large-cap
    - Mid/small-cap
    - Multi-cap
    - Sector Fund
  - Gold fund
  - Money market fund
  - Debt fund

1. Types of funds based on the nature of mutual funds

The three major types of mutual funds are open-ended, closed-ended and interval funds.

- Open-ended funds: Investors can buy and sell units whenever they wish to. The unit value is based on the NAV of that particular day. Open-ended funds are available throughout the year for a subscription and they do not have a fixed maturity date, except units of ELSS funds as they are locked in for three years from the date of investment.

- Closed-ended funds
  - Closed-ended funds have a stipulated maturity period. These mutual funds are available for subscription during a specified period at the time of the scheme's launch, i.e., New Fund Offer (NFO). Investors cannot buy units once the NFO is over and have a lock-in period. If any investor wishes to exit, they can do so only once the funds get listed on the stock exchange.
  - If an investor is in urgent need of money, he can sell the units to buyers available in the market and earn money. In such a

'I will tell you the secret to getting rich on Wall Street. You try to be greedy when others are fearful. And you try to be fearful when others are greedy.'—Warren Buffett

transaction, the price of the unit is based on the demand-supply ratio and might differ from the NAV.

- Interval funds
  - o This type is a combination of open-ended and closed-ended, which means the funds are partly open and closed over a long term.
  - o Example: A fund is open for transaction between 1 January and 15 January or between 1 July and 15 July, and will operate as a closed fund at other times. Investors can enter or exit during the open period.

2. Types of funds based on the goal of the investment:

I. **Equity funds:** People can invest through these funds in equities such as company shares, share warrants and derivatives, i.e. futures and options.

A. Diversified funds

1.1.1 As per the market cap

a) Investments can be done in various sectors and in shares of companies of specific market-cap categories.

b) The funds can be further classified into large-cap, mid-cap and small-cap.

A. Large-cap mutual funds

- Investment is done in shares whose market capitalization is equal to or more than that of the last company in the BSE 100 index.

- Large companies are better equipped to handle the ups and downs in the market as compared to others.

- As the companies are backed by huge capital and market experience, their share prices are relatively stable. Investing in large-cap mutual funds helps brings stability to one's portfolio.

- 80–100 per cent of investment is done in such large companies.

- Returns are usually certain as compared to direct equity investments

- This alternative is suitable for long-term investment in the form of SIPs.

'No price is too low for a bear or too high for a bull.'—Unknown

B. Mid-cap mutual funds

- Investment is done in shares of medium and small companies. Even here, investors get good returns on their capital investment.

C. Small-cap/Micro-cap mutual funds

- Here, investments are done in small companies. The share prices may see huge fluctuations. Just like large-cap funds, even these funds offer regular returns.

- Mid-cap and small-cap stocks tend to display greater volatility compared to large-cap stocks, but they also offer higher growth potential over the long term. In light of this, it is generally advisable for investors to diversify their investments across different market capitalizations.

D. Flexi-cap mutual funds

- Investment is done in shares of large-cap, medium-cap, small-cap and micro-cap companies. Investors are free to choose the companies as well as the proportion of investment in each category.

- It offers variety and flexibility to the investor.

- Risk is low and returns are usually high.

- The funds experience higher deviation as compared to large-cap funds.

- They are suggested for long-term investment.

The conservative investor primarily allocates the majority of their funds to large-cap funds. The balanced investor allocates 75 per cent of their funds to large-cap funds while allocating the remaining 25 per cent to mid-cap and small-cap funds. On the other hand, the aggressive investor allocates 75 per cent of their funds to small-cap and mid-cap funds, with the remaining 25 per cent allocated to large-cap funds.

These allocation strategies enable investors to match their investment decisions with their risk tolerance, growth expectations and personal objectives.

1.1.2 Thematic equity funds

- Infrastructure funds

> 'One of the funny things about the stock market is that every time one person buys, another sells, and both think they are astute.'—William Feather

- Focused funds: In this type, investment is done in a maximum of thirty shares as against fifty shares in the other types.

- Dividend yield funds: These funds invest in shares of high dividend-yielding companies.

- Value fund: Investment is done in value shares, meaning, shares of companies whose market value is less than their real value.

- Opportunity funds, MNC funds

- Dynamic plan funds, PE ratio funds, long/short funds

- International funds

- Arbitrage funds

1.1.3 Index funds

These are schemes based on the NSE Fifty (fifty shares) Index or the Sensex (thirty shares), where the ratio of investment in shares of companies is fixed.

1.1.4 Sector funds

Only companies from one sector are included in this type of fund. The sectors could be:

- IT

- FMCG—items of daily use

- Pharmaceuticals—medicines

- Financial services—banking and finance

- Power—electricity and energy

In this way, investment can be done in various sectors.

1.1.5 Equity-Linked Savings Schemes (ELSS)—Tax-Saving Schemes

- If an investment offers good returns along with tax deductions, then it is always considered beneficial. ELSS is one such type of mutual fund and is one of the best alternatives for investment.

- ELSS is the most popular among mutual fund investments. These funds invest in the equities of companies.

'Little disciplines compounded over time make a huge difference.'—Orrin Woodward

- Individuals and HUFs can get a deduction up to Rs 1,50,000 under section 80C of the Income Tax Act 1961.

- ELSS investments have a lock-in period of three years.

- Since these are open-ended funds, you can invest in them at any time but cannot withdraw before three years from the date of investment.

- Investors have two options: dividend or capital appreciation.

- You can invest small amounts through a monthly SIP in an ELSS.

- After the lock-in period of three years is over, investors have the option of keeping their money invested in the same scheme.

- Long-term capital gains on equity shares and units of equity-oriented mutual funds up to Rs 1 lakh are not taxable. Gains exceeding Rs 1 lakh are taxed at a rate of 10 per cent. That means capital gains up to Rs 1 lakh are tax-free per year. Overall, ELSS is the best option among mutual funds for tax saving.

ELSS vs Other Tax-Saving Schemes

1. Lock-in period

- ELSS has the lowest lock-in period, of just three years.

- This period is very small, compared with those of other tax-saving schemes
  - o PPF: fifteen years
  - o EPF: up to retirement
  - o NPS: up to the time investor turns sixty
  - o Other tax-saving schemes: the general tenure is more than five years

- **Withdrawal in case of financial emergency**
  - o Investors can withdraw a part of their investment in ELSS in case of a financial emergency.
  - o Except for PPF, other schemes do not allow withdrawal before the maturity of the tenure.

'Even the intelligent investor is likely to need considerable willpower to keep from following the crowd.'—Benjamin Graham

    o   EPF: No withdrawal while you are employed except under some special circumstances.

    o   NPS: No withdrawal until the investor turns sixty but withdrawal is allowed under some special circumstances.

2. Debt-based schemes

These mutual fund schemes invest in the following types of instruments that offer guaranteed returns: government bonds, debentures of private and government companies, commercial papers, bonds of financial institutions, certificates of deposit, money market instruments, etc.

The sub-categories are as follows:

a. Tenure: less than one year	b. Tenure: one year to four years	c. Variable tenure	d. Tenure: more than seven years
• Overnight • Liquid • Ultra-short duration • Low duration • Money market, etc.	• Short duration • Medium duration, etc.	• Dynamic bonds • Corporate bonds • Credit risk • Banking and PSUs, etc.	• Long duration • Gilt • Gilt Fund—ten years • Floater, etc.

Investing money in liquid funds will fetch better returns than if you kept the money in your savings account.

• Those who want to keep their risk to a minimum can opt for debt funds instead of equity funds.

• The returns on debt funds are less than those from equity funds.

• Choose a debt fund to suit your investment tenure. Think of ultra-short-duration and low-duration schemes for low tenure.

• Just because a debt fund gave good returns once does not guarantee similar returns from it in the future too. Compare it with the prevailing rate of return in the market and decide whether you will invest in one.

• **Balanced funds:** Fund managers try to achieve a balance by investing in debt, equity and gold funds. Sub-types of balanced funds include monthly income schemes, capital guarantee plans, balanced fund plans, etc.

- **Gold ETFs:** The mutual funds in this plan invest in gold. The value of the units in a gold exchange traded fund (ETF) varies according to the fluctuations in the gold market.

Precautions to Be Taken While Investing in NFOs

- Many mutual fund advisers and financial experts advise buying funds through NFOS. But it is difficult to predict their performance while they are new to the market.

- Understand the difference between an IPO and an NFO: The listing price of the shares in an IPO is determined by the demand for them in the market, the IPO price of the equity shares, future predictions of profits of the company, etc. The price of the share can vary once the company is listed. But increase in NAV is based on the increase in the price of the shares in which mutual funds are invested.

- The NAV is pre-decided at Rs 10 per unit in an NFO, and it does not vary due to rise or fall in demand for the fund, or for any other reason.

- Many investors believe that NFOs are available at a lower cost than existing plans, but this is not true.

- Suppose you invest Rs 10,000 in an NFO that is valued at Rs 10 per unit and another person invested Rs 10,000 in a plan whose NAV is Rs 20 per unit. In both cases, the increase in NAV is based on the portfolio performance. Here, the percentage growth is more important than the value of the NAV. That is why it will not be wise to invest in a fund just because its NAV is low.

- It is important to diversify one's portfolio. If a sector is not performing well and is giving low returns, another well-performing sector can cover for it. Usually, NFOs are sector-specific or category-specific, such as mid-cap, small-cap, etc. That is why understanding the objectives of the NFO before investing in it is essential, as this is often overlooked.

'Learn every day, but especially from the experiences of others. It's cheaper!'—John Bogle

- Mutual fund companies launch various types of NFOs to increase their AUM (assets under management) and achieve their performance objectives. But not all plans are beneficial for you. That is why it is important to learn about the past performance of the fund house that is offering the NFO while making one's own investment decision or on the advice of a financial adviser.

Checks to Be Made While Investing in Mutual Funds

Every mutual fund advertisement carries a disclaimer: 'Mutual funds are subject to market risks. Please read all scheme-related documents carefully before investing.'

What are these scheme-related documents? It is important to know that. The disclosure information published by mutual funds consists of three parts:

1. Scheme information document (SID)

2. Statement of additional information (SAI)

3. Key information memorandum (KIM)

1. Scheme information document (SID)

- All the details about the scheme, based on the guidelines set by the Association of Mutual Funds in India, are mentioned in this document.

- The document can run into multiple pages as every minute detail is mentioned in it. The following points in it hold high importance:

  o Objectives of the scheme, investment goals and ratio of investments.

  o History of the fund house and various investment alternatives offered by the fund house.

  o Details about the fund management team, leaders, their educational qualifications and relevant experience.

'Bills travel through the mail at twice the speed of checks.'
—Steven Wright

o   Management expenses, fees for early withdrawal, and ways to redeem investments.

o   Crisis management and planning thereof.

o   Information about tax eligibility and deductions.

2.   Statement of additional information (SAI)

● Any changes in the fund's objectives are recorded in this document.

● The structure of the fund and the legal formalities are also mentioned. In short, the information that is briefly mentioned in the SID is talked about in detail here.

3.   Key information memorandum (KIM)

● This contains the summary of the SID and the SAI.

● Asset management companies have to oblige investors if they ask for such information, and without charging them for it.

The following information needs to be considered before making any type of investment, whether done through someone or by oneself online:

● **Objective of investment:** Confirm whether the mutual fund scheme is aligned with your financial objectives or not.

● **Fund manager:** Who is going to manage this fund? What is his educational and professional background?

● **History:** Other schemes managed by the fund house and the returns thereof.

● **Risk:** What are the risks involved in this investment and what are the solutions for it?

● **Various expenses:** What are the entry load, exit load, fund management charge, taxation, etc.?

● **Investment limit:** What is the minimum and maximum limit for both investment and withdrawal?

We will look at the concept of a systematic investment plan (SIP) in the next chapter.

> 'God, grant me the serenity to accept the things I cannot change, the courage to change the things I can and the wisdom to know the difference.'—Serenity Prayer

Systematic Investment Plan (SIP)

- SIP is a way of investing in mutual funds. Instead of investing a large sum in mutual funds in one go, it is better to invest small amounts in it regularly over a period of time and reduce the risk.

- Investment done through SIP follows a disciplined path. Investors can choose between monthly, quarterly or half-yearly investments and take advantage of the ups and downs of the market.

- Investors have the option to buy mutual fund units from a variety of mutual fund schemes by way of the SIP.

- It is hugely popular among investors. In India, about 6.42 crore people regularly invest through SIPs.

- You can definitely achieve your financial goals if you too invest regularly in SIPs.

Prominent Benefits of the SIP

1. Expert help

The fund manager/company is responsible for investing the money in the right companies.

2. A disciplined way of investing

A pre-determined sum is deducted every month once we start investing through SIPs. That is why the SIP helps one develop financial discipline and the habit of regularly investing.

3. The big power of starting small

- You don't need a large sum of money to begin investing in SIPs. You can begin with as little as Rs 500 to Rs 1000 every month.

- Through SIPs, those who have just started to earn can begin their investment journey.

- Many a time, it is difficult to save a large sum in order to invest. It can also feel risky to invest a large part of one's savings all at once. But even a small amount invested in SIPs can give good returns.

> 'In the short run, the market is a voting machine. But in the long run, it is a weighing machine.'—Benjamin Graham

- Also, SIPs work in favour of those who do not want to take the risk of investing in the share market directly and yet want to benefit from the highs and lows of the share market.

4. Finalizing financial objectives

- It is important to invest keeping in mind your financial objectives and bringing your dreams to reality.

- Example: If, currently, you are between twenty and thirty years of age and want to save significant wealth by the time you retire, you can take the SIP route. By investing Rs 5000 per month and achieving a minimum return of 12 per cent, your investment over thirty years will yield Rs 1.76 crore. With a total investment of Rs 18 lakhs, you can expect remarkable returns of Rs 1.54 crore.

5. The magic of compounding

- Investing regularly for a long period of time can help one earn at a compounded rate of return.

- The same magic of compounding works when you invest regularly through SIPs.

6. Tenure and flexibility

- You can stop investing in mutual funds if you feel the need to do so.

- Your fund value is calculated as the product of NAV multiplied by the number of units you hold. You can withdraw the amount left after the deduction of taxes and charges, if any.

7. Transparency

- Investment in SIPs or mutual funds is absolutely transparent.

- You can check the value of your investments at any point and can also know which sector the fund manager is investing in.

The SIP, thus, has multiple benefits. That is why, if you are thinking of investments, you can become a smart investor with the SIP.

> *'Hastily taken decisions always result in heavy losses.*
> *Take your own time before putting money in any stock.'*
> —Rakesh Jhunjhunwala

Mistakes Made While Investing in SIP

The SIP is a popular choice for many when it comes to investment. We have learnt about its benefits, but there are a few mistakes that need to be avoided in order to achieve our financial objectives through the SIP.

1. Don't start SIP with a large amount

- Many people invest a large amount in a mutual fund at one go without understanding its implications. Imagine if you want to jump into the water, you would first check how deep it is. This works in a similar way.

- Don't begin with a large sum. You can start small with monthly investments as you may find it difficult sometimes to pay large amounts through SIP every month.

- Investing in a mutual fund without checking its current market condition can lead to financial loss.

- This is true, especially for beginners. They should consult a financial adviser before investing.

2. Not selecting the right mutual fund

- Since there are numerous options to choose from, make sure you select the right fund if you are planning to invest through SIPs.

- Everyone expects high returns so that they can fulfil their financial needs.

- While selecting a mutual fund, find out about the mutual fund company's history and market standing, as selecting the wrong fund can lead to financial loss.

3. Stopping the SIP mid-way

- It is important to keep your money invested for a long time to earn good returns.

- Stopping the SIP when the market is down can lead to financial loss.

- Investors need to have patience as market volatility can send them through an emotional roller coaster.

- Even if your portfolio is seen to be in the red (negative performance), it is important not to give up. Remember, in the same way that the market went down, it is bound to spring back too. Don't lose heart because of these ups and downs. Regular and consistent investment can create wonders.

Can Cryptocurrencies Compete with Shares?

- The popularity of various cryptocurrencies, such as Bitcoin and Dogecoin, has been growing rapidly in India since the last few years. Cryptos are an emerging asset class and have not yet gained common acceptance like equities, commodities and mutual funds have.

- Bitcoins have been in existence for over a decade now. The CEO of Tesla and one of the world's richest businessmen, Elon Musk, fell in love with bitcoins and he invested in them. This led to the whole world noticing them.

- Bitcoin's value has experienced significant fluctuations over the past three years. On 13 March 2021, the price of one bitcoin stood at Rs 3.82 lakh. It then soared to a high of Rs 47.87 lakh per unit on 12 November 2021, only to drop sharply to Rs 13.43 lakh on 25 November 2022. As of 30 June 2023, the price has settled at Rs 25.11 lakh per bitcoin.

- These new, unregulated currencies were gaining popularity in India and the government predicted a financial crisis about them.

What is Cryptocurrency?

- Cryptocurrency is virtual money backed by cryptography. It is designed to be used as a medium of exchange. Cryptocurrencies are built on blockchain technology, which guarantees transparency and helps to track every transaction. Blockchain technology is revolutionizing the way the world transacts. Crypto currencies such as Bitcoin and Ethereum are just a few of the products of this technology.

- Cryptocurrencies came into force in order to be free from government interference as well as any kind of manipulation. Cryptos have free portability across geographical borders, divisibility and transparency because of its digital structure.

- Cryptocurrencies can be bought via crypto exchanges. Most of the e-commerce websites in India do not accept payment through cryptos and they are barely used for retail transactions.

'You must never delude yourself into thinking that you're investing when you're speculating.'—Benjamin Graham

Investment in Crypto

● Investment experts term cryptocurrencies as an extremely risky asset class. Wild price swings are common in them.

● Investors in cryptocurrencies must have proper knowledge and understanding of the risks involved before investing in them.

● The lack of regulatory protection discourages many keen investors from investing in cryptocurrencies. There are some other risks that cryptocurrencies face, such as the possibility of hacking, permanent loss in case of a forgotten password, malware attacks and scams.

● The value of any currency is decided by the demand and supply situation of goods and services. That is why there is a globally accepted formula for how much money should be in circulation and central banks all over the world follow it diligently. Since nothing of this sort backs cryptocurrency as of now, it is a risky proposition to invest in them.

● Even if bitcoin or other cryptocurrencies can be bought and sold in small amounts, it is best for small investors to stay away from them.

● There are hundreds of cryptocurrencies listed in the crypto exchanges. Their future would depend on the way they are managed and are able to build trust. As the objective of using these instruments is more personal than social, this chain can break any time and can leave investors high and dry (many such instances are already in the news).

● **Crypto scams:** You might be reading crypto scam news articles coming from all parts of India regularly. Innocent, ignorant, ill-informed common people are regularly duped by conmen on the pretext of investing in cryptos.

● Modus operandi of crypto Ponzi scheme:

  o Fraudsters promise a staggering 100 to 200 per cent returns on the investments. Gullible people who aspire to get rich quickly fall prey to such schemes. Crypto is something new that they cannot understand. Fraudsters take these investors to sleek offices and hold grand events at five-star hotels where they explain the complex process of blockchain technology, deliver

'People who live far below their means enjoy a freedom that people busy upgrading their lifestyles can't fathom.'—Naval Ravikant

motivational speeches and explain how they are earning huge returns. A few investors also get returns initially, cementing their faith in the scheme.

o Money received from new participants is used for marketing and paying initial scheme members. One fine day, this circus stops and fraudsters run away with the money.

Is cryptocurrency legal in India?

● This question does not have a plain 'yes' or 'no' answer, as the government and the central bank, i.e., the Reserve Bank of India (RBI) still has not expressly endorsed it. In 2018, the RBI came out strongly and somewhat banned them in India. In 2020, the Supreme Court of India reversed the RBI ban.

● Then, Indian banks tried to limit transactions with crypto exchanges. But later, the RBI mentioned that banks cannot quote its 2018 ban to customers as it was overruled by the Supreme Court. It paved the way for crypto trading to continue in India.

● The government has not issued any specific clarification for cryptocurrencies to be considered legal in India.

Taxation: The Government of India announced the income tax on gains arising from virtual digital assets at a flat rate of 30 per cent without any exemptions or deductions in the Union Budget of 2022. If traders face any loss from the virtual digital asset trading or investment, it cannot be set off against other income.

● Virtual Digital Assets (VDAs) comprise cryptocurrencies, non-fungible tokens (NFTs) and similar tokens, and other assets that the government may specify.

● For example, if a person has gains of Rs 20,000 arising out of transfer of Bitcoin and a loss of Rs 10,000 out of transfer of Ethereum, then she has to pay taxes on the gains of Rs 20,000 on Bitcoin. The loss of Ethereum will not be used to set off the gains of Bitcoin and it will not be carried forward to the next year for set-off against income.

● The new taxes imposed on VDAs seem to be aimed at discouraging investment in such assets.

What will you do?

● As cryptocurrency is not regulated by any central government authority in India, it is better to not invest in them. Investors should wait and watch till more clarity on them emerges.

Money Works

Money Works

लोभमूलानि पापानि संकटानि तथैव च |
लोभात्प्रवर्तते वैरं अतिलोभात्विनश्यति ||

—सुभाषित

*(Greed is the root cause of all sins. It creates jealousy and
being overly greedy leads to destruction.)*

To protect ourselves from being cheated is entirely our own responsibility

How we respond when someone tries to cheat us is very important. Otherwise, we will be blaming ourselves later on. Scamsters have updated themselves with the various advancements of the modern age. They will succeed in cheating you if you fail to conduct thorough research and stay vigilant regarding your financial choices.

If you deposit your money in a cooperative bank which then goes bankrupt, the government can help you financially—to an extent. But don't rely entirely on government policies to come to your aid if you are a victim of financial fraud. Here, we will discuss what you should and should not do as an individual to protect yourself from fraud.

How do you safeguard yourself from financial fraud? The answer to this is easy in theory but difficult to implement in practice. We will first look at the means used by scamsters to defraud others:

1. Ponzi schemes

2. Pyramid schemes

3. Frauds promising returns from the share market

4. Fraudulent calls

5. Frauds on social media

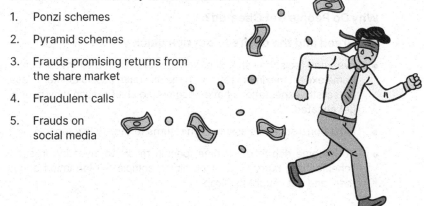

'Don't think money does everything or you are going to
end up doing everything for money.'—Voltaire

353

Ponzi Schemes

The Crown Jewel of Deceit—Charles Ponzi

The reason why fraudulent financial schemes are called Ponzi schemes is as interesting as any tale from the *Panchatantra* or the *Arabian Nights*. Some brands gain so much popularity that the brand itself becomes the generic identity of the item in question. Example: Brand names such as Bisleri and Xerox not only represent the products of the companies by the same name but are also used generically to refer to bottled water and photocopying, respectively. This is how the term 'Ponzi', coined after the conman Charles Ponzi, has come to be used for any fraudulent scheme.

How Charles Ponzi Swindled People

- Charles Ponzi, an Italian by birth, launched a fraudulent financial scheme in the US in 1920 assuring unbelievably huge returns.

- Under the scheme, investors were guaranteed returns of 50 per cent in forty-five days and 100 per cent in ninety days.

- Over a period of time, investors started losing millions of dollars, leading to colossal losses for many. All such schemes have since that time been referred to as Ponzi schemes.

- Even 100 years after this episode, the greed to earn quick money and the urge to become rich overnight are still leading people to invest in such fraudulent schemes. Unfortunately, we are no exception to this in India.

Why Do People Get Cheated?

1. Greed and the desire to get rich quickly

- Everyone feels they should earn huge returns on their investments. Some expect maximum returns in the minimum possible time. These unrealistic expectations have become the chief reason why people get cheated.

- Most Ponzi schemes assure high returns for a very low tenure.

- To become rich in quick time, people resort to investing in such schemes in a hurry without obtaining complete information about them and get caught in a trap.

> 'The quickest way to double your money is to fold it in half and put it in your back pocket.'—Will Rogers

2. Your blind faith

- Your faith, innocence, goodness, ignorance or shrewdness can play an important role in determining whether you are the type that will get cheated.

- You will save yourself from deceit if you have the confidence to ask basic questions about a scheme, check the scheme manager's past records and think about the offer from all angles before investing.

3. Social pressure

- Many people have the 'fear of missing out' when their friends, relatives and big names in society invest in a certain scheme and they don't.

- Without any preliminary information, people invest in a scheme that has become suddenly popular out of fear of losing an opportunity to earn big money and end up losing their money.

- Some jobs are not meant to be 'outsourced'. Thinking is one such job that you have to do for yourself. Whatever others decide to invest in, you must not invest in it without first studying it.

4. Attractive advertisements + aggressive salespersons

- The salespersons appointed to sell Ponzi schemes are extremely cunning and sharp at their job. They indulge in sweet talk, and sometimes you may know them personally too.

- Many salespersons are unaware of both the product they are selling and the wrong intentions behind their sale. This means a fool is engaged in fooling others.

- In many instances, a known face may promote Ponzi schemes to you.

5. Short-term memory

- These days there is a lot of hype and discussion about current events. But we tend to completely ignore significant events of the past.

> 'Facts are threatening to those invested in fraud.'
> —DaShanne Stokes

- Instead of learning from others' mistakes people think it is better to learn from their own! This attitude gets them into trouble.

- We get to read about financial frauds every other day in the newspapers or see reports on them on television and social media. We are not cautious even after knowing how fraudsters operate.

Let us look at one such fraud.

The Self-Certified Stock Guru Scam[1]

The number of investors in the share market has grown to a record high as people believe it can give good returns. However, studying the market and taking financial experts' advice is important to maximize returns. The markets that had dipped during Covid-19 rose to a new record high, thereby attracting many young investors. While the past generations looked at the share market as a gamble, today's generation feels it is one of the best options to build wealth. Although this is a welcome move, the opportunity comes with a signboard that says 'Caution: Wet Floor'. This is because swindlers who claim to be stock gurus could be around you. In 2010, the number of such self-proclaimed experts was high in Maharashtra and this had led to many such financial frauds.

Who Were These Stock Gurus?

A couple was the architect of the Stock Guru scam. They resided in Ratnagiri, in the coastal belt of Maharashtra, under fake identities. They had mingled well with the local middle-class community. Even before their Stock Guru scam, they had started a film institute that assured 100 per cent placement. But they fled with all the money they had collected as fees. They had run similar Ponzi businesses in different cities and duped their customers.

The Stock Guru Scheme

- The same couple launched the Stock Guru scheme in the year 2010.

- Under this scheme, investors were assured a monthly return of 20 per cent on their investments. At this, many investors were blinded by greed and fell for the scam.

- The scheme targeted the poor and financially illiterate at first. But as the scheme gained popularity, even literate and successful businessmen were attracted to it.

'Fraud is the daughter of greed.'—Jonathan Gash

- The way the couple duped their investors so easily was rather different from the usual method employed by fraudsters. Their company did indeed give 20 per cent returns for the first six months and even repaid the capital in the seventh month.

- Wasn't it great that the per-month return was 20 per cent? Investors were confident that the scheme was great and started investing even more in it than they did before.

- What happened next? The cycle continued until about 2 lakh investors had invested approximately Rs 1100 crore in the scheme.

How Stock Guru Tricked People

- Their manner of operating might have appeared different, but actually, the swindlers used a well-known trick. The company used the new investors' money to pay the old investors returns assured to them. In short, the money in the left pocket was shifted to the right pocket.

- The investors spread the word about the company since they were getting good returns, and this led to more investors and more investments in the company.

- As the number of investors started increasing, the company played its next card—it announced that its offer was for a limited period only.

- Investors now started putting all their savings into the company to earn high returns.

- No company will be able to pay 20 per cent monthly returns on crores of rupees. The company simply shut shop overnight and the founders were nowhere to be seen.

What Happened to the Stock Guru Couple?

- A few investors filed a police complaint while others took to complaining on social media when they came to know of the scam.

- They created a Facebook group and the mass media took note of it. The police department broke into action mode as the scam made 'Breaking News' headlines on all news channels.

'Who is going to believe a con artist? Everyone, if she is good.'
—Andy Griffith

- Finally, the couple was arrested in November 2012, and the police recovered bank drafts worth Rs 20 crore, land, expensive watches, and vehicles from them.

A Ponzi scheme entails the collection of money from new investors to pay returns or capital to the old investors

- Those who run the Ponzi scheme assure customers of high returns on their investment.

- Marginal-income earners and middle-class people are their main victims. Ignorant but innocent people from all economic classes are their primary targets.

- They make tall claims such as, 'Your money will be invested in schemes that carry the least risk', or 'Not many people understand the way we operate.'

- In reality, the money is not invested anywhere and is just circulated among investors. A prerequisite for this is to keep adding new investors regularly.

- A few alert or smart people realize that no real business is taking place and start a chain of discussion, leading to the government inquiring into the scheme.

- The number of new investors falling for the scheme decreases and the old investors start demanding a return of their investments.

- Once the cycle is interrupted, these scamsters vanish into thin air.

- Those who have lost their money repent and seek legal help.

'Youth is easily deceived because it is quick to hope.'—Aristotle

Highlights of Ponzi Schemes

1. Assured high returns

- Bank savings deposits offer about 4 per cent returns and term deposits 6–7 per cent per annum. The best-performing mutual funds in the share market offer 12–15 per cent annual returns.

- Ponzi schemes offer upwards of 10 per cent returns per month, i.e., 120 per cent per annum. When you hear something like this, the following doubts must occur to you:

- Which business model offers eight times more returns than other popular alternatives? How will they succeed when large organizations recording consistent performance over the years could not achieve this? If what they are saying is true, why isn't everyone investing in the scheme and leaving aside their daily work?

2. Assured returns without any risks involved

- Except for government-led schemes, every investment scheme has a degree of risk associated with it.

- Words like '100 per cent safe and guaranteed returns' and 'one-of-its-kind investment opportunity' should raise an immediate red flag in your mind.

3. Complex, difficult-to-understand schemes

- You should avoid investing in a scheme that you are not able to understand, does not feel trustworthy and fails to produce sufficient information.

4. Fear of missing out on a golden opportunity

- Try to stay away from schemes that promote themselves as a 'once-in-a-lifetime opportunity', 'limited period offer', etc.

- These words make you invest in a hurry without asking a lot of questions.

- In your greed for 20–30 per cent returns, you may end up losing 100 per cent of your capital.

- More than for you, this is a golden opportunity for the scamsters.

- When investing in schemes that guarantee high returns, it is important to make sure that at least the principal amount is safe.

5. Unregistered schemes

- Those who run Ponzi schemes do not care for any government licences. Registered companies have to present financial statements and many other documents and details of their schemes to the government.

- If the scheme is unregistered, the promoters are answerable to no one. That is how they are able to operate Ponzi schemes.

- RBI and SEBI are government regulatory bodies and their websites contain a lot of information. Investors can easily access information about a company if it is registered with the Registrar of Companies (ROC), up to what year the financial statements have been submitted, who the promoters of the company are, and so on (website: https://www.mca.gov.in).

- You can read reviews on the web about a particular scheme, its managers and the way it is managed.

- You should be flooded with doubts before you invest your hard-earned money in anything. Even the gods cannot come to the rescue of the people who have blind faith in others despite having access to tons of information on the web.

> 'It's discouraging to think how many people are shocked by honesty and how few by deceit.'—Noël Coward

Precautions to Take to Safeguard Yourself from Ponzi Schemes

1. Hard work and patience are the best solutions to protect yourself from financial fraud.

2. There is nothing wrong with aspiring to live a rich lifestyle, but it is wrong if you are careless about it. Remember, there is no shortcut that allows you to earn a lot in a short period of time. That is why you should practise caution.

3. The least you should do is wonder how and why someone would offer you hefty returns. Ask yourself this simple question: Why would anyone bear a loss to help me earn profits? No one does that! We have all heard the story of the monkey that stepped on her baby to save herself from the floods.

4. Avoid investing in schemes that ask for a large sum to be committed at once and offer huge returns. An example of an advertisement for one could read: 'Invest with us. We will operate your demat account on your behalf and offer 10 per cent monthly returns.'

5. Think of it this way. If you invest Rs 10,000 in a year and you are fortunate to earn a maximum rate of return of 18 per cent, you will receive Rs 18,000 as returns on your investment. But when someone offers you double the money in a year, hold on. Beware of such offers. And if a scheme offers you three or four times these returns it could very well be a Ponzi scheme.

6. It is important to know the basic facts about what you are investing in and read all the financial documents, legalities, rules and regulations associated with it before investing.

   - Take expert advice if you feel the need to do so and make informed decisions before making any financial commitment.

   - No schemes offer easy returns without any risk involved.

   - You should also know the ways by which to exit from financial schemes and the tenure of capital repayment if it offers high returns.

7. Don't fall for any schemes that promise to make you rich overnight. Learn the ABC of financial literacy.

> 'The secret of your future is hidden in your daily routine.'
> —Mike Murdock

The Banning of Unregulated Deposit Scheme Bill 2019 bans all Ponzi schemes in India; people found guilty of operating them are liable to financial penalties and rigorous imprisonment.

2. Pyramid schemes

● Getting rich by way of investing can be a boring and time-consuming process for some people. Everyone wants to become rich as soon as possible.

● Many investment schemes offering unrealistic or fake assurances are rolled out to exploit this sentiment among the people.

● People often misunderstand that multi-level marketing (MLM) schemes and pyramid schemes are one and the same thing. MLM seems good on paper. MLM schemes thrive on a basic plank of how much marketing money can be saved if products and services are advertised just by word of mouth instead of going the traditional advertising way or by using celebrity endorsements. Whereas pyramid schemes are fraud schemes which use MLM as just a marketing tool to reach the maximum number of gullible people.

● We will understand the difference between both of them.

Particulars	Multi-Level Marketing (MLM)	Pyramid Scheme
Nature	A type of marketing.	A financial scheme designed to cheat people.
Product and services	Salespersons are paid commission on sales of products and services.	Either the products and the services don't exist or are sold at exorbitant prices. Commission is paid to agents on signing up new members.
Operator company's income	The money earned by selling products and services, and the enrolment fees earned from new members.	Since the money earned from new members is used to pay the old members, there is no real income.

'Never stand begging for that which you have the power to earn.'
—Miguel de Cervantes

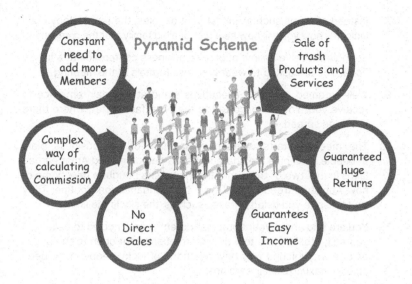

How a Pyramid Scheme Operates

1. Your friend, colleague, relative or acquaintance come to you with an out-of-this-world business opportunity.

2. The business looks easy. All you have to do is sell a few products in your free time. Along the way, you get a few more people to do the same.

3. The calculations showing how you will earn huge profits on a regular basis are always kept ready. You are also entitled to a commission on the sales done by the people in your chain.

4. It is constantly hammered into you that earning a side income in this way is always easy.

5. You need to invest something to earn such high returns. The promoters may charge 'just' Rs 40,000 to Rs 50,000 as an enrolment fee.

6. Sometimes you are given products worth that amount to sell immediately upon your joining the scheme.

'If you're having financial trouble, it is because you have the wrong information.'—Grant Cardone

7. Instead of terms such as investment or sales, the terminology used indicates how you will now be a part of a big family that the company is.

8. Soon you receive an invitation to a business conference at a luxury hotel. You are asked to wear business formals to the meeting.

9. Well-groomed, polished executives stand at the main entrance to receive you. You are escorted to the breakfast buffet, where there is a huge spread.

10. The meeting starts with an explanation of the business plan. Relatable examples are shared—how a person named Amar earned lakhs in just two or three months; how Asha bought a new home or how Abhishek freed himself from his mundane work routine. They try to inspire you using phrases such as 'the sky is the limit'.

11. You are told about your untapped potential or exhorted to believe in yourself, etc. You are told this information is not open to the public as of now, which is why only a handful of lucky people have been able to maximize their earnings.

12. You start believing in your luck since such an opportunity has come to you. You are then taken to the main conference room.

13. Someone good at making presentations shows how sales and commission work at the company. While this is happening, a person of superstar stature enters the room.

14. We are informed that this person is the highest earner in the company for that year. He carries himself with full confidence and starts narrating his story—he had used a bicycle two years back and now he moves around in a Mercedes.

15. 'There is a businessman within you. Unleash your real potential and see where this business takes you. I want to see each one of you driving a Mercedes in the next two years . . . ' This is the typical kind of motivational speech heard at these conferences.

16. Everyone applauds when the speaker finishes his talk. By the end of it, people are desperate to get out of their seats and rush towards the registration counter to pay Rs 40,000–50,000 and become a member.

17. Eventually, you opt to become a member of the company. You start finding it difficult to meet the targets or to get new members to

'I'm only rich because I know when I'm wrong . . . I basically have survived by recognizing my mistakes.'—George Soros

sign up. In the end, you believe you are not made for this business and give up the dream of being a rich person. The money paid goes down the drain.

18. Every new member is told to get just three people to sign up for membership and help them get three each. But it doesn't work that way. While most of them lose the money they paid for their membership, they also mess up their relations with those they introduce to the scheme.

19. Only the people sitting at the top of the pyramid get to make financial gains through this. That is why it is better to stay away from such schemes.

20. When someone you know wants to talk about a one-of-its-kind business opportunity, beware. By now you will have understood what should be done with a business model that is based on getting new members to sign up. Remember, it is just a matter of time before these pyramids collapse, leading to financial loss to its members.

We will look at how pyramid schemes use the multi-level marketing model to cheat people.

Scam 1: Speak Asia Scam[2]

- Many people lost their hard-earned money by investing it in a multi-level marketing scam run by a company named Speak Asia in 2013. Investors were assured a return of Rs 52,000 from investing just Rs 11,000. The registration charge was Rs 1000, and the balance Rs 10,000 was towards annual fees, magazines and training provided by the company.

- Once a member, one had to get surveys filled out by others. Each form was potentially worth thousands of rupees, depending on how many surveys they could get done. Also, members had to bring in new members to do the same job. The more members you added, the higher your income would be.

- The data to be filled in the form was so simple that it could be copied from sites like Wikipedia.

- Investors should have sensed that something was wrong here. But once you are possessed by the idea of getting rich quickly, your capacity for rational thinking goes for a toss.

> *'Never interrupt your enemy when he is making a mistake.'*
> —Napoleon Bonaparte

- Speak Asia had changed their business name on three or four occasions previously. All the addresses provided by the company were fake. They did not pay any investors and duped nearly 2.4 crore Indians of about Rs 2273 crore.

- The promoters of the company were arrested once the scam was uncovered in the year 2013. They had to face court trials after their arrest.

- The court ordered them to return the money they had taken from investors. However, many investors have still not got back their money.

Scam 2: Saradha Chit Fund Scam[3]

The Saradha Chit Fund scam was brought to light in the year 2013 and was covered by the news channels for many months as breaking news. There were some startling revelations made by the Central government, the West Bengal government, the CBI and other investigating agencies.

Expansion of Saradha Group

- The Saradha Group consisted of more than 239 companies that were operational in tours and travels, immovable assets, housing development, resorts, hotels, entertainment and media.

- Before the scam was uncovered in April 2013, the Group had collected more than Rs 4000 crore from depositors.

- It had created a name for itself in the film industry with the help of big celebrities. It had also invested in popular football clubs and media brands and was a leading event sponsor during prominent festivals such as Durga Puja in West Bengal.

- It had spread its wings to the neighbouring states of Orissa, Assam and Tripura and had more than 17 lakh depositors.

Modus Operandi

- Sudipto Sen founded the Saradha Group in the year 2000. His first depositors were from the rural community of West Bengal who were assured high returns. Sen capitalized on the fact that banking facilities were not in full swing in West Bengal, as they were in states such as Maharashtra and Gujarat.

- Initially, the Group started collecting deposits against secured debentures and redeemable preference bonds.

'We learn from failure, not from success!'—Bram Stoker

- As per the Companies Act applicable then, no company could raise capital from more than fifty people without issuing a proper prospectus and balance sheet. Its accounts had to be audited and it also had to have explicit permission to operate from the market regulator SEBI, the apex organization that regulates the capital market. Hence, SEBI started questioning the transactions of the Saradha Group. As the inquiries began, the Group changed the way they operated and set up multiple companies to mislead SEBI.

What Was the Scam?

- Saradha Group was actively engaged in raising capital for all its subsidiary companies. The group floated various investment schemes to raise capital for investments in tourism packages, forward travel, hotel booking, timeshare credit transfer, real estate, infrastructure finance, motorcycle manufacturing, etc.

- Some investments were promoted as chit funds since they are regulated by the state government and not by the Central government.

- The schemes were targeted at marginalized communities staying in the remote Naxalite areas of eastern India.

- The investors would get assured returns at the rate of 50 per cent annually, meaning the deposited money would double in one and a half years.

- The company had appointed agents to collect the money. The agents were paid commissions of 25–40 per cent on the money they collected from members they had connected to the group.

- Celebrities and famous personalities from various industries, including television, sports, films and politics, were seen actively promoting the brand. The Bengali media would constantly carry investment-related advertisements for the Group. The Group also maintained close relations with whichever political party formed the state government.

- The scheme went the same way other scams go. The money collected from new depositors was used to pay the old depositors, the agents and for advertisements. Problems started to surface the day new deposits began to dry out. The Group did not have the money required to pay the promised returns to their depositors.

> 'The first step towards change is awareness. The second step is acceptance.'—Nathaniel Branden

- The downfall of the Saradha Group began in the year 2012. That was the time when its investors started filing complaints as they had not received the promised returns.

What Happened Next

- When the scam was brought to light, Sudipto Sen and his trusted aide Debjani Mukherjee fled after making an eighteen-page statement to the CBI. Thousands of collection agents and investors demanded that Sen should be arrested for cheating.

- The first complaint on behalf of the depositors was filed at the Bidhannagar Police Commissioner's office. Finally, Sen and Mukherjee were both arrested in Kashmir on 18 April 2013. The state government had set up a special task force for this. Many high-profile politicians were later arrested in connection with this case. Even after all this, most of the depositors did not get their money back.

Salient Features of Pyramid Schemes

The Securities and Exchange Commission (SEC) regulates capital markets in the US, just the way SEBI does the capital markets in India. These are the chief features of pyramid schemes, according to SEC:[4]

1.   Constant need to add new members

- All pyramid schemes use new ways of marketing to trap people. Specific information is shared via social media, Internet advertisements, company websites, group presentations and conference calls. That is because the pyramid will grow only when new members are constantly added to the base.

- If a scheme expects you to just add new members without selling any product or service, be cautious about it.

2.   Sale of trash products and services

- The products sold by pyramid schemes are so expensive, unnecessary, or of such low quality that no one has a need for them.

- Example: In 2010, the MLM company named eBiz asked its members to sell computer lesson CDs at Rs 7500. The lessons were created using freely available information, under the pretext of expanding

> 'Smart people learn from their mistakes. But the real sharp ones learn from the mistakes of others.'—Brandon Mull

digital literacy. The members would earn a commission if they got three more people to sell the CDs.[5]

● These companies use attention-grabbing names and sell 'energy' mattresses, stones that bring you peace, weight-loss programmes, cancer cures, ancient secrets, powders made with ancient wisdom, revitalizing pills, beauty products, etc. These products are mostly not certified.

● No one outside the so-called extended family of members is interested in buying these products.

3. Guaranteed huge returns

● Each member must get six people to join the scheme and help them to get six members each. This way, six becomes thirty-six, which in turn becomes 216, and the chain continues. A member who sets off a chain gets commissions on the entire chain. This feels like a dream, but if it actually became a reality, the entire population of India would be covered in just twelve steps and the world population in thirteen steps.

4. Guaranteed easy income

● No one offers anything for free to anyone. No one can earn money without putting in mental or physical effort.

● If someone is offering you a commission to get more people to sign up for a membership, for posting advertisements on random websites and filling survey forms that make no sense, be cautious, as the person could be part of a pyramid scheme.

No Pyramid Scheme Can Sustain Forever

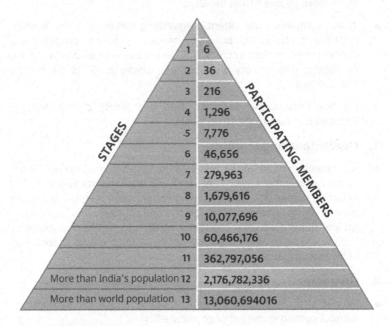

STAGES		PARTICIPATING MEMBERS
	1	6
	2	36
	3	216
	4	1,296
	5	7,776
	6	46,656
	7	279,963
	8	1,679,616
	9	10,077,696
	10	60,466,176
	11	362,797,056
More than India's population	12	2,176,782,336
More than world population	13	13,060,694016

5. No direct sales

● Genuine MLM companies earn income from direct sales of products and services. If the membership fees make up most of a company's earnings, then it could very well be a pyramid scheme.

6. Complex way of calculating commissions

● If the commission earned on the products and services you sell is being calculated in a complex way, you should be cautious about it.

All pyramid schemes are bound to collapse after a point in time. Scamsters are always on the lookout for new ways to cheat others and for new scapegoats. They may even be somewhere around you. So stay cautious and safe. Don't just be literate, be educated! Don't just learn the ABC of a language, learn the ABC of financial literacy too.

> ''Money can't buy friends, but you can get a better class of enemy.'
> —Spike Milligan

Frauds Promising Returns from the Share Market

People have contrasting points of view when it comes to the share market—they think that investors either make a fortune from it or lose everything. Many want to earn a lot of money with the least amount of effort and many want to exploit people who have this mindset. Although a lot of awareness is being created to save people from getting cheated, there comes a moment when greed gets the better of 'gyaan' and people fall into the pit they are led to by scamsters as follows:

1. Fake Experts

- Investors who have their own demat accounts may find that their personal details are sold, and they receive calls from tier II cities such as Indore, Surat, Rajkot and Faridabad making tall offers.

- A telecaller disguised as a stock market expert or an adviser makes you an offer to invest in equity or derivative products. He assures mouth-watering short-term returns from regularly offered 'hot tips'. You have to subscribe to their investment schemes and you have to pay joining fees. You either get tips or you hand them your money for investment.

- They promise that the money will be invested to maximize gains. You are given positive updates on your portfolio. After a few days, you do not receive regular updates. Then one fine day, you cannot reach the caller despite repeated attempts to contact him. Your hard-earned money has vanished!

2. Pump and Dump Stocks

- You receive a text message with content like '100 per cent returns from intraday and multi-bagger stocks' or 'Earn 200 per cent profit in three months.' You are being bombarded with spam text messages containing a link to subscribe to their investment schemes. You fall prey to these unsolicited offers promising unbelievable returns.

- They lure small and new investors to put money in highly manipulated and rigged penny stocks recommended as future multibaggers. The share prices are artificially inflated by operators giving fake buy

'I'm not interested in cars and my goal is not to make people envious. Don't confuse the cost of living with the standard of living.'—Warren Buffett

alerts. Once they reach the targeted levels, fraudsters dump their holdings to leave naive investors disappointed.

- There are some other luring techniques and fraud types such as organizing workshops to teach technical analysis but not hosting it after receiving payment or charging exorbitant fees but not teaching anything of value, sending online investment newsletters with fake information and fake testimonials, posting screenshots of their non-existent stock portfolio and asking for the subscription fee to get investment tips.

- **Common red flags you must pay attention to**

  o   Someone offering guaranteed returns

  o   Investment schemes that sound too good to be true

  o   Pressure to transfer money immediately or you will miss the so-called golden opportunity

  o   'Everyone is buying, do not miss this lifetime opportunity' pitches

- SEBI has taken strict action against fraudsters from time to time. Such investigations will keep happening, but as a responsible citizen, it is important for you to be cautious. Let us recap a few points we have learnt:

1.   Understand the difference between courage and greed. You should realize what risk is involved in every type of investment. You should always have full knowledge about the products you are investing in.

2.   Pay attention to common red flags as mentioned above.

3.   Don't discuss your transactions with anyone and block the numbers of strangers who call you to get information about your finances.

4.   Prior to placing your trust in any individual or company or their recommendations, ask as many questions as possible and thoroughly examine all relevant aspects.

5.   You should not invest in any scheme or fund run by an entity not registered with SEBI.

6.   Get into a legal agreement with your financial adviser and stay true to the terms mentioned in the agreement. Do not opt for hidden transactions.

7.   Never make cash payments to any stockbroker.

8. Keep an eye on your investments, and when in doubt, get them cleared as early as possible by trusted sources.

9. Never let anyone else use your trading account. Don't be under the notion that someone else can make better use of it and help you earn more.

10. Trust Your Instincts: If something appears suspicious or raises doubts, trust your instincts and take a step back. Better to be safe than sorry when it comes to money!

Conclusion

The number of fraudsters in the stock market is on the rise at a rapid pace with the advancement of technology. You have to be alert ! Always remember: 'Vigilance is the key to navigating the stock market's treacherous waters'—Peter Lynch.

Fraud Calls

In this method of cheating, people get phone calls asking for their bank account details. The callers use various tactics to get this information; sometimes they sound like professionals, and sometimes they try to frighten or threaten people too.

- 'Congratulations Sir, you have won a reward of Rs 1 crore. Please share your UPI ID and UPI PIN for us to send it to your account.'

- 'Congratulations Madam, we have increased the credit limit on your credit card. Please send an SMS to the given number.'

- 'Sir, you have won Rs 2 lakh. Please accept the request we have sent to your UPI ID and pay the processing charges.'

- 'Sir, we have noticed a few suspicious transactions in your account. We have sent you an OTP, please share it with us to secure your account.'

- 'Madam, your credit card has been used without your knowledge. Please share your CVV number so that we can secure the card.'

With advancements in technology, the scamsters who make these calls have been able to cheat many people. People must stay cautious. These calls can frighten ordinary, unsuspecting people. Senior citizens are often the prime targets. Educate them about such calls so they may stay safe.

Follow the instructions published by banks to secure your online transactions. Never share your debit or credit card details, CVV numbers, OTPs, net banking or mobile banking passwords. These days, most people prefer to make digital transactions. Take the necessary precautions while using Google Pay, PhonePe, PayTM and other UPI (Unified Payments Interface) apps.

'You will never reach your destination if you stop and throw stones at every dog that barks.'—Winston Churchill

Frauds on Social Media

- Generally speaking, problems of any kind have a psychological effect on people too.

- People who are active on social media, those who are always looking for social acceptance, those who live in the virtual world or those who find themselves alone often become magnets to problems.

- They are easy targets for fraudsters, not just on social media but in real life too.

- Social media has become a hub for cyber criminals.

How to Stay Safe

- Don't share your problems with everyone. Ill-intentioned people use this as an opportunity to become close to you and cheat you in some way.

- Don't share your personal details, such as phone number, address, bank details or passwords with anyone.

- Get into real and meaningful conversations with your family members.

- Remember, only your close ones will step forward to help you in your hard times. Let the seniors and youngsters in your family know that you will always be there for them, as both age groups can become easy targets for fraudsters.

> क्षणशः कणशश्चैव विद्यामर्थं च साधयेत् ।
> क्षणत्यागे कुतो विद्या कणत्यागे कुतो धनम् ॥
>
> *'Knowledge should be gained through minute by minute efforts.*
> *Money should be earned utilizing each and every resource.*
> *If you waste time, how can you get knowledge? If you*
> *waste resources, how can you accumulate wealth?'*

Financial Resolutions

You would have your own financial resolutions. Add to your list another—'financial planning'. How is financial planning done? Let us look at a few easy yet important points which can ease your process of financial planning.

Making your Personal Financial Budget

1. Calculate your net worth. It is the total value of the assets you own minus your loans and payables.

2. Your net worth is a measure of your financial health, indicating how much money would be left if you had to sell your assets at market price to pay your liabilities.

3. Every financial decision should be taken keeping in mind the goal of increasing your net worth, either by adding to your assets or by decreasing your liabilities.

4. Preparation of a monthly budget would be an important step in financial management. Plan your budget. Avoid unnecessary expenses. Every penny saved is a penny earned.

5. Prepare a monthly budget based on your income and expenses. Consider both your and your partner's income.

6. Maintain a diary and develop the habit of recording your daily expenses and earnings in it. Ask your family to follow the same discipline.

7. Audit your expenses and find out where you are spending most.

8. Create a financial calendar and mark all the important dates for investment, loan repayment and other known expenses.

9. Stay updated by reading financial news, articles, information on various websites, blogs, etc.

10. Plan your financial objectives based on your earnings, expenses, assets and liabilities. This will help you to track your financial progress.

> 'The man who does not read good books has no advantage over the man who can't read them.'—Mark Twain

Financial Planning for Purchases and Expenses

1. Develop the habit of saying 'No'. We often spend a lot of money just because we cannot say no to our friends, relatives, etc. A single 'no' can help in saving a lot of money.

2. Challenge yourself to save as much money as possible in a month.

3. Curtail your desire to splurge on shopping. This is the biggest step in controlling your expenses.

4. Control yourself from buying expensive and branded items. Remember that needs are more important than status. That is why you must buy only what is needed.

5. Make a list before you set out to shop and stick to it.

6. Don't buy just because you saw an offer on a product you do not need.

7. Unsubscribe from websites that send offers to you by email. We buy products that are on sale without giving any thought to it.

8. Control your excessive spending at beauty parlours and on cosmetics.

9. Pre-decide the time you will spend watching television and films or web series on OTT apps. This will save you both time and money.

10. Learn the art of reusing your belongings. Preserving gift wrapping, packing boxes, old stationery, etc. can help you save a lot of unnecessary expenses. Items no longer in use can be sold on resale websites or in a resale market. You can make gifts at home using your own creativity.

11. Always buy 'energy efficient' products. This helps in saving on electricity consumption and thus, money.

12. Control your usage of electricity. Use LED lighting wherever possible.

13. Instead of chilling out at a mall, go to a nearby garden. The mall could act as a magnet leading you to unnecessary purchases.

Utility Bills

1. Pay all your bills on time to avoid penalties and late fees.

> 'The best weight you'll ever lose is the weight of other people's opinions of you.'—Lesley Bradshaw

2. Try to pay your bills online to avail yourself of discounts and cashback offers.

3. Install a solar roof if possible. That will help reduce your expenses towards gas and electricity.

4. Stop paying subscription fees for magazines you do not read.

5. Stop paying membership fees for club and gym memberships you no longer use.

6. If you undertake vacation trips on a regular basis, start planning your next trip at the earliest and avail yourself of early-bird discounts.

Commute

1. Look for fuel-efficient options when buying a vehicle. This will help you save both fuel and money.

2. The life of the vehicle can be stretched when it is serviced regularly and maintained properly.

Health and Financial Planning

1. Health is wealth! Since expenses on health can mess up your finances, take care of your health.

2. Stay away from addictions. That is where the most money is spent and your health is also at risk.

3. Develop habits such as regular exercise, yoga and walking. The money spent on gyms, yoga workshops or in pursuing sports is an investment for your health.

4. Carry a water bottle from your home instead of buying bottled water every time you go out. A lot of money is spent on water, which can be easily saved.

5. Cleanliness is very important. Many diseases can be kept at bay and medical expenses avoided if one has developed habits of hygiene. Having said that, avoid spending a lot on unnecessary hygiene products too.

> '*The chief difference between a fool and a wise man is that the wise man learns from his mistakes, while the fool never does.*'—Phil Fisher

Habit of Saving

1. Start saving from this very moment. This resolution is to be followed not tomorrow but right now!

2. Set aside a part of your monthly income as an emergency fund to handle financial contingencies.

3. Open a different account in which to save your emergency funds. This money will come in handy since you won't have to ask anyone for money when financial emergencies arise.

4. Remember, saving is a respectable way to lead your life. Once you have an emergency fund, understand various investment options and start investing a certain sum every month.

Check Your Bank Accounts Regularly

1. You can check whether your financial planning is on track or not by looking at your bank accounts.

2. You will also come to know about the various bank charges from your account statement.

3. You can look at the rates of recurring deposits and fixed deposits and plan your finances accordingly.

4. Compare the interest paid by various banks online. If the rate at your bank is lower than at other banks, you can move your deposits to another bank for higher returns.

Alternative Ways of Investment

1. Everyone invests in traditional instruments such as the recurring deposit, fixed deposit, gold, real estate, etc. Always choose an alternative that offers a good rate of return.

2. Learn about how you can invest in the share market.

3. Find out whether your investments are exempted from taxation and if yes, up to what amount.

> 'Everyone wants to ride with you in the limo, but what you want is someone who will take the bus with you when the limo breaks down.'—Oprah Winfrey

Loan/Credit Card

1. Plan in such a way that you can repay your loan in the shortest possible tenure in order to save on interest.

2. Prepare a repayment timetable so that the instalments are paid on time. This also helps in planning for faster repayment of the loan.

3. Check the interest rates levied on the credit card you use. It can vary from 15 per cent to 42 per cent per annum.

4. Start saving for the down payment if you plan to buy a new home.

5. Check the interest rates at two or three banks when applying for a home loan.

6. If you have already taken a home loan, start planning for pre-payment of it.

7. Don't bring losses upon yourself by falling for misleading offers and schemes.

8. Use websites that help you compare insurance and loans and make informed decisions. Read blogs around it. This would help you in arriving at the right decision.

9. Avoid use of the credit card as much as possible. Your credit card spends should be a small fraction of your total expenses.

10. Before becoming a guarantor to someone taking a loan, make sure you know the person well. Learn to say no.

Insurance

1. Insurance is a provision to help you face financial uncertainties. Learn about various types of insurance policies.

2. Banks and insurance companies sell multiple types of insurance policies these days. They include life insurance, vehicle insurance, accident insurance and health insurance.

3. Buy term insurance. This is the cheapest and one of the most important policies to buy.

Financial Provisions for Children, and Financial Literacy

1. Consider future costs you have to incur for your children, such as higher education and marriage expenses while planning your finances.

2. If you start planning for your children's rising cost of education from the beginning, you will not feel the burden later on.

3. Teach your kids the importance of savings at an early age.

4. Many banks offer a 'zero balance account' or a higher-interest account for children. Make good use of that.

5. If we plan for the children's education expenses when they are very young, we will not feel the burden of having to take an education loan when they grow up.

6. Open a separate savings account for them. You may invest in Sukanya Samruddhi Yojana meant for the girl child.

Retirement Planning

1. Whether your retirement is near or far, it is important to plan for your life after retirement.

2. If you have never planned for your retirement to date, do it at the earliest.

3. Take note of your financial needs in the future while planning your retirement.

4. Set aside a part of your income towards retirement funds whenever possible.

5. Government employees who joined public service before the year 2004 are eligible to get a pension. But what about the others? They have to plan for their retirement.

6. Mutual funds and insurance companies have various retirement plans. You can also invest in PPF and NPS to create provisions for your post-retirement life.

Summary

1. Develop the habit of reading. Remember, reading helps you understand your life better. There are many websites specializing in the topic of personal finance. Reading those can add to your financial knowledge.

2. Maintain a financial planning diary and keep it with you at all times. Check the list of your savings and expenses whenever possible. This will help you control your expenses.

> 'A wise person should have money in their head, but not in their heart.'—Jonathan Swift

3. Learn to accept your mistakes as that is the first step towards rectifying them.

4. Never stop trying. Don't feel bad if you do not succeed. Those who keep trying are the ones who eventually become successful.

5. Time is precious; that is why those who are able to plan their time well can plan everything else equally well.

6. If you have a habit of comparing yourself to others, you will always find someone ahead in the race. Instead of comparing yourself with others, improve yourself and grow financially.

7. Being rich does not guarantee financial freedom. The concept of 'being rich' differs from person to person and from situation to situation.

8. Money is just a means to fulfil your needs and not the need itself. That is why you must find out what you really want from it.

9. . . . and finally, never forget how Money Works as explained in this book!

'If you want to be in the 1 per cent, don't do what the
99 per cent do.'—Grant Cardone

Final Thoughts

हतो वा प्राप्यसि स्वर्गम्, जित्वा वा भोक्ष्यसे महिम्।

तस्मात् उत्तिष्ठ कौन्तेय युद्धाय कृतनिश्चय: ॥

(श्रीमद्भगवद्गीता, द्वितीय अध्याय, श्लोक ३७)

(Oh, Arjun, son of Kunti, you will achieve heaven if you die in
the battlefield or will rule the earth if you win the battle.
Therefore, resolve to stand and fight!)

The teachings of Lord Shri Krishna say we should fulfil our
duties with equal excitement, whatever the situation. Our
actions are in our control. We can bring a sea change in
our financial situation based on our continuous efforts,
hard work, perseverance, constant learning and honesty.
My best wishes for your journey towards financial success
and happiness.

Acknowledgements

First and foremost, I am grateful to the management team of Arthasakshar. com for giving me the opportunity to author my first book.

To Smita Gune, Vazir Advertisers, who helped compile and edit this book. Her valuable guidance proved to be a navigation system for minimizing errors.

To Prakash Tikare of Media Tree, who provided meaningful illustrations for this book.

To Rishikesh Lokapure, who helped me translate this book from Marathi to English without losing the context and sensitivity of the topic.

To all my clients who taught me financial literacy—practically. I stay indebted to them forever.

To the Arthasakshar family—Manasi Joshi, Uday Pingale, Prasad Bhagwat, Aditi Kapadi, Atul Kotkar, CA Shruti Shah and Omkar Gandhe, who are part of Arthasakshar website family.

I am thankful to Sharad Ashtekar of Madhushree Publications, publisher of the Marathi version *Arthasakshar Vha*! I am also thankful to the Penguin Random House team: Vaishali Mathur, Radhika Marwah, Aparajita Pant and Ralph Rebello.

I am also very thankful to CA Vinayak Kamurti, Dhanashree Abhyankar, Seema Dudhane, Vishal Shirke, Shantanu Phadke, Pandurang Dhebe and the article students. They took charge of the office, which allowed me to focus on writing this book. Without their active cooperation, this book would not have been possible.

To my mentors and teachers for life—CA S.B. Zaware, CA S.N. Puranik, CA Shashikant Barve, CA Chandrasekhar Chitale, CA M.N. Kulkarni, Prashant Barate, CA Sarosh Irani, CA Manoj Solanki, C.S. Suraj Padhiar. My respect for them goes beyond words.

To my friends and well-wishers—Makrand Ranade, CA Saurabh Kulkarni, CA Dheeraj Dandaghawal, Preeti and Arpan Gadiya, Pravin Tekale, Santosh Kamurti, Amit Deshpande, Nilesh Bagore, CA Parag Gandhi, Suvarna Mule, CA Amit Kalantri, Sagar Gandhi, CA Sameer Sheikh, CA Ashish Bihani, CA Pratik Dhatrak and Rohan Unde. I am at a loss for words when it comes to thanking you all.

To my wife, Durga, who has been a constant support and the one who pushed me to finish this book. You looked after everyone and everything at home. To my mother, my father and other family members—words are not enough to express my gratitude to you all.

Notes

Part 1: Introduction to Financial Literacy

1. Justin Kruger and David Dunning, 'Dunning-Kruger Effect, Unskilled and Unaware of It: How Difficulties in Recognizing One's Own Incompetence Lead To Inflated Self-Assessments', *Journal of Personality and Social Psychology*, 1999, https://www.researchgate.net/publication/12688660_Unskilled_and_Unaware_of_It_How_Difficulties_in_Recognizing_One's_Own_Incompetence_Lead_to_Inflated_Self-Assessments.

2. 'The World's Real-Time Billionaires', *Forbes*, https://www.forbes.com/real-time-billionaires/#783166613d78.

3. Number of births every day in India, key data—collection and analysis of disaggregated data for evaluating evolving risks and opportunities for children is key to all UNICEF programming, https://www.unicef.org/india/key-data.

4. 'Five Stages of Grief', Wikipedia, https://en.wikipedia.org/wiki/Five_stages_of_grief.

5. 'HUL, ITC, and USL Now Have 432 Officials Earning More than Rs 1 Cr a Year', *Business Standard*, 18 July 2022, https://www.business-standard.com/article/companies/hul-itc-and-usl-now-have-432-officials-earning-more-than-rs-1-cr-a-year-122071800539_1.html.

Part 2: Financial Planning

1. 'Why Shopping Makes You Feel High', Neurotracker, https://www.neurotrackerx.com/post/shopping-makes-feel-high.

2. Lauren Szeto, 'Confessions of a Shopaholic: 4 Brain Chemicals That Cause Impulse Buys', Nova, 21 July 2020, https://novamoney.com/blog/4-chemical-messengers-that-dictate-the-way-you-spend.

3. The Pleasure of Walking Tall, published by First Federal Savings & Loan Association of St. Petersburg, FL in St Petersburg Times, 1963, Source: https://www.oneidiot.in/2020/08/18/the-pleasure-of-walking-tall/.

Part 3: Insurance

1. 2023 Global Medical Trends Survey, 12 October 2022, https://www.wtwco.com/en-in/insights/2022/10/2023-global-medical-trends-survey-report#:~:text=The%202023%20Global%20Medical%20Trends,most%20regions%20(Figure%201).

Part 5: Investment

1. Dhirendra Kumar, 'Rs 1 Lakh in 1984 Is Worth Just Rs 7,451 Now: Are You Saving Enough to Beat Inflation?', the *Economic Times*, 6 March 2017, https://economictimes.indiatimes.com/wealth/plan/how-can-inflation-affect-our-retirement-planning/articleshow/57451629.cms?from=mdr.

Part 6: Shares and Mutual Funds

1. Amit Mudgill, 'Stocks That Made Investors Crorepatis amid Devastating COVID Pandemic', the *Economic Times*, 4 June 2021, https://economictimes.indiatimes.com/markets/stocks/news/stocks-that-made-investors-crorepatis-amid-devastating-covid-pandemic/articleshow/83227514.cms?from=mdr.

2. Navdeep Singh, 'Sensex Ends Flat but M-Cap of All BSE-Listed Stocks Crosses Rs 300 Lakh Crore-Mark for First Time', the *Economic Times*, 5 July 2023, https://economictimes.indiatimes.com/markets/stocks/news/sensex-ends-flat-but-bse-m-cap-crosses-rs-300-lakh-crore-mark-for-first-time/articleshow/101515440.cms?utm_source=contentofinterest&utm_medium=text&utm_campaign=cppst.

3. 'Top 10 Wealth Creators (1995–2020)' Motilal Oswal 25th Annual Wealth Creation Study—2020, https://www.motilaloswal.com/site/rreports/HTML/637443115602580742/index.htm.

4. Ralf Dahrendorf, *Class and Class Conflict in Industrial Society* (Stanford, CA: Stanford University Press, 1959);

   Ulrike Malmendier, 'Roman Shares', https://eml.berkeley.edu/~ulrike/Papers/Roman_Shares_published_090605.pdf;

   David Kessler, Peter Temin, *Money and Prices in Early Roman Empire*, Working Paper Series, Department of Economics, Massachusetts Institute of Technology, 14 April 2005, https://dspace.mit.edu/bitstream/handle/1721.1/63816/moneypricesinear00kess.pdf.

5. Andrew Odlyzko, 'Newton's Financial Misadventures in the South Sea Bubble', The Royal Society Publishing, 29 August 2018, https://royalsocietypublishing.org/doi/10.1098/rsnr.2018.0018;

   'South Sea Company', Wikipedia, https://en.wikipedia.org/wiki/South_Sea_Company.

6. Brad M. Barber, Yi-Tsung Lee, Yu-Jane Liu, Terrance Odean, and Ke Zhang, 'Do Day Traders Rationally Learn About Their Ability', published at https://faculty.haas.berkeley.edu/odean/papers/

Day%20Traders/Day%20Trading%20and%20Learning%20110217.
pdf.

7. Fernando Chague, Rodrigo De-Losso, and Bruno Cara Giovannetti,
    'Day Trading for a Living?', August 2019, published at https://www.
    researchgate.net/publication/334630772_Day_Trading_for_a_Living.

8. 'Analysis of Profit and Loss of Individual Traders Dealing in Equity
    F&O Segment', SEBI Study, Department of Economic and Policy
    Analysis, https://www.sebi.gov.in/reports-and-statistics/research/
    jan-2023/study-analysis-of-profit-and-loss-of-individual-traders-
    dealing-in-equity-fando-segment_67525.html.

9. 'Largest Economies by Nominal GDP in 2023', World Economic
    Outlook Database, April 2023;

    International Monetary Fund, https://www.imf.org/en/Publications/
    WEO/weo-database/2023/April. 'The World in 2050' Report,
    published by PWC, February 2017, https://www.pwc.com/gx/en/
    research-insights/economy/the-world-in-2050.html.

10. Demographic Dividend—United Nations Population Fund, https://
    www.unfpa.org/data/IN;

    Atul Thakur, 'India Enters 37-Year Period of Demographic Dividend',
    the Economic Times, 22 July 2019, https://economictimes.indiatimes.
    com/news/economy/indicators/india-enters-37-year-period-of-
    demographic-dividend/articleshow/70324782.cms?from=mdr.

11. 'The World's First Investment Fund', Exchange History NL,
    https://www.beursgeschiedenis.nl/en/moment/the-world's-first-
    investment-fund/;

    Ritu Kant Ojha, 'Who Was Abraham van Ketwich and Why Modern
    Mutual Fund Managers Both Admire and Envy Him', Medium, 30
    September 2018, https://medium.com/@ritukantojha/who-was-
    abraham-van-ketwich-and-why-modern-mutual-fund-managers-
    both-admire-and-envy-him-81643b1d73e5.

12 'Indian Mutual Fund Industry's Average Assets Under Management
    (AAUM) stood at Rs 44.82 Lakh Crore (INR 44.82 Trillion)', https://
    www.amfiindia.com/indian-mutual.

Part 7: Financial Frauds to Beware Of

1. 'Stockguru.India allegedly dupes 2 lakh investors of over Rs 1,000
    crore', Moneylife, 9 April 2011, https://www.moneylife.in/article/
    stockguruindia-allegedly-dupes-2-lakh-investors-of-over-rs1000-
    crore/15461.html;

'Stock Guru Scam—Lesson to Learn', Wisdomtimes, https://www.wisdomtimes.com/blog/stock-guru-scam-lesson-to-learn/.

2. Sarmistha Neogy, 'Speak Asia: A Primer', *Business Standard*, 20 January 2013, https://www.business-standard.com/article/companies/speak-asia-a-primer-111052000146_1.html; Vivek Sinha and Gaurav Choudhury, 'Inside SpeakAsia Ponzi Scam: How 2.4 Million Indians Lost Savings', *Hindustan Times*, 29 December 2013, https://www.hindustan-times.com/india/inside-speakasia-ponzi-scam-how-2-4-million-indians-lost-savings/story-INMz4WAdcat2ydKrPkZcaL.html.

3. 'Saradha Scam Case: Key Things You Need Know', MoneyControl, 22 March 2021, https://www.moneycontrol.com/news/india/saradha-scam-case-key-things-you-need-know-6677201.html; 'Saradha Chit Fund Scam: All You Want To Know', the *Times of India*, 4 February 2019, https://timesofindia.indiatimes.com/india/sardha-chit-fund-scam-all-you-want-to-know/articleshow/67831731.cms.

4. 'Beware of Pyramid Schemes Posing as Multi-Level Marketing Programs', U.S. Securities and Exchange Commission, 1 October 2013, https://www.sec.gov/oiea/investor-alerts-bulletins/investor-alerts-ia_pyramidhtm.html.

5. 'Ebiz.com Uses MLM Route to Dupe Students with IT Package Offer', Moneylife, 1 December 2010, https://www.moneylife.in/article/ebizcom-uses-mlm-route-to-dupe-students-with-it-package-offer/11807.html.

Bibliography

1. *I Can Do Financial Planning*, Swapna Mirashi, Reserve Bank of India

2. 'Capacity Building for Financial Literacy Programmes', Reserve Bank of India College of Agricultural Banking, Pune

3. *The Psychology of Money: Timeless Lessons on Wealth, Greed, and Happiness*, Morgan Housel, Jaico Publishing House

4. *Sketchbook of Wisdom*, Vishal Khandelwal

5. Arvind Paranjpe, Mantra Guntavanukicha Mantra Guntavanukicha, Rajhans Prakashan